BUDDHIST COSMOLOGY

BUDDHIST COSMOLOGY

Science and Theology in the Images of Motion and Light

W. RANDOLPH KLOETZLI

MOTILAL BANARSIDASS PUBLISHERS
PRIVATE LIMITED • DELHI

Reprint: Delhi, 1989, 1997, 2007
First Published: Delhi, 1983

ISBN: 978-81-208-0463-0

MOTILAL BANARSIDASS
41 U.A. Bungalow Road, Jawahar Nagar, Delhi 110 007
8 Mahalaxmi Chamber, 22 Bhulabhai Desai Road, Mumbai 400 026
203 Royapettah High Road, Mylapore, Chennai 600 004
236, 9th Main III Block, Jayanagar, Bangalore 560 011
Sanas Plaza, 1302 Baji Rao Road, Pune 411 002
8 Camac Street, Kolkata 700 017
Ashok Rajpath, Patna 800 004
Chowk, Varanasi 221 001

PRINTED IN INDIA
BY JAINENDRA PRAKASH JAIN AT SHRI JAINENDRA PRESS,
A-45 NARAINA, PHASE-I, NEW DELHI 110 028
AND PUBLISHED BY NARENDRA PRAKASH JAIN FOR
MOTILAL BANARSIDASS PUBLISHERS PRIVATE LIMITED,
BUNGALOW ROAD, DELHI 110 007

TO
MY PARENTS

TABLE OF CONTENTS

PREFACE

The following pages grow out of an interest I developed in the cosmologies of Buddhism when I first read the popular Buddhist text known as *The Lotus of the True Law* (*Saddharma-puṇḍarīka*). The boldness of imagery, the certainty of statement and the fantastic scenarios which accompany the sermons of the cosmic Buddha in this text were startling and incomprehensible and required an explanation. None was to be found. Because of the central place which these speculations occupy, I imagined—correctly—that this was a topic worthy of future research and—incorrectly—that such research could be accomplished expeditiously. Bright hopes dimmed.

After many years of trying to unravel these mysteries, three facts became apparent :

(1) There were actually two discrete strands within these cosmological materials; those emphasizing time or motion as the basic cosmological metaphor and those emphasizing images of space and light.

(2) All phases of Buddhist cosmological speculation were closely related and each could not be understood apart from the others.

(3) The cosmologies of Buddhism did not exist in isolation, but were closely related to the broader scientific and theological speculations which captured the imagination of the entire Classical world—particularly the ancient sciences of mathematics and astronomy.

As a result of bringing these various perspectives to bear on the problem of Buddhist cosmology, a coherent and convincing picture began to emerge. In the pages that follow, Buddhist cosmological speculation is presented in terms of four major moments : (1) the single world system, (2) the "cosmology of thousands," (3) the "cosmology of innumerables," and (4) the cosmologies of the Pure Land sects. The "cosmology of thousands" and the "cosmology of innumerables" are the two major strands of what I have termed the mathematical cosmologies. They are the primary focus of this work for two reasons. First, they have provided the key with which to understand the intention behind the other Buddhist cosmologies. Second, it is the mathematical cosmologies which present the scientific basis of all Buddhist cosmological speculation in sharpest relief.

This work, then, is divided as follows. Chapter I presents the major moments of cosmological speculation in the history of Buddhist philosophy, their perception in modern scholarship and the major problems with these perceptions. Chapter II presents the outlines of the single world system with some general insights into the intention behind this perception of the universe. While the single world system is not the primary concern of this work, it is presented here in some detail in order to serve as a convenient reference and to show its relationship to other phases of Buddhist cosmological speculation. Chapters III-IV present the outlines of the "cosmology of thousands," provide the first effort at interpreting the central concept of this cosmology and analyze the key moments in the drama of salvation which are central to this cosmology. Chapters V-VI present the structures of the "cosmology of innumerables" together with the radically changed drama of salvation to be found here. It is these chapters which constitute the core of this study and establish a clear distinction between the cosmologies of the Hīnayāna and those of the Mahāyāna as well as the scientific basis underlying each. Chapter VII summarizes the key differences between the drama implicit in the two mathematical cosmologies, presents additional suggestions which cannot be fully developed in this work and attempts to expose the most basic issues which confront us in the study of the Buddhist cosmologies. Finally, Chapter VIII presents a discussion of available bibliography both as a summary of materials reviewed in this study and as a resource for future research.

As a result of the publication of this work, I am able to formally acknowledge the debts I owe to those who have provided encouragement and shaped my interests along the way. My debts are indeed great. My parents to whom this work is dedicated provided a home in which religion was a focus of personal concerns. At Wittenberg University, I was exposed to a healthy theological and philosophical reexamination of Western religiosity and introduced to the study of "comparative religions." I continue to feel a great debt of gratitude for my teachers during those years, especially to the memories of Milton Kleintop and Margaret Ermarth. In 1964, I entered the University of Chicago to study the History of Religions. Among the persons I recall with gratitude and affection from this period are Joseph Haroutunian, Joseph Sittler, Frank Reynolds and J.A.B. van Buitenen. In addition it was an undeniable privilege to have been exposed to two of the great minds of the twentieth century—Paul Tillich and Mircea Eliade.

Following my years in the university, I became a civil servant, a position I have found more challenging than I had imagined. It is no small debt that I acknowledge to the U. S. Department of Labor for providing me with a livelihood as well as with an opportunity to make a contribution, however small, over a period of ten years. During these years, my interest in scholarship has been kept alive in large part as a result of the encouragement of Alf Hiltebeitel. As a result, I am unable to fully acknowledge the debt which I owe to Alf both as a friend and as a teacher. It is almost certain that had it not been for his steady encouragement, this study would never have been completed. The catholicity of his interests, his grasp of detail which is so important in coming to terms with the Indian materials, and his aggressive pursuit of bibliography have opened many avenues for me. Without his encouragement and example, this research would have foundered at many more points than it did.

Finally, I would like to express my gratitude for everyone who has been my friend over the years of this research despite obstacles I placed in the way. In particular, I would like to acknowledge a special debt to Catherine Romano who listened at length to the tangled details of this project and who despite prudent doubts, had the sensitivity to celebrate with me when the threads finally became apparent.

LIST OF FIGURES

ABBREVIATIONS

Background	Teresina Rowell, "The Background and Early Use of the Buddha-Kṣetra Concept;" *The Eastern Buddhist* 6 (1934) : 199-246, 379-430; 7 (1935) : 131-69.
BEFEO	*Bulletin de l'école français d'Extrême-Orient.*
Cosmogony	Louis de La Vallée Poussin, "Cosmogony and Cosmology (Buddhist)," *Encyclopaedia of Religion and Ethics*, ed. James Hastings, 13 vols. (Edinburgh : T & T Clark, 1908-27) : 2, 129-38.
Enseignement	*L'enseignement de Vimalakīrti* (*Vimalakīrtinirdeśa*), trans. and ann. Étienne Lamotte (Louvain : Bibliothèque du Muséon, 1958)
ERE	*Encyclopaedia of Religion and Ethics*, ed. James Hastings, 13 vols. (Edinburgh : T & T Clark, 1908-27).
Histoire	Étienne Lamotte, *Histoire du bouddhisme indien* (Louvain : Bibliothèque du Muséon, 1958).
Hôbôgirin	*Hôbôgirin; dictionraire encyclopédique du Bouddhisme d'après les sources chinoises et japonaises*, ed. Paul Demiéville, 4 fasc. (Tokyo : Maison franco-japonais, 1929).
Kośa	*L'Abhidharmakośa de Vasubandhu*, trans. and ann. Louis de La Vallée Poussin, anastatically reproduced with a new preface by Étienne Lamotte, 7 vols. (Brussels : Mélanges chinois et bouddhiques, 1971).
Kosmógraphie	Willibald Kirfel, *Kosmographie der Inder* (Bonn : K. Schroeder, 1920).
Marche	"La marche de la concentration héroïque (*Śūraṃgamasamādhisūtra*)," trans. and ann. Étienne Lamotte, *Mélanges chinois et bouddhiques*, Vol. 13 (1965).
Mythologie	Madeleine Biardeau, "Études de mythologie hindoue : Cosmogonies purāṇiques," Parts 1-3, *Bulletin de l'école français d'Extrême-Orient* 54 (1968) : 19-45; 55 (1969) : 59-105; 58 (1971) : 17-89;

"Bhakti et avatāra," Part 4, *Bulletin de l'école français d'Extrême-Orient* 63 (1976) : 111-263.

Siddhi — *La Siddhi de Hiuan-tsang* (*Vijñaptimātratāsiddhi*), trans. and ann. Louis de La Vallée Poussin, 2 vols. (Paris : Librarie Orientaliste Paul Geuthner, 1928-48).

Système — Pierre Duhem, *Le système du monde; Histoire des doctrines cosmologiques de Platon à Copernic*, 10 vols. (Paris : Hermann, 1971).

Traité — *Traité de la grande vertu de sagesse de Nāgārjuna* (*Mahāprajñāpāramitāśāstra*), trans. and ann. Étienne Lamotte (Louvain : Bibliothèque du Muséon, Vol. 18 [1949]; Publications de l'Institut Orientaliste de Louvain, Vols. 2, 12 [1970, 1976]).

CHAPTER I

BUDDHIST PHILOSOPHY AND THE MAJOR MOMENTS OF COSMOLOGY

La tradition bouddhique baigne
dans le merveilleux.
—Lamotte, *Histoire*, p. X

Cosmological Agnosticism—A Paradox

A common and widely recognized aspect of the Buddha's teaching centers about the rejection of speculations concerning the beginning and end of the world, the limited or unlimited nature of its extension in space, and a variety of questions which relate the soul to the body and to the cosmos. The so-called fourteen difficult questions (*caturdaśāvyākṛtavastūni*)[1] are a systematic presentation of these speculations in summary fashion : (1-4) Are the world and the self eternal ? Non-eternal ? Both eternal and non-eternal ? Neither eternal nor non-eternal ? (5-8) Are the world and the self finite ? Infinite ? Both finite and infinite ? Neither finite nor infinite ? (9-12) Does the Tathāgata (i.e. one

1. For a list of the sources and variations in the *avyākṛtavastu*, see *Traité de la grande vertu de sagesse de Nāgārjuna* (*Mahāprajñāpāramitāśāstra*), trans.—and ann. Étienne Lamotte (Louvain : Bibliothèque du Muséon, Vol. 18 [1949]; Publications de l'Institut Orientaliste de Louvain, Vols. 2, 12, [1970, 1976]), p. 154, n. 1. (Hereafter cited as *Traité*, *Mppś* or *Śāstra*.) See also Louis de La Vallée Poussin, "Agnosticism (Buddhist)," *Encyclopaedia of Religion and Ethics*, ed. James Hastings, 13 vols. (Edingburgh : T & T Clark, 1908-27) : 1, 220-25. (Hereafter cited as *ERE*.) Idem, *Nirvāṇa* (Paris : Gabriel Beauchesne, 1925), pp. 85-129. The Buddha's response to Mālunkyāputta's curiosity concerning these questions is recorded in the *Cūla Mālunkyāsutta* of the *Majjimanikāya*. *The Collection of Middle Length Sayings*, trans. Isaline Blew Horner, 3 vols. (London : Luzac & Co., Ltd., 1954) : 2, 97-101. It is commented upon further in the *Mahāprajñāpāramitāśāstra* in a discussion of the perfection (*pāramitā*) of patience (*kṣānti*). Lamotte, *Traité*, pp. 913 ff. Additional bibliography relating to this discussion is available in Tiruppattur Ramesshayyer Venkatachala Murti, *The Central Philosophy of Buddhism: A Study of the Mādhyamika System* (London : George Allen and Unwin Ltd., 1955), pp. 36-54.

who has attained *nirvāṇa*) exist after death ? Does he not exist after death ? Does he both exist and not-exist after death ? Does he neither exist nor not-exist after death ? (13-14) Is the vital principle the same as the body ? Is it different from the body ?

The Buddha refused to answer these questions because they were vain and had no significance for salvation. All of the proposed alternatives are rejected by tradition as false or heretical. The scholastic difficulties inherent in apparent corollaries of two of these positions shed additional light on the implications of these "cosmological" questions. If the universes are limited in number, and since each of the innumerable Buddhas saves by himself an immense (*aprameya*) and incalculable (*asaṅkhyeya*) number of beings, the totality of beings would be exhausted in the course of time. If there are not always new beings, their number would be exhausted. If, on the other hand, the universes are infinite in number, the Buddha would not be omniscient.[1] The *Brahmajālasutta* of the *Dīghanikāya* echoes these sentiments

1. Lamotte, *Traité*, pp. 529-30. For additional discussion of the problem of the Buddha's omniscience, see ibid., p. 13, n. 4; 146-61, 1735-55; *L'Abhidharmakośa de Vasubandhu*, trans. and ann. Louis de La Vallée Poussin, anastatically reproduced with a new preface by Etienne Lamotte, 7 vols. (Brussels : Mélanges chinois et bouddhiques, 1971), chap. iii, p. 101, n. 2; and Padmanabh S. Jaini, "On the *Sarvajñatva* (Omniscience) of Mahāvīra and the Buddha" in *Buddhist Studies in Honour of I. B. Horner*, eds. L. Cousins, A. Kunst, and K. R. Norman (Boston : D. Reidel Publishing Co. 1974), pp. 71-90. The first of these heretical positions is apparently assumed by Gosāla and the Ājīvikas. Moreover, the Ājīvika doctrine of the bodhisattva is closely tied to this point of view. Since a finite number of beings would be exhausted in the course of time as each passed into *nirvāṇa*, certain beings must return after extinction in order to maintain the world. These are the bodhisattvas who re-enter time. Arthur Llewellyn Basham, *History and Doctrine of the Ājīvikas : A Vanished Indian Religion* (London : Luzac & Co., Ltd., 1951, Reprint MLBD 1981), pp. 260-61. According to La Vallée Poussin, "There is no beginning to transmigration · · ·; there will be no end to it : on these two points all Buddhist schools agree. But, · · · it must be observed that there is an end to transmigration for the Arhats, who rightly say at the time of dying, 'This existence is for me the last one.' · · · The problem . . . will probably have to be solved as it has been by the Samkhya : the number of souls being infinite, there will never come a time when all have attained Nirvāṇa." Louis de La Vallée Poussin, "Ages of the World (Buddhist)," *ERE* 1:187-90.

by condemning a wide range of theories,[1] including theories that the world is (a) limited in space, (b) unlimited, (c) unlimited at the sides and limited towards the top and bottom, and (d) neither limited nor unlimited. Thus, a prominent feature of the Buddha's teaching came to be characterized by a systematic agnosticism with regard to the "cosmological" questions.

Despite the aversion of various elements of the Buddhist community to speculations on issues of cosmology, they occupy a prodigious place. The oldest Buddhist sources[2] represent the universe in terms of the *cakkavāla/cakravāla*, a single, circular world system surrounded by a mountain of iron (*cakravāla*) from which its name is derived. Above this circular surface is a series of four meditations (*dhyāna*) or "meditation realms" as they are generally designated. The successive divisions of the meditation realms into seventeen heavens mark the progress of the *śrāvaka* or one who has undertaken the religious vocation toward the state of *arhat*, the Buddhist saint. Detachment from all the meditation realms through the practice of meditation eventuates in the extinction of *nirvāṇa*.

The majority of scholars have either limited their discussion of Buddhist cosmology to the single world system or have placed their greatest emphasis on it owing to the more readily available descriptions of these materials and the apparent coherence of these descriptions. Other aspects of Buddhist cosmology have been all but neglected. The reasoning has apparently been that even if these descriptions of the single world system did not really make any more sense than the seemingly more bizarre cosmologies which proliferated in the Buddhist Sanskrit traditions, at least they were orderly and could be represented in diagram drawn to scale. Almost without exception, discussions of the "*cakravāla-*

1. Dīghanikāya, *Dialogues of the Buddha*, trans. T. W. Rhys Davids, 3 vols. (London : Oxford University Press, 1899-1921), 1.23 ff. For a discussion of the *Brahmajālasutta*, see Nalinaksha Dutt, "The Brahmajāla Sutta in the Light of Nāgārjuna's Expositions," *Indian Historical Quarterly* 8 (1932) : 706-46. Other heretical positions are briefly described in Narendra Nath Bhattacharyya, *History of Indian Cosmogonical Ideas* (New Delhi : Munshiram Manoharlal, 1971), pp. 75-76.

2. According to Louis de La Vallée Poussin, these include the Sūtras of the *Dīrgha* and the *Madhyamāgama*, notably *Dīrgha* 30. Other sources are listed in La Vallée Poussin, *Kośa*, chap. III, p. 138, n. 1.

cosmology" are little more than catalogues of names and measurements, altogether lacking in interpretation.

While there is a vast secondary literature describing the *cakravāla* in every cultural setting permeated by Buddhism, our research has relied on the descriptions of the *cakravāla* found in the *Abhidharmakośa* (hereafter *Kośa*). The *Kośa* has been chosen as much for the rich detail which it provides as for the exhaustive annotations provided by La Vallée Poussin's translation. The *Kośa* is a compendium of *abhidharma* or philosophical teachings of the Vaibhāṣika sect of Kashmir at the beginning of our era, compiled and commented upon by Vasubandhu around the fifth century A.D.[1]

Although the oldest tradition apparently limited its interest to a single world system, a grandiose cosmic structure developed on the perimeter of this single universe. Traces of themes associated with multiple world systems appear in texts of the Pāli Canon.[2] A 10,000 world system is mentioned in the Jātakas, though with little elaboration, and in a more systematic way in Buddhaghoṣa. Since it is apparent that the 10,000 world system is part of a larger category of cosmological speculation characterized by the fact that it is dominated by the numerology of "thousands," it will be treated as a variant of the "*sāhasra*-cosmology" or "cosmology of thousands." Themes associated with thousands of worlds are most pronounced in the Sarvāstivādin texts. The *trisāhasramahāsāhasralokadhātu* is the most prominent

1. La Vallée Poussin, *Kośa*, "Preface," and chap. viii, pp. 222-25.

2. A clear statement in the Pāli tradition affirming the existence of many worlds can be found in Buddhaghoṣa's *Atthasālinī* (sec. 160) which states that four things are infinite : space, the number of universes, the number of living beings and the wisdom of the Buddha. *The Expositor Buddhaghoṣa's Commentary on the Dhammasangaṇi, The First Book of the Abhidhamma Piṭaka*, trans. Maung Tin, 2 vols. (London : Oxford University Press, 1920-21), 1:213-14. For non-Indian speculations concerning the plurality of worlds see Pierre Duhem, *Le système du monde; Histoire des doctrines cosmologiques de Platon à Copernic*, 10 vols. (Paris : Hermann, 1971), 1-230-41, and the system of Suhrawardi as discussed by Henry Corbin in *Avicenna and the Visionary Recitals*, trans. Willard R. Trask (New York : Pantheon Books, Inc., 1960) and idem, *Terre céleste et corps de resurrection* (Paris : Buchet-Chastel, 1961). Plato's arguments against the existence of more than one world are discussed in Francis MacDonald Cornford, *Plato's Cosmology* (New York : Liberal Arts Press, 1957), pp. 41-43.

expression of the "*sāhasra*-cosmology", although the precise meaning of this term is extremely problematic. It may be translated provisionally as scholars have done to date as "triple chiliocosm" or "three thousandth great thousandth universe" or even "The Thrice-a-thousand Mighty Thousandfold World-system." While these translations provide a certain literalness, they convey little if any meaning.

The materials describing the *trisāhasramahāsāhasralokadhātu* are few, scattered and sparse in their detail. Yet they are consistent and occur in such diverse contexts both within and without Buddhism that its significance cannot be doubted. Use of certain Hellenistic materials has been valuable in deciphering the meaning of the *trisāhasramahāsāhasralokadhātu* since the juxtaposition of threes and thousands finds even wider currency here. References to the *trisāhasramahāsāhasralokadhātu* within Buddhism are scattered in the most fragmentary manner throughout the Pāli texts, the *Kośa* and other Sanskrit literature as well as in the Chinese and Japanese texts. What we have identified as the "*sāhasra*-cosmology" is not a theme of Western scholarship as such since these cosmologies are generally blurred with those of the Mahāyāna in discussions concerning the field of a Buddha (*buddhakṣetra*). In short, they have not been recognized heretofore as a discrete strand of cosmological speculation and certainly not as one with a coherent drama of salvation which we will characterize as the drama of the single *buddhakṣetra* and which we can relate provisionally to the Sarvāstivādin school.

Finally, the cosmology of the Mahāyāna is characterized by innumerables of world systems distributed throughout the ten regions of space. As such, I have termed this the "*asaṅkhyeya*-cosmology" or "cosmology of innumerables." Although certain of these world systems lack the presence of a Buddha,[1] most are Buddha-fields (*buddhakṣetra*) where a fully and perfectly enlightened Tathāgata resides and teaches the law for the benefit of countless beings. Generally speaking, there are three types of *buddhakṣetras* : pure (*viśuddha*), impure (*aviśuddha*) and mixed (*miśraka*). For the most part, Sukhāvatī is the most prominent among the "pure" lands, although in some texts it is clearly

1. *L'enseignement de Vimalakīrti* (*Vimalakīrtinirdeśa*), trans. and ann. Étienne Lamotte (Louvain : Bibliothèque du Muséon, 1958), p. 395.

subordinated to others. Sahā[1] is the most important of the "impure" lands, although, from another perspective, Sahā may be considered a "mixed" land, alternately ornamented (pure) and unornamented (impure).[2] This "mixed" land Sahā is our universe. It is located in the region of the South and is the field of the Buddha Śākyamuni.

While the Sarvāstivādins recognize a single *buddhakṣetra* defined as a *trisāhasramahāsāhasralokadhātu*, a full and dramatic use of the *buddhakṣetra* is reserved for the Mahāyāna. As such, it is difficult to overstate the role which the *buddhakṣetra* plays throughout nearly every phase of Mahāyānist cosmology. Taken in its broadest significance, the plurality of *buddhakṣetras* which characterize the "*asaṅkhyeya*-cosmology" presents a dramatic vision of the Buddha who illuminates the cosmos, whose yogic facility endows it with reality, and whose skill-in-means (*upāya*) makes the cosmos itself an agent of salvation. As with the vastness of all the Indian cosmologies, the monumental scope of the "*asaṅkhyeya*-cosmology" is finally an intimate psychology. This "intimate immensity" has a flavor or tone which it contributes to Budddism, in particular to the Mahāyāna, and it is this sense of the miraculous and supernatural more than the actual structure of these cosmologies which has been duly noted by scholars.

Because of the fantastic imagery and intense numerological

1. The meaning of Sahā as a designation of this world is unclear. Kern translates the phrase *iyaṃ sarvāvati lokadhātu* as "this all-embracing world" and apparently understands it to refer to Sahā. See *The Lotus of the True Law* (*Saddharmapuṇḍarika*), trans. Hendrik Kern (Sacred Books of the East, Vol. 21; New York : Dover Publications, Inc., 1963), p. 232. The term *sahā* is an adjective which is generally translated as "enduring," "suffering" or "supporting." See Louis de La Vallée Poussin, "Cosmogony and Cosmology (Buddhist)," *ERE*, 2:138, n. 1. A valuable summary of scholarship to that time relating to the meaning of Sahā can be found in Eugène Burnouf, "Sahālokadhātu" in his *Introduction à l'histoire du bouddhisme indien*, 2 vols. (Paris : Imprimerie royale, 1844), 1:594-97. A discussion of the term Brahmā Sahāmpati can be found in Jean Przyluski, "Brahmā Sahāmpati, "*Journal asiatique* 205 (1924) : 155-63. According to Eitel, Sahā is the "capital of the chiliocosmos." See Ernest John Eitel, *Handbook of Chinese Buddhism; A Sanskrit-Chinese Dictionary*, 2nd ed. (Tokyo : Sanshusha, 1904).

2. "Butsudo" in *Hôbôgirin: dictionnaire encyclopédique du Bouddhisme d'après les sources chinois et japonais*, ed. Paul Demiéville (Tokyo : Maison franco-japonais, 1929-37), p. 200.

speculations which they contain, these cosmologies have frequently been judged to be lacking in all logic. Some scholars have gone so far as to maintain that the Mahāyāna is totally lacking in any systematic cosmology.[1] Still others have condemned the seemingly bizarre exaggerations of these cosmologies as "rubbish."[2] Aversion to the fantastic numbers which dominate these cosmologies is not limited to contemporary students of India. Al-Biruni is quoted as follows :

> If those dreamers had more assiduously studied arithmetic, they would not have invented such outrageous numbers. God takes care that their trees do not grow into heaven.[3]

Even the more generous have been startled by the boldness of imagery and the fantastic scenarios which dominate these cosmologies. La Vallée Poussin has been most subdued, alluding to it simply as the "Great Cosmology." Kirfel brands it the "fantastic speculations" of a later period. Suzuki repeatedly calls attention to a "Mahāyāna supernaturalism"; Mus to "un Mahāyānisme flamboyant"; and with more than a trace of humor, Richard Robinson has termed it "Mahāyāna space fiction."

A number of works provide an introduction to various aspects of the "*asaṅkhyeya*-cosmology".[4] However, the major text used both to identify and characterize the "*asaṅkhyeya*-cosmology"

1. According to McGovern, the Mahāyāna was more concerned with the ultimate nature of reality than with cosmology, and what opinions there were, were never developed in a systematic manner. "From the absolute standpoint the universe was completely non-existent—why, therefore, would one bother to classify the fictitious." William Montgomery McGovern, *A Manual of Buddhist Philosophy*, Vol. 1 : *Cosmology* (New York : E. P. Dutton & Co., 1923), p. 14.

2. "In no sphere has the Indian imagination been more extravagant than in this (i.e., numerology; in this case associated with the hells). Japan has taken on some of this rubbish as may be seen from Genshin's description of the Buddhist hells; but, after all, the Japanese mind has never lost itself very seriously in such morbid speculations." August Karl Reischauer, *Studies in Japanese Buddhism* (New York : AMS Press, Inc., 1970), p. 203, n. 4.

3. La Vallée Poussin, *Kośa*, chap. iii, p. 189, n. 2.

4. Included in this category are the following survey materials : Lamotte, *Enseignement*, Note I—"Les buddhakṣetra," pp. 395-404; La Vallée Poussin, "Cosmogony"; "Butsudo," Hôbôgirin, pp. 198-203; and Teresina Rowell, "The Background and Early Use of the Buddha-Kṣetra Concept," *The Eastern Buddhist* 6 (1934) : 199-246, 379-430; 7 (1935) : 131-69.

has been the *Mahāprajñāpāramitāśāstra* of Nāgārjuna (hereafter cited as *Mppś* or *Śāstra*). The text of the *Mppś* reveals a complex debate between the Sarvāstivādins and an emerging Mahāyāna. In fact, the *śāstra* takes the forms of a detailed refutation of the Abhidharma portion of the Sarvāstivādin canon.[1] The Sarvāstivādins embracing the position of the Hīnayāna, and the Mahāsaṅghikas, primary representatives of this emerging Mahāyāna, opposed each other on all the major points of Buddhology, a fact of particular significance in the emergence of the mathematical cosmologies which are our primary concern. The *Mppś* bears witness to this controversy in several ways. Most notable is the juxtaposition of the created Buddhas (*nirmāṇa-buddha*) associated with the "*sāhasra*-cosmology" and the Buddhas of the ten regions (*daśadigbuddha*) integral to the "*asaṅkhyeya*-cosmology." Correspondingly, a distinction is made regarding the nature of the miraculous powers inherent in these differing views of the Buddha. As we shall see, there is a close and important relationship between the *nirmāṇabuddha* and the powers of multiplication (*nirmāṇa*) while the *daśadigbuddha* are associated with the exercise of the miraculous powers of illumination (*raśmiṛddhibala*).

The *Mppś* takes the form of an extensive commentary on the *Pañcaviṃśatisāhasrika-prajñāpāramitāsūtra.*[2] The first volume which is more than 600 pages in translation, is reserved for commentary on the Prologue (*nidāna*) of the *Pañcaviṃśati.* Of particular interest is a mytheme which occupies a position of special prominence in the *Mppś* and which constitutes the fundamental drama of the "*asaṅkhyeya*-cosmology." The mytheme involves four basic elements : (a) the entrance of Śākyamuni into concentration (*samādhi*); (b) the exercise of Śākyamuni's miraculous power of illumination; (c) the rendering of homage to Śākyamuni by the Buddhas of the ten regions; and (d) the transformation of Sahā into a "pure land.". While this mytheme occurs in a number of places in a variety of forms, the *Mppś* devotes nearly

1. Lamotte, *Traité*, 3: xiii.

2. *The Pañcaviṃśatisāhasrika-Prajñāpāramitā*, ed. Nalinaksa Dutt (London : Calcutta Oriental Series, No. 28, 1934). *The Large Sutra on Perfect wisdom, with the Divisions of the Abhisamayālaṅkāra*, trans. Edward Conze, Part I (London Luzac & Co., 1961, Rep. 1979 MLBD); Parts II-III (Madison : College Printing and Typing Co., 1964).

200 pages to commentary upon it, bringing together a wealth of material to assist in its interpretation.

A second text which has been important in our interpretation of the "*asaṅkhyeya*-cosmology" is the *Lotus of the True Law* (*Saddharmapuṇḍarīka*); hereafter *Lotus* or *Lotus Sūtra*. The themes of faith and rebirth found in the *Lotus* are also found in the Pure Land sects. However, the setting of the drama of rebirth in the *Lotus* is placed solidly within the framework of the "*asaṅkhyeya*-cosmology." Miraculous displays of light and predictions by Śākyamuni that various individuals will become Buddhas in a future aeon in one of the pure lands are testimony to this fact. Thus we read :[1]

> ". . . the Lord addressed the complete assembly of monks : I announce to you, monks, I make known to you that the monk Kāśyapa, . . . shall do homage to thirty thousand kotis of Buddhas. . . . In his last bodily existence in the world Avabhāsa . . . in the age . . . Mahāvyūha . . . he shall become a Tathāgata . . . by the name Raśmiprabhāsa. . . ."

In addition to numerous statements concerning the future destiny of beings, the *Lotus* contains some compelling observations on the mathematical sciences of the day and their relationship to cosmological speculation which provide support for this work in key places.

As the mytheme of the *Mppś* and the drama of rebirth in the *Lotus* point up, it is difficult to draw a clear line between the "*asaṅkhyeya*-cosmology" and the pure land cosmologies since, as we shall see, the latter presuppose the former. However, at a certain moment, the theologies of faith emerged from the general background of the "*asaṅkhyeya*-cosmology" taking with them only the Buddha-field Sukhāvatī as testimony to their cosmological heritage. The descriptions of Sukhāvatī are manifold and vary widely in content and detail. The *Smaller Sukhāvatīvyūha* provides the following details :

> Then Bhagavat addressed the honoured Sāriputra and said, 'O Sāriputra, after you have passed from here over a hundred thousand koṭis of Buddha countries there is in the Western

1. Kern, *Lotus*, p. 142.

part a Buddha country, a world called Sukhāvatī (the happy country). And there a Tathāgata, called Amitāyus, an Arhat, fully enlightened, dwells now, and remains, and supports himself, and teaches the Law.

...that world Sukhāvatī is adorned with seven terraces, with seven rows of palm-trees, and with strings of bells. It is enclosed on every side, beautiful, brilliant with four gems, viz. gold, silver, beryl and crystal.

...in that world Sukhāvatī there are lotus lakes, adorned with the seven gems, viz. gold, silver, beryl, crystal, red pearls, diamonds, and corals as the seventh. They are full of water which possesses the eight good qualities,...they are strewn with golden sand.

...in that Buddha country there are heavenly musical instruments always played on, and the earth is lovely and of golden colour.

...The very name of hells is unknown in that Buddha country, and likewise that of (descent into) animal bodies and of the realm of Yama.

...And again, O Sāriputra, of those beings also who are born in the Buddha country of the Tathāgata Amitāyus as purified Bodhisattvas, never to return again and bound by one birth only, of those Bodhisattvas, also, O Sāriputra, the number is not easy to count, except they are reckoned as infinite in number.

Then again all beings, O Sāriputra, ought to make fervent prayer for that Buddha country. And why ? Because they come together there with such excellent men. Beings are not born in that Buddha country of the Tathāgata Amitāyus as a reward and result of good works performed in this present life. No, whatever son or daughter of a family shall hear the name of the blessed Amitāyus, the Tathāgata, and having heard it, shall keep it in mind, and with thoughts undisturbed shall keep it in mind for one, two, three, four, five, six or seven nights,—when that son or daughter of a family comes to die, then that Amitāyus, the Tathāgata, surrounded by an assembly of disciples and followed by a host of Bodhisattvas, will stand before them at their hour of death, and they will depart this life with tranquil minds. After their death they will be born in the world Sukhāvatī, in the Buddha country of the same Amitāyus

> the Tathāgata. Therefore, then, O Sāriputra, having perceived this cause and effect, I with reverence say thus, Every son and every daughter of a family ought with their whole mind to make fervent prayer for that Buddha country'.[1]

Here we are told that rebirth in Sukhāvatī does not come about as the result of good works, but simply through mindfulness of the name of the Buddha. This is the celebrated "easy path" of the Pure Land sects, the path of faith. Elsewhere it is stated that rebirth in Sukhāvatī is made possible by the vows of the bodhisattvas to save all beings. The eighteenth vow is the most famous :[2]

> If, after my obtaining Buddhahood, all beings in the ten quarters should not desire in sincerity and trustfulness to be born in my country, and if they should not be born only by thinking of me for ten times, except those who have committed the five grave offences and those who are abusive of the true Dharma, may I not obtain the Highest Enlightenment.

While modern scholars are generally familiar with the elements of faith associated with this tradition, there is only a vague understanding of the cosmological setting and meaning of the key elements in this drama of salvation. Among those themes which can be amplified through an understanding of the cosmological setting are the significance of the hour of death, the precise mechanism of rebirth, the meaning of having one birth remaining, the symbolism of the trees and waters, the absence of mountains, and indeed the very significance of designating Sukhāvatī a "pure" land.[3] All of these specific themes receive considerable

1. "Smaller Sukhāvatī-Vyūha," trans. Friedrich Max Müller in *Buddhist Mahāyāna Texts,* ed. Edward Byles Cowell (Sacred Books of the East, Vol. 49; New York : Dover Publications, Inc., 1969, Rep. MLBD), pp. 91-99.

2. Alfred Bloom, *Shinran's Gospel of Pure Grace* (Tucson : University of Arizona Press, 1965), pp. 2-3.

3. Much information about the Pure Land sects including many theological issues are treated in "Butsudo," "Jôdô," etc., *Hôbôgirin.* For related devotional themes, see Hans Haas, *Amida Buddha : Unsere Zuflucht* (Göttingen : Vandenhoeck und Ruprecht, 1910). For studies of the Japanese Pure Land sects, see Bloom, *Shinran* ; and Harper Havelock Coates and Ryugaku Ishizuka, *Honen the Buddhist Saint* (Kyoto : Chion-in, 1925). An excellent discussion of the Tendai and Pure Land traditions can be found in Allan A. Andrews, *The Teachings Essential for Rebirth* (Tokyo : Sophia University,

clarification from an understanding of the "other power" of the Buddha which is at the heart of the drama of rebirth in Sukhāvatī. Themes associated with the "other power" of the Buddha are grounded in the "*asaṅkhyeya*-cosmology"; cosmological speculations which belong to the Indian background of the Pure Land traditions.

Thus, it is convenient to distinguish three discrete phases of Buddhist cosmological speculation : (1) the single world system or "*cakravāla*-cosmology," (2) the numerological or mathematical cosmologies focusing on the thousands of worlds and innumerables of Buddha-fields, and (3) the cosmologies of the Pure Land sects which concentrate on the drama associated with a particular Buddha-field, generally Sukhāvatī. As we have seen, the weight of scholarship has fallen either on cataloguing the details of the "*cakravāla*-cosmology" or on examining the role of faith which results in rebirth in Sukhāvatī in the Pure Land cosmologies. It has regarded the second phase with a sense of wonderment and general amazement and has all but dismissed the "mathematical cosmologies" as frivolous.

While those scholars who have focused on the drama of rebirth have all but ignored the overall cosmological structures in which rebirth occurs, they have nevertheless been closest to understanding the meaning of all the Buddhist speculations. They rightly perceive that at the core lies a drama of salvation. It is this drama of salvation implicit in all the Buddhist cosmologies which is the primary concern of this work and which alone provides the unifying force to bring together the fragmented source materials and fragmented scholarship. These dramas alone allow for the integration of the scientific and theological bases for these cosmologies and emerge clearly only when both components are understood. In an effort to uncover the drama implicit in all three phases of Buddhist cosmological speculation, this work will focus on the "mathematical cosmologies" and their scientific and theological setting.

From this survey of the major moments of Buddhist cosmological speculation and of the resources used to approach them, it is clear that modern scholarship in these areas has been inhibited

1973). A discussion of the Pure Sukhāvatī in terms of a "nostalgia" for paradise can be found in Henri de Lubac, *Amida* (Paris : Éditions du Seuil, 1955).

by several factors. Primary among them is the sentiment echoed by a number of scholars that Buddhism is fundamentally agnostic with regard to cosmology. This conviction has spread largely as a result of the celebrated discussion of the "difficult questions" by La Vallée Poussin, Oldenberg, Stcherbatsky and others. The references to cosmological speculation found in the Buddhist texts are consequently judged to be devoid of religious significance; meaningless accretions at best derivative in their import. The major difficulty with this view is that in minimizing the significance of the Buddhist cosmologies in this manner, it is impossible to account for the rich development of cosmological themes in the Buddhist literature. Moreover, it does not do justice to the important position these cosmologies occupy in the mind of the Buddhist believer. As Winston L. King has noted :[1]

> Theravada Buddhism is almost unthinkable without its cosmology. . . . Should one attempt to remove it by some sort of theological surgery, the remaining corpus might well be a corpse instead ! And so strong is the rootage of this cosmology in the tradition that the majority of orthodox monks and laity even today would resist any attacks upon or alterations in the Mount Meru cosmology (i.e., the "*cakravāla*-cosmology"). For them this cosmology represents the clear teaching of the Buddha as interpreted by the orthodox commentators, and this is the end of the matter.

Similar statements can be made about the significance of cosmology for Mahāyānist believers, though it would reference the pure lands and the powers of the celestial Buddhas rather than the Mount Meru cosmology. It is my hope that the apparent paradox between this cosmological agnosticism on the one hand and the abundance of cosmological themes on the other can be resolved by understanding the general intention behind all the Buddhist cosmologies.

The consistent preference to concentrate on the single world system to the near exclusion of other phases of Buddhist cosmology has also acted to inhibit an understanding of the overriding concerns of Buddhist cosmological speculation. One factor which

1. Winston L. King, *A Thousand Lives Away : Buddhism in Contemporary Burma* (Cambridge, Massachusetts : Harvard University Press, 1964), pp. 108-09.

partially accounts for the aversion of scholars to those cosmologies other than that of the single world system is that materials relating to the "mathematical cosmologies" are in such great disarray, totally lacking in systematic presentation or interpretation. Therefore, it has been one of the goals of this work to focus considerable attention on the Buddhist literature and relevant secondary materials with the hope of being able to present a coherent picture of these "mathematical cosmologies." The distinction which we have established between the "*sāhasra*-cosmology" and the "*asaṅkhyeya*-cosmology" is the key to unravelling the logic of these traditions. As a result, we have found that not only can the "mathematical cosmologies" be presented in a coherent and compelling manner, but that it is precisely these mathematical and numerological cosmologies which provide the link between the single world system and the Pure Land cosmologies.

Cosmology and Classical Science

The failure to appreciate the relationship between the Buddhist cosmologies and the scientific environment in which they were conceived, i.e. the mathematical and astronomical sciences of Antiquity, has provided yet a third obstacle to meaningful interpretation. It is this shortcoming more than any other which has precluded a satisfactory understanding of the mathematical cosmologies and has caused the single world system to be regarded as essentially discontinuous with other phases of Buddhist cosmological speculation. If it is true that each of the Buddhist cosmologies is grounded in a particular scientific perception of reality, it is also true that in each case the scientific basis is interpreted for the benefit of a theological vision, and it is this relationship between science and theology which must be understood. Toward this end, we will suggest that the underlying theology of these cosmologies centers around a drama of salvation. This drama finds its expression in terms of a journey of the soul.

The contemporary Buddhist community itself has apparently felt the need to reconcile its cosmologies with some "real" basis as evidenced by a number of apologetic efforts to find the views of modern science reflected therein. In one such effort, we are told that the *cakravāla* is the equivalent of a solar system, while a "lesser chiliocosm" is equated with a galaxy, a "middle chiliocosm" with a "cluster of galaxies" and the "triple chiliocosm" with a "metagalaxy."[1] We are told further that the Buddha's vision of endless time and infinite space correctly anticipated the vision of modern science, a fact which is offered as further proof of the Buddha's omniscience.[2] The countless succession of worlds which the Buddhists posit as arising and disappearing throughout time are also said to support the anticipations of modern science that countless worlds are capable of sustaining life.[3]

> Does not science, with its ever-expanding vision of illimitable worlds, many of which may be inhabited, and its ever-lengthening time-scale, accord with the Buddhist cycle theory ? Who can longer speak of our little earth as the one and only "world" that had an absolute beginning in time ? Is it not far more likely that the history of the physical universe is endless, an infinitely long and beginningless process in which matter or energy forms achieve and lose a patterned existence over and over again; that worlds are born and die without cessation ? Such a view, says the contemporary Buddhist, is both Buddhistically and scientifically true at the same time.

The fact that the islands of the world disk do not correspond to existing continents leads to the rationalization that "perhaps some 2500 years ago in the Buddha's day the continents on earth were in different relation to each other, so that the traditional Buddhist cosmology might have been quite correct."[4] Apart from this current apologetic enthusiasm which has all but lost sight of the theological meaning of these cosmologies, no systematic effort exists which attempts to discern their scientific basis. When we see arguments such as these being taken seriously, we may wonder if the Buddhists themselves have not lost sight of the meaning of these traditions.

It is precisely because the scientific component of these cosmologies has either been completely overlooked or has been treated in the sparest manner that these cosmologies have defied orderly

1. Kullatissa Nanda Jayatilleke, "The Buddhist Conception of the Universe" in *The Message of the Buddha*, ed, Ninian Smart (London : George Allen & Unwin Ltd., 1975), pp. 93-96.
2. King, *Thousand Lives*, p. 107.
3. Ibid., pp. 110-11.
4. Ibid., p. 109.

description and meaningful interpretation. As a result, it is not only their scientific meaning which has been obscured, but their theological meaning as well. Each of these cosmologies—the motions and measurements of the *cakravāla*, the thousands of the "*sāhasra*-cosmology" and the innumerables of the "*asaṅkhyeya*-cosmology"—derives its intention from its scientific setting and can be understood only as a result of familiarity with the sciences of the day.

As we have seen, it is the mathematical cosmologies which are the key to understanding all phases of Buddhist cosmological speculation and which consequently constitute the primary concern of this book. More than the other phases, they also present the relationship between science and theology in sharpest relief. The "thousands" and "innumerables" of these cosmologies are the basis for the Buddhist critique of science, particularly the mathematical sciences of Antiquity. As we shall see, these mathematical sciences are the springboard for all the theological interpretations of the issues of time, space, measurement, mind and omniscience emerging out of these cosmologies.

While the relationship between mathematics and these cosmologies is clear, and while it is to be expected that familiarity with the mathematical sciences of the time might be of some value in understanding the materials of this research, it is an occasion for more than a little wonder that the full extent of the differences between the "*sāhasra*-cosmology" and the "*asaṅkhyeya*-cosmology" did not emerge until reading Archimedes' curious treatise "The Sand Reckoner."[1] From the outset, it was clear that this was a major clue in deciphering both the use of thousands in astronomical measurement as well as the meaning of the *asaṅkhyeya*.

Because of our use of Archimedes as well as other non-Buddhist and non-Indian materials, it should be noted that pursuit of the scientific basis of the Buddhist cosmologies has carried us deep into issues of Hellenistic culture. This has occurred partly because there is a clear commonality of concern between the cosmologies of the Hellenistic world and those of Buddhism, partly because the history of cosmological speculation is better documented in the West and partly because the relationship between science and cosmology is better understood with regard

1. See *The works of Archimedes*, ed. Thomas Little Heath (New York : Dover Publications, Inc., 1912), pp. 221-32.

to the Hellenistic materials as opposed to the Indian cosmologies. While the ability to interpret Buddhist materials using Hellenistic categories certainly implies a common cultural heritage, this work makes no effort to systematically argue for such influences, much less the direction of such influences. As a result of pursuing these connections, however, it has become apparent that the great theological and metaphysical interpretations of the movements of the planets and the starry heavens which characterize the Hellenistic cosmologies are shared by all the Indian cosmologies, not least by the Buddhist.

For the most part, all of the Classical interpretations of the heavenly motions had several basic concerns in common. Primary among these was the measurement of time based on the motions of the planets and the subsequent calculation of the beginning and end of the world. Doctrines of creation, transmigration, causality, eschatology, and the relationship of the present to the past and the future were all associated with the measurement of time provided by the movements of the planets.

In contrast to the irregular movements of the planets, the perfect, circular motion of the stars provided a brilliant example of the divine order of the cosmos. Because the stars possess motion, they are animated, i.e., they possess a soul. Because their motion is perfectly circular, their lives are eternal. Therefore, they are gods. According to Alcmaeon of Croton, man is not eternal, because, unlike the stars, he is unable to connect the end of his life to the beginning.[1] This perfect motion is thus the great teaching—of perfect divine order and of eternal life.

Since the animation of both the stars and the planets finds its expression in a great display of light, it is light which is the expression par excellence of the soul and of the teaching of the soul's immortality. Exposure to the Hellenistic materials has been instrumental in suggesting the importance of the mysticism of light which is clearly present in the Buddhist cosmologies. Many works touch on these themes of mystical light in various cultural

1. For a discussion of the figure of Alcmaeon of Croton with an emphasis on the significance of circular motion in Greek thought, see William Keith Chambers Guthrie, *A History of Greek Philosophy*, 4 vols. (Cambridge : Cambridge University Press, 1962, 1965, 1969, 1975), 1:341-59.

contexts, but none offers a richer interpretation of their significance than the writings of Henry Corbin.[1]

As we have already suggested, not only do the cosmologies of Buddhism share in these general concerns, but the key moments in the drama of salvation occur in conjunction with the great displays of light. As such, it is difficult to determine where theological cosmology ends and an outright mysticism of light commences. It is light which "fixes" the Buddhist saints in the path of enlightenment. The miraculous displays of light are also associated with the spiritualization of death and spiritualized rebirth in a pure land. As the drama of the "*asaṅkhyeya*-cosmology" makes clear, it is the unique power of the Buddha to command the extraordinary displays of light which accomplish these acts. Finally, we shall suggest that the Buddhist cosmologies contain the suggestion that man too possesses an interior light, a divine spark, a particle of light containing within it the Buddha-nature, the seed of rebirth and transformed being.

However, it is one of the curiosities of the Buddhist literature that almost no direct reference is made to any of these heavenly bodies. Moreover, the role played by the luminaries in the Buddhist materials has either gone totally unrecognized or has not been presented in any convincing manner. As a result, it is possible to state that it is one of the "discoveries" of this work that the luminaries do in fact play a significant role in these cosmologies. The role of the heavens, their association with the teaching, the images used to represent them and the scholastic dilemmas posed with regard to the limited or unlimited nature of the starry realm are all major concerns of this work.

In the most general sense, it may be said that the luminaries collectively orient man. Thus, from one perspective, the "teaching" may be regarded as an orientation.[2]

To the extent that it does involve an orientation, it is for the

1. Works by Corbin referenced in this context include *Avicenna; Terre céleste;* and *L'homme de lumière dans le soufisme iranien* (Paris : Éditions Présence, 1971).

2. For a discussion of this understanding of "oriental" philosophy, see Corbin, *Avicenna*, esp. pp. 16-17, 151-64. For a discussion of the religious significance of orientation in general, see Mircea Eliade, *The Sacred and the Profane*, trans. Willard R. Trask (New York : Harper & Brothers, 1961), passim.

purpose of a journey; a journey begun by the soul in the realm of darkness and eventuating in its return to the realm of light. Here again, the writings of Corbin and Franz Cumont[1] reveal the structures of such mystical journeys in the Hellenistic cosmologies; journeys which, as we shall see, have unmistakable Buddhist counterparts. Stated in its simplest terms, the journeys of the soul found in these Buddhist cosmologies find their expression in the stages of meditation, and as such, are related to the more general themes of ecstatic flight and mystical ascent.[2]

Every journey, of course, involves a "beyond." Buddhism, perhaps more than any other tradition is relentless in its assertion of the beyond. For Buddhism, "beyond" means ultimately "beyond the cosmos." Because "cosmos" refers to those structures of space and time which transform chaos into a "world," i.e., structures which support and sustain life, it must not be understood primarily as the physical universe, but rather as structured reality at every level, whether physical or spiritual. As such, "cosmos" is the world at every level: whether universe, village, domicile, body or soul. Moreover, the meanings of each of these levels are frequently interrelated. Thus, the body may be understood as the abode or domicile of the soul while the universe may be regarded as the body of the deity.[3] The interchangeability of

1. See Franz Cumont, *Astrology and Religion Among the Greeks and Romans* (New York : Dover Publications, Inc., 1960); idem, *After Life in Roman Paganism* (New York : Dover Publications, Inc., 1959); idem, *The Mysteries of Mithra* (New York : Dover Publications, Inc., 1956); and idem, *Oriental Religions in Roman Paganism* (New York: Dover Publications, Inc., 1956).

2. For a discussion of the significance of ecstatic flight and mystical ascent, see Mircea Eliade, *Shamanism : Archaic Techniques of Ecstasy*, trans. Willard R. Trask (New York : Pantheon Books, 1964), esp. pp. 477-82; idem, "Symbolisms of Ascension and 'Waking Dreams'," in *Myths, Dreams and Mysteries : The Encounter Between Contemporary Faiths and Archaic Realities*, trans. Philip Mairet (New York]: Harper & Row, Publishers, 1967), pp. 99-122; idem, "Briser le toit de la maison," in *Studies in Mysticism and Religion Presented to Gershom G. Scholem* (Jerusalem : Hebrew University, 1967), pp. 131-39. Themes of ascent emphasizing the significance of the "fifth direction" and the "pole mystique du nord" are found in Paul Mus, *Barabadur, esquisse d'un histoire du Bouddhisme* (Hanoi : Bulletin de l'école français d'Estrême-Orient, 1935).

3. An indication of the polyvalence of the term "cosmos" together with its religious significance can be found in Eliade, *The Sacred and the Profane*,

self and world is a commonplace of both the Hindu and Buddhist traditions. One example of this which will occupy an important place in this work is the similarity in the issues raised by the innumerables of beings, the innumerables of worlds and the innumerables of Buddhas.

Because of the radical manner in which Buddhism understands all of structured reality—whether world, domicile or self—as expressions of conditioned existence, the thrust of all Buddhist ontology is directed toward defining the precise relationship between the Buddha and the world primarily in negative terms. The focus of the Buddhist dramas of salvation, then, is to go beyond the world, realize the non-reality of the self and achieve the extinction of *nirvāṇa*. Since it is the house which is symbolic of the cosmic structures at every level, the Buddhist affirmation of the "beyond" finds its symbolic expression in the breaking of the roof of the house/body/cosmos. According to the *Nidāna-Kathā*, the Buddha, after his illumination, proclaims his victory over "the builder of houses."

> Long have I wandered, long,
> Bound by the chain of life
> Through many births,
> Seeking thus long in vain,
> The builder of the house. And pain
> Is birth again, again.
> House-maker, thou art seen !
> No more a house thou'lt make.
> Broken are all thy beams.
> Thy ridge-pole shattered !
> From things that make for life
> my mind has past :

esp. pp. 20-65; idem, *Cosmos and History*, trans. Willard R. Trask (New York : Harper & Brothers, 1959), esp. pp. 6-16; idem, *Patterns in Comparative Religion*, trans. Rosemary Sheed (Cleveland : World Publishing Co., 1963), esp. pp. 367-87. The interpenetration of the meanings of "world," "self," and "deity" in the Vedic, Upaniṣadic and Purāṇic materials are examined in the following excellent monographs : Jan Gonda, *Loka : World and Heaven in the Veda* ((Amsterdam : Noord-Hollandsche U. M., 1966), and idem, *The Meaning of the Sanskrit Term Dhāman* (Amsterdam : Noord-Hollandsche U. M., 1967).

The end of cravings has been
reached at last ![1]

The astronomical themes of motion and light are here transformed into the mytho-philosophic themes of journey and soul and integrated into a great drama of salvation. The power of mathematics which allows the astronomers to measure the motions of the heavens also enables the faithful to comprehend the theological and mystical implication of these measurements. The precise manner in which these themes are reflected in the Buddhist cosmologies will emerge in the Chapters which follow.

1. For discusstion of this theme in Buddhism together with other symbolisms of ascent and transcendence, see Eliade, "Briser." Buddhist imagery which conveys a similar sense of departure from an abode or the realm of abodes is evident when we read that an individual possessed of the 32 marks has two choices : if he remains in the house, he will become a cakravartin king; if he leaves the house, he will become a Buddha. See Lamotte, *Traité*, p. 272. The characterization of the *nirvāṇa* of the bodhisattva as "non-abiding" (*apratiṣṭhita nirvāṇa*) would appear to be the scholastic culmination of this theme of transcending all abodes. See below, Chapter IV, p. 82, n. 2; Chapter V, p. 110, n. 2.

CHAPTER II

THE *CAKRAVĀLA* OR SINGLE WORLD SYSTEM
THE MONASTIC GUIDE TO BRAHMĀ'S PURE REALM

The stars turn about Meru as in a whirlpool

The basic outlines of the single world system of the "*cakravāla*-cosmology" are generally agreed upon throughout a broad spectrum of Buddhism and are a prominent feature of the Pāli texts as well as the Buddhist Sanskrit literature. The *Mppś* and the *Kośa*, for instance, are in almost complete agreement with the details of the Pāli Canon and the Commentaries in this regard.[1] Moreover, the single, circular world system is not unique to the Buddhist traditions. It is a prominent feature of the Hindu and Jain cosmologies as well, though with many important differences in detail. In addition, it has a wide dispersion throughout the Classical world in general.[2] It is not possible to discuss all the

1. The following materials have been of use in reconstructing the outlines of the "*cakravāla*-cosmology" : Willibald Kirfel, *Die Kosmographie der Inder* (Bonn : K. Schroeder, 1920), pp. 178-207; Étienne Lamotte, *Histoire du bouddhisme indien* (Louvain : Bibliothèque du Muséon, 1958), pp. 34-36; Lamotte, *Traité*; Louis de La Vallée Poussin, "Ages of the World (Buddhist)," *ERE*, 1 : 187-90; idem, "Cosmogony"; idem, *Kośa*, esp. chap. iii, pp. 138-217; idem, "Vasubandhu et Yaçomitra; Troisième Chapitre de l'Abhidharmakoca : Kārikā, Bhāṣya et Vyākhyā; Avec une analyse de la Lokaprajñapti et de la Kāraṇaprajñapti de Maudgalyāyana," *Mémoires de l'académie royale de Belgique*, 2e sér, Tome 6, Fasicule II (January 1919); and McGovern, *Manual*. Thai sources for reconstructing the *cakkavāla* cosmology include : George Coedes, "The Traibhumika Buddhist Cosmology and Treaty [sic] on Ethics," *East and West* 7 (June, 1957) : 344-52 ; and George Coedes and Charles Archaimbault, *Les trois mondes* (*Traibhumī Brah R'van*) (Paris : Publications de l'école français d'Extrême-Orient, 1973). A Japanese resource includes Genshin's *Ōjōyōshū* or "Teaching Essential for Rebirth" whose early chapters include much detail on the heavens and hells of this world. See August Karl Reischauer, "Genshin's Ojo Yoshu : Collected Essays on Birth into Paradise," *Transactions of the Asiatic Society of Japan*, 2d series 7 (1930) : 16-98.

2. See Kirfel, *Kosmographie*, pp. 28*-36*; Duhem, *Système*, passim., esp. volumes 1 and 2. The idea of a single circular world system is also clearly

instances of its occurrence, though reference will be made to a variety of non-Indian uses in the course of this dissertation for purposes of illustration and comparison.

The richness of detail contained in the "*cakravāla*-cosmology" places any comprehensive treatment beyond the reach of this work. Moreover, the different positions which these. structures occupy in the Pāli and Sanskrit texts suggest substantially different views of its place in these two traditions. Stated briefly, it appears that the Pāli *cakkavāla* is intended as a more or less practical guide to the *bhikku* in his meditations, while the Sanskrit *cakravāla* is part of a more self-consciously speculative system. While the basic structure of the *cakravāla* is the same in both traditions, certain discrepancies in detail do occur. Since it is not our goal to record all the variations in the detail of the *cakravāla* but rather to provide an overview of its basic structure and imagery, we will restrict ourselves to the testimony of the *Kośa.*

The *cakravāla* is represented as a disk ringed with a series of seven circular, golden mountain ranges. These mountain ranges are arranged concentrically with Mt. Meru at the center[1] and the *cakravāla* wall of iron at the perimeter. Proceeding outward from the center, the mountains are known as Meru, Yugandhara, Īṣadhāra, Khadirıka, Sudarśana, Aśvakarṇa, Vinataka,. Nimindhara and Cakravāla.[2] Mt. Meru has a height of 80,000 yojanas and each of the mountain ranges is one-half the height of the preceding range. All of the mountains except the *cakravāla* ring are excrescences of the golden earth. The *cakravāla* ring is made of iron.[3] The waters of the various seas (*sītā*) fill the regions

reflected in the calculations of Archimedes and Aristarchus of Samos (see below, Chapter VI) and in Plato's "Myth of Er" (see below, p. 46, n. 3).

1. Disagreements regarding the size and shape of Mt. Meru can be found in Kirfel, *Kosmographie*, pp. 15*, 16*-17*, 187, and LaVallée Poussin, *Kośa*, chap. iii, pp. 143, 161, n. 3. A Buddhist representation of Mt. Meru shaped as the seed vessel of a lotus can be found in Alicia Matsunaga, *The Buddhist Philosophy of Assimilation* (Tokyo : Charles E. Tuttle Co., 1969), p. 39.

2. Variations on this sequence can be found in Kirfel, *Kosmographie*, p. 186. A completely different tradition regarding the names of the ring mountains is found in the *Lotus Sūtra* and is discussed in Lamotte, *Enseignement*, p. 104, n. 41.

3. La Vallée Poussin, *Kośa*, chap. iii, p. 142.

between the mountain ranges. The mountains penetrate these waters in an extent equal to their height. These *sītā* are possessed of the following eight qualities : cold, clear, swiftly flowing, pleasant to the taste, fresh, inoffensive in smell, offensive to neither the throat nor the stomach.[1]

The inhabited land masses are situated in the great ocean (*mahāsamudra*) which flows about the seventh mountain range. The four land masses located at the points of the compass are spoken of as islands (*dvīpa*), and are known as Pūrvavideha in the East (Eastern Videha), Jambudvīpa in the South, named after the Jambu tree which is found there, Aparagodānīya in the West (Western Pasturage) and Uttarakuru in the North (Northern Kuru-land).

All of this rests on a layer of golden earth (*kāñcanamayībhūmi*), a substance whose significance is elusive but whose importance cannot be doubted. As noted, all of the mountains of the *cakravāla* are composed of excrescences of this golden earth with the exception of the *cakravāla* wall which is said to be made of iron. While the islands do not appear to be composed of the golden earth, the "diamond throne" (*vajrāsana*) situated in the middle of Jambudvīpa is said to rest on the golden earth.[2] The Hindu cosmologies found chiefly in the Purāṇas apparently invert these images by stating that the *lokāloka* mountain which surrounds the circular world is composed of the golden earth. No ring mountains are to be found in the Purāṇas, although a series of seven ring islands occur in their place.[3]

1. Ibid., p. 144, 144, n. 3. Other bodies of water also possess the eight qualities, including lake Anavatapta, the rivers flowing therefrom and the lakes of Sukhāvatī. According to Orphic doctrine, the soul, upon dying, goes to Hades where it is given the following instructions. "Thou shalt find to the left of the house of Hades a spring, and by the side of it standing a white cypress. To this spring approach not near. But thou shalt find another, from the lake of Memory flowing forth, and there are guardians before it. Say, 'I am a child of Earth and starry Heaven. This ye know yourselves. But I am parched with thirst and I perish. Give me quickly the cold water flowing forth from the lake of Memory.' And of themselves they will give thee to drink from the holy spring, and thereafter among the other heroes thou shalt have lordship." William Keith Chambers Guthrie, *The Greek and Their Gods* (Boston : Beacon Press, 1955), p. 322.

2. LaVallée Poussin, *Kośa*, chap. iii, p. 145, n. 4.

3. Kirfel, *Kosmographie*, pp. 57-127.

The golden earth of the *cakravāla* rests in turn on a circle of water (*ābmaṇḍala*). The layer of water is represented as being 1,120,000 yojanas in thickness. However, as a result of the churning of this layer of water (presumably by the wind) causing it to foam, the upper 320,000 yojanas are transformed into golden earth.[1] The layer of wind (*vāyumaṇḍala*) supports the water and in turn rests on empty space.

The wind in turn is endowed with specific and unique properties. According to the Buddhists, the seed (*bīja*) of the new universe is the wind, a wind endowed with special agencies which have their principle in the acts of beings. The "instrumental cause" (*nimitta*) of this wind is the wind of the Rūpadhātu.[2] Presumably the winds of the Rūpadhātu are those which create the heavenly bodies :

> The winds which create (*nirma*) the moon, sun and the stars in the sky (*antarikṣe*) are produced by the collective force of the actions of beings. All the stars turn about Meru as though caught in a whirlpool.[3]

We read further that the waters which fall on the earth have many potentialities and that when they disappear, they are replaced by jewels. The waters are thus regarded as the cause and the jewels as the effect. The gold, silver, jewels and the earth formed in this manner are united and put into a heap by the winds which are produced by the force of acts. As a result, they come to constitute the mountains and the continents.[4] This sequence of events is understood to be in contrast to the Sāṅkhya School within Hinduism which maintains that the world is created as the result of the transformation of a primordial substance.[5]

The four islands of the *cakravāla* are distinguished from each other in a number of ways; particularly with regard to the size, shape and duration of life of their inhabitants. Uttarakuru is square, measuring 2,000 yojanas on a side, and life there has a duration of 1,000 years. (Avara) Godānīya is shaped like a

1. LaVallée Poussin, *Kośa*, chap. iii, p. 140.
2. Ibid., p. 210.
3. Ibid., p. 156.
4. La variété de monde nait de l'acte. Ibid., chap. iv, p. 1.
5. Ibid., chap. iii, p. 143. Elsewhere, in discussing the atomic nature of the material world, we are told that it is the wind which agglomerates the atoms and holds them together. Ibid., chap. i, pp. 89-94.

full-moon measuring 7,500 yojanas around with a diameter of 2,500 yojanas and life there is equal to 500 years. Pūrvavideha has the shape of a half-moon with three sides said to be 2,000 yojanas in length and a fourth which is 350 yojanas in length. Duration of life there is equal to 250 years. Jambudvīpa too measures 2,000 yojanas on three sides, but its fourth side is only 3-1/2 yojanas long. It is said to be shaped like a chariot.[1] Jambudvīpa provides an important exception to the super-human and unchanging durations of life found in the other islands. The length of human life in Jambudvīpa at the beginning of the Kalpa is incalculable, but diminishes to only ten years by the end of the Kalpa, a fact whose significance is explored more fully in Chapters III and IV. Suffice it to say that because of these irregular life expectancies, resembling in many ways doctrines associated with the *yugas* in the Purāṇic materials, the inhabitants of Jambudvīpa are particularly aware of the workings of karma. It is only in Jambudvīpa during a time of declining life that a Buddha will appear.[2] In addition to the four main islands,

1. Ibid., chap. iii, p. 145.

2. Clearly, Jambudvīpa resembles Bhārata in the later Brāhmaṇic period. According to Kirfel : "Alle Texte stimmen darin überein, dass in den acht Landschaften ausser Bhārata keine yugāvasthā, Abstufung der Zeitalter sei, also nur das Krtayuga, das goldene Zeitalter, herrsche, wahrend in Bhārata das Krta-, Treta-, Dvāpara- und Kali-yuga einander folgen. Bhārata ist also eine karmabhūmi, d.h. hier allein wirkt das aus den Handlungen resultierende karman · · · während die Wesen in allen übrigen Landschaften und auch die andern Kontinenten ein Göttergleiches Leben führen. Infolgedessen heissen diese Landschaften und Kontinenten bhogabhūmi,' Länder des Genusses.' Weil aber in Bhārata eine Erlösung aus dem Kreislauf des Samsāra möglich ist, word es das beste unter allen Ländern genannt." Kirfel, *Kosmographie*, p. 58. The cosmological distinction between *karmabhūmi* and *bhogabhūmi* is an important one and is not restricted to the islands of the world disk. The distinction between pure and impure lands involves similar considerations, though with important differences as well. A pure land, in the last analysis, is one in which karmic reality has been suppressed or otherwise overcome by the presence of a Buddha or the Buddha-nature. While the Pure Land sects of China and Japan stress the unique place of Sukhāvatī in affording access to salvation, Sukhāvatī does not occupy a prominent place in the *Śāstra*. For the *Mppś* it is only in an "impure" or "mixed" land such as Sahā that the *prajñā* and *upāya* of the bodhisattvas is uncommonly sharp. See Lamotte, *Traité*, pp. 572ff. Moreover, it is only in Sahā that the bodhisattvas multiply the artifices of salvation (*upāya*). See Lamotte, *Traité*,

the *Kośa* recognizes eight intermediate islands, two of which are similar in shape, though smaller, to each of the four main islands.[1] The shape of the faces of the inhabitants of each of the islands is said to resemble the shape of the island.

Moving north in Jumbudvīpa, one encounters three mountains in the shape of ant-hills, then three more, a third set of three and finally Mt. Himavat. Beyond Himavat, but this side of Gandhamādana, there is the lake Anavatapta whence issue the four great rivers—Gaṅgā, Sindhu, Vakṣu, and Sītā.[2] The waters of Anavatapta are also endowed with the eight qualities. Only men possessed of the miraculous powers are able to go there.[3] Near the lake is the Jambu tree. Our continent receives its name either from the tree or its fruit which is also known as Jambu.[4]

As already noted, the "diamond throne" (*vajrāsana*) is directly in the middle of Jambudvīpa. It is here that the bodhisattva sits in order to become *arhat* and Buddha.[5] Another distinguishing feature of Jambudvīpa is that all the hells are situated beneath this island. The *Kośa* distinguishes eight hot hells and eight cold hells.[6]

Finally, a number of scattered references are made to various attributes of Jambudvīpa. It is only the men of Jambudvīpa who break or destroy the roots of good.[7] The beings of Jambudvīpa,

p. 575. Clearly Sahā shares many of the attributes of Bhārata, although this is not due to the *yugāvasthā*, but rather to the skills of the bodhisattvas.

For a clear statement that the length of human life is regulated by the positions of the planets, see al-Biruni, *The Chronology of Ancient Nations*, trans. Dr. C. Edward Sachau (Frankfurt : Minerva GMBH, 1969) pp 90-92, 94-98.

1. LaVallée Poussin, *Kośa*, chap. iii, p. 146.
2. Ibid., p. 147.
3. Ibid., p. 148.
4. Ibid.
5. Ibid., p. 145. The bodhisattva sits on the *vajrāsana* to realize the *vajropamasamādhi* in order to become *arhat* and Buddha (ibid., chap. iv, p. 231, n. 1). There are many types of *vajropamasamādhi* (ibid., pp. 227-29). The *vajropamasamādhi* belongs to the fourth dhyāna (ibid., chap. viii, p. 195). A broad spectrum of throne symbolism is examined in Jeannine Auboyer, *Le trône et son symbolisme dans l'Inde ancienne* (Paris : Presses Universitaires de France, 1949).
6. La Vallée Poussin, *Kośa*, chap. iii, pp. 148-56.
7. Ibid., p. 145.

Pūrvavideha and Avaragodānīya possess eight organs.[1] The rupture of the wheel occurs in Jambudvīpa.[2] According to the *Kośa*, the marks are produced in Jambudvīpa.[3] In the *Mppś*, on the other hand, there is a debate regarding whether the bodhisattva develops the marks (i.e. the thirty two marks of a mahāpuruṣa) only in Jambudvīpa or in Avaragodānīya and Pūrvavideha as well. The Sarvāstivādin position is the former while the Mahāyānists embrace the latter position.[4]

In its vertical dimensions, we find a series of heavens superimposed one upon another beginning at the level of Mt. Meru and extending upward to the farthestmost point of the universe. These heavens are arranged in three great divisions : (1) those belonging to the six classes of the gods of desire (*kāmadeva*) belong to the realm of desire (*kāmadhātu*) which includes the mountains and the waters of the *cakravāla* together with the five classes (*gatis*) of beings (*sattva*) of the Kāmadhātu; (2) those seventeen heavens belonging to the realm of form (*rūpadhātu*) which are grouped into four classes of meditation realms (*dhyāna*); and (3) the four "infinities" of the realm of non-form (*ārūpya-dhātu*).

Two classes of gods dwell on Mt. Meru; the Caturmahārāja-kāyika and the Trāyastriṃśa. Four classes of Caturmahārāja-kāyika gods inhabit the four terraces (*pariṣaṇḍa*) extending half-way up Meru. The Caturmahārājakāyikas are the most numerous among the gods and also inhabit the palaces (*vimāna*) of the sun, moon and stars.[5] The ruler of the Trāyastriṃśa is Indra or Śakra whose abode rests atop Mt. Meru. The Tuṣita heaven is the fourth of the heavens of the Kāmadeva. It is distinguished by the fact that it is in the Tuṣita that the bodhisattva is born immediately prior to being born as a Buddha in Jambudvīpa. We are also informed that the duration of life in the Tuṣita corresponds to the ages in which a Buddha appears.[6]

While all seventeen heavens of the Rūpadhātu are known collectively as the Brahmaloka, the precise abode of the great

1. Ibid., chap. iv, p. 174.
2. Ibid., pp. 210f.
3. Ibid., p. 223.
4. Lamotte, *Traité*, pp. 249, 294-96.
5. La Vallée Poussin, *Kośa*, chap. iii, p. 159.
6. Lamotte, *Traité*, p. 268, 268, n. 1.

god Brahmā is an occasion for debate as well. The concensus of the *Kośa* is that Brahmā resides in the Brahma-purohita heaven, protected by his belvidere.[1] The gods superior to the Trāyastriṃśa reside in aerial-palaces (*vimāna*).[2] The five uppermost of these seventeen heavens are known collectively as the abodes of the pure ones (*śuddhāvāsika*). The uppermost of these is the Akaniṣṭha.[3] The Akaniṣṭha is the place of *nirvāṇa*. Once the *arhat* detaches himself from the Akaniṣṭha abode by practicing the *vajropamasamādhi*, he may pass into extinction upon dying.

In addition to the heavens of the Kāmadhātu and the Rūpadhātu, there are also the four infinities of the Ārūpyadhātu. The *Kośa* is quite emphatic that these are not abodes : "there are no abodes above the Akaniṣṭha."[4] Moreover, one cannot be reborn in the *ārūpyas* as such. If the *śrāvaka*, as a result of his concentrations achieves the second "infinity" while in the third *dhyāna*, he will be reborn in the third *dhyāna* in possession of the second "infinity."[5] Despite the fact that the infinities are not "above" the *dhyāna* realms, the fourth infinity is nevertheless designated as the *bhavāgra* or pinnacle of being. The *Kośa* makes the following additional distinction : the saint who obtains *nirvāṇa* at the *bhavāgra* is consecrated to concentration while the saint obtaining it in the Akaniṣṭha is consecrated to vision.[6]

All the various divisions of the vertical cosmology are interpreted in terms of the progress of the saint as he pursues the path of liberation. As such, it is further divided into nine successive stations of meditation (*navānupūrvavihāra*), corresponding to the nine spheres of existence, i.e., Kāmadhātu, the four *dhyānas* of the Rūpadhātu and the four *samāpattis* of the Ārūpyadhātu.[7]

1. La Vallée Poussin, *Kośa*, chap. iii, pp. 4, 18.
2. Ibid., p. 164.
3. Ibid., chap vi, p. 213.
4. Ibid., chap. iii, p. 4. Au-dessus des Akaniṣṭhas, il n'y a plus des residences (*sthāna*), Ibid., p. 168.
5. With regard to the Ārūpyadhātu, the *Kośa* states : "Cette sphère d'existence n'est pas située au-dessus du Rūpadhātu; mais on dit qu'elle est au-dessus parce qu'elle est supérieure au Rūpadhātu au point de vue de recueillement." Ibid., chap. ii, pp. 132-33.
6. Ibid., chap. vi, p. 214.
7. Lamotte, "Marche," pp. 18, 21.

The accompanying exhibits show the world disk and a horizontal cross-section representing Mt. Meru, seven rings of mountain ranges and the *cakkavāla* ring. These drawings are reconstructions from the Pāli Abhidhamma.[1] A series of additional exhibits reveal the richness and detail of the vertical portions of the "*cakravāla*-cosmology." The details presented are taken from the *Abhidharmakośa*.

1. This diagram of the *cakkavāla* is reproduced from Daniel John Gogerley, *Ceylon Buddhism* (London : Kegan Paul, Trench, Trubner & Co., Ltd., 1908).

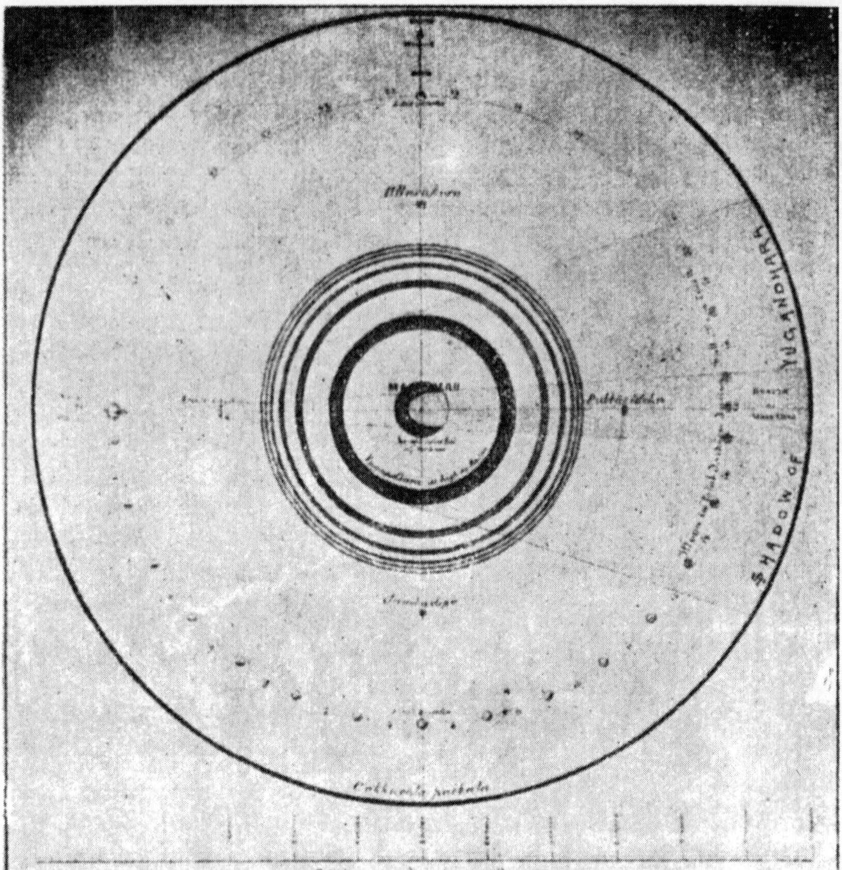

Fig. 1.—The Cakkavāla

- III. Ārūpya-dhātu — Caturārūpya Brahmaloka
  - IV. Naivasañjñānāsañjñā
  - III. Ākiñcanya
  - II. Vijñānānantya
  - I. Ākāśānantya
- II. Rūpadhātu — Brahmaloka
  - IVth Dhyāna
    - 8. Akaniṣṭha (Śuddhāvāsika)
    - 7. Sudarśana (Śuddhāvāsika)
    - 6. Sudṛśa (Śuddhāvāsika)
    - 5. Atapa (Śuddhāvāsika)
    - 4. Avṛha (Śuddhāvāsika)
    - 3. Bṛhatphala
    - 2. Puṇyapraveśa
    - 1. Anabhraka
  - IIIrd Dhyāna
    - 3. Śubhakṛtsna
    - 2. Apramāṇaśubha
    - 1. Parīttaśubha
  - IInd Dhyāna
    - 3. Ābhāsvara
    - 2. Apramāṇābha
    - 1. Parīttābha
  - Ist Dhyāna
    - 3. Mahābrahma
    - 2. Brahmapurohita
    - 1. Brahmakāyika
- I. Kāmadhātu
  - 5. Kāmadeva
    - 6. Paranirmitavaśavartin (Devaloka)
    - 5. Nirmāṇarati (Devaloka)
    - 4. Tuṣita (Devaloka)
    - 3. Yāma (Devaloka)
    - 2. Trāyastriṃśa (Meru) (Devaloka)
    - 1. Caturmahārājakāyika (Meru)
      - —Sadāmattas (Meru)
      - —Mālādharas (Meru)
      - —Karoṭapāṇis (Meru)
  - 4. Manuṣya
  - 3. Preta
  - 2. Tiryagyoni
  - 1. Naraka

Kāñcanamayībhūmi
Ābmaṇḍala
Vāyumaṇḍala
Ākāśa

Fig. 2.—The Vertical Cosmology[1]

1. This chart is a composite of information presented in Lamotte, *Histoire*, p. 35; idem, *Traité*, pp. 434, 434, n. 2, 435, 435, n. 2, 1264, n. 2; La Vallée Poussin, *Kośa*, chap. iii, pp. 138 ff. For a description of the mythologies associated with these heavens, see La Vallée Poussin, *Kośa*, chap. iii, pp. 159-69; Lamotte, *Traité*, pp. 604-16; Kirfel, *Kosmographie*, pp. 195-98. For the mythologies of the hells not shown here, see La Vallée Poussin, *Kośa*, chap. iii, pp. 148-56; Lamotte, *Traité*, pp. 951-68; Kirfel, *Kosmographie*, pp. 199-206. For variations in the names and numbers of these heavens, see La Vallée Poussin, *Kośa*, chap. iii, pp. 2, n. 5, 3, n. 1 and Kirfel, *Kosmographie*, pp. 190-95. For materials relating to the class of beings known as *yakṣas*, see Ananda K. Coomaraswamy, *Yakṣas* (Washington, D.C. : Freer Gallery of Art, 1931). For traditions which include the Asuras among the *gatis*, see Paul Mus, *La lumière sur les six voies* (Paris : Institut d'ethnologie, 1939). For an outline of the meditations culminating in arhatship of which this cosmography is the "path," see below, Chapter IV.

- **III. Realm of Non-Form**
  - IV. Neither Consciousness nor Not-Consciousness
  - III. Realm of Nothingness
  - II. Infinity of Intellect
  - I. Infinity of Space
- **II. Realm of Form**
  - IVth Meditation
    - Abodes of the Pure Ones:
      - 8. Not Youngest
      - 7. Well-Seeing
      - 6. Beautiful
      - 5. No Heat
      - 4. Effortless
    - 3. Abundant Fruit
    - 2. Merit-Born or Merit -Begetting
    - 1. Cloudless
  - IIIrd Meditation
    - 3. Complete Beauty
    - 2. Immeasurable Beauty
    - 1. Limited Beauty
  - IInd Meditation
    - 3. Radiant Gods
    - 2. Immeasurable Splendor
    - 1. Limited Splendor
  - Ist Meditation
    - 3. Great Brahmās
    - 2. Brahmā-priests
    - 1. Retinue of Brahmā
- **I. Realm of Desire**
  - 5. Gods of Desire
    - 6. Rulers over Things Created by Others
    - 5. Those Who Have Their Pleasure in Creation
    - 4. Blissful Gods
    - 3. Yāma
    - 2. Gods Who Have the Thirty-Three at Their Head
    - 1. Four Great Kings
      - —Always Drunk
      - —Bearing Garlands
      - —Bowl in Hand
  - 4. Mankind
  - 3. Ghosts (Abode is Yama; below Meru; not to be confused with Yāma)
  - 2. Animals (Special Abode is the Exterior Ocean)
  - 1. Damned (Abodes are the Hells)

Golden Earth
Circle of Water
Circle of Wind
Space

Fig. 3.—The Vertical Cosmology

Dhātu	Division	Heaven	Extent
III. Ārūpyadhātu		IV. Naivasañjñānāsañjñā	
		III. Ākiñcanya	
		II. Vijñānānantya	
		I. Ākāśānantya	
II. Rūpadhātu	IVth Dhyāna	8. Akaniṣṭha	
		7. Sudarśana	
		6. Sudṛśa	
		5. Atapa	
		4. Avṛha	1,000×1,000×1,000 worlds
		3. Bṛhatphala	
		2. Puṇyapraveśa	
		1. Anabhraka	
	IIIrd Dhyāna	3. Śubhakṛtsna	
		2. Apramāṇaśubha	1,000×1,000 worlds
		1. Parīttaśubha	
	IInd Dhyāna	3. Ābhāsvara	
		2. Apramāṇābha	1,000 worlds
		1. Parīttābha	
	Ist Dhyāna	3. Mahābrahma	
		2. Brahmapurohita	4 island universe
		1. Brahmakāyika	
I. Kāmadhātu	5. Kāmadeva	6. Paranirmitavaśavartin	80,000 yojanas
		5. Nirmāṇarati	80,000 yojanas
		4. Tuṣita	80,000 yojanas
		3. Yāma	80,000 yojanas
		2. Trāyastriṃśa (Meru)	80,000 yojanas
		1. Caturmahārājakāyika (Meru)—4th pariṣaṇḍā	16,000 yojanas
		Sadāmattas (Meru)—3rd Pariṣaṇḍā	8,000 yojanas
		Mālādharas (Meru)—2nd pariṣaṇḍā	4,000 yojanas
		Karoṭapāṇis (Meru)—1st pariṣaṇḍā	2,000 yojanas
	4. Manuṣya		
	3. Preta		
	2. Tiryagyoni		
	1. Naraka		
		Kāñcanamayībhūmi	1,203,450 yojanas
		Ābmaṇḍala	1,203,450 yojanas
		Vāyumaṇḍala	without measure
		Ākāśa	

Fig. 4.—The Universe in Lateral Expanse (A)[1]

1. La Vallée Poussin, *Kośa*, chap. iii, pp. 138-41, 159-60, 169; problems ibid., p. 145, n. 1.

Dhātu	Division	Heaven	Measure
III. Ārūpyadhātu		IV. Naivasañjñānāsañjñā	
		III. Ākiñcanya	
		II. Vijñānānantya	
		I. Ākāśānantya	
II. Rūpadhātu	IVth Dhyāna	8. Akaniṣṭha	
		7. Sudarśana	
		6. Sudṛśa	
		5. Atapa	
		4. Avṛha	without measure
		3. Bṛhatphala	
		2. Puṇyapraveśa	
		1. Anabhraka	
	IIIrd Dhyāna	3. Śubhakṛtsna	
		2. Apramāṇaśubha	1,000 x1,000 x1,000 worlds
		1. Parīttaśubha	
	IInd Dhyāna	3. Ābhāsvara	
		2. Apramāṇābha	1,000 x1,000 worlds
		1. Parīttābha	
	Ist Dhyāna	3. Mahābrahma	
		2. Brahmapurohita	1,000 worlds
		1. Brahmakāyika	
I. Kāmadhātu	5. Kāmadeva	6. Paranirmitavaśavartin	1,280,000 yoganas
		5. Nirmāṇarati	640,000 yojanas
		4. Tuṣita	320,000 yojanas
		3. Yāma	160,000 yojanas
		2. Trāyastriṃśa (Meru)	80,000 yojanas
		1. Caturmahārājakāyika (Meru)—4th pariṣaṇḍā	16,000 yojanas
		Sadāmattas (Meru)—3rd pariṣaṇḍā	8,000 yojanas
		Mālādharas (Meru)—2nd pariṣaṇḍā	4,000 yojanas
		Karoṭapāṇis (Meru)—1st pariṣaṇḍā	2,000 yojanas
	4. Manuṣya		
	3. Preta		
	2. Tiryagyoni		
	1. Naraka		

Kāñcanamayībhūmi	1,203,450 yojanas
Ābmaṇḍala	1,203,450 yojanas
Vāyumaṇḍala	without measure
Ākāśa	

Fig. 5.—The Universe in Lateral Expanse (B)[1]

1. Ibid.

Dhātu	Division	Realm	Duration of life
III. Ārūpyadhātu		IV. Naivasañjñānāsañjñā	80,000 kalpa
		III. Ākiñcanya	60,000 kalpa
		II. Vijñānānantya	40,000 kalpa
		I. Ākāśānantya	20,000 kalpa
II. Rūpadhātu	IVth Dhyāna	8. Akaniṣṭha	16,000 kalpa
		7. Sudarśana	8,000 kalpa
		6. Sudṛśa	4,000 kalpa
		5. Atapa	2,000 kalpa
		4. Avṛha	1,000 kalpa
		3. Bṛhatphala	500 kalpa
		2. Puṇyapraveśa	250 kalpa
		1. Anabhraka	125 kalpa
	IIIrd Dhyāna	3. Śubhakṛtsna	64 kalpa
		2. Apramāṇaśubha	32 kalpa
		1. Parīttaśubha	16 kalpa
	IInd Dhyāna	3. Ābhasvara	8 kalpa
		2. Apramāṇābha	4 kalpa
		1. Parīttābha	2 kalpa
	Ist Dhyāna	3. Mahābrahma	1 kalpa
		2. Brahmapurohita	1/2 kalpa
		1. Brahmakāyika	1/4 kalpa
I. Kāmadhātu	5. Kāmadeva	6. Paranirmitavaśavartin	* 16,000 yrs. day.. =1,600 yrs.
		5. Nirmāṇarati	* 8,000 yrs. day = 800 yrs.
		4. Tuṣita	* 4,000 yrs. day = 400 yrs.
		3. Yāma	* 2,000 yrs. day = 200 yrs.
		2. Trāyastriṃśa (Meru)	* 1,000 yrs. day = 100 yrs.
		1. Caturmahārajakāyika (Meru)	* 500 yrs. day = 50 yrs.
	4. Manṣuya		(Kuru-1,000 yrs.; Godānīya-500 yrs.; Videha-250 yrs.; Jambudvīpa — varies)
	3. Preta		500 yrs. day=1 month
	2. Tiryagyoni		1 antarakalpa maximum
	1. Naraka		varies accorcing to ḥell

Kāñcanamayībhūmi
Ābmaṇḍala
Vāyumaṇḍala
Ākāśa

Fig. 6.—The Durations of Life[1]

*Each of the divine years shown in the left-hand column consists of days which are equivalent in duration to the number of human years shown in the right-hand column. 360 such days make up a divine year.

1. Ibid., pp. 171-74.

Dhātu	Division	Realm	Height
III. Ārūpyadhātu		IV. Naivasañjñānāsañjñā	
		III. Ākiñcanya	
		II. Vijñānānantya	
		I. Ākāśānantya	
II. Rūpadhātu	IVth Dhyāna	8. Akaniṣṭha	16,000 yojanas
		7. Sudarśana	8,000 yojanas
		6. Sudṛśa	4,000 yojanas
		5. Atapa	2,000 yojanas
		4. Avrha	1,000 yojanas
		3. Bṛhatphala	500 yojanas
		2. Puṇyapraveśa	250 yojanas
		1. Anabhraka	125 yojanas
	IIIrd Dhyāna	3. Śubhakṛtsna	64 yojanas
		2. Apramāṇaśubha	32 yojanas
		1. Parīttaśubha	16 yojanas
	IInd Dhyāna	3. Ābhāsvara	8 yojanas
		2. Apramāṇābha	4 yojanas
		1. Parīttābha	2 yojanas
	Ist Dhyāna	3. Mahābrahma	1-1/2 yojanas
		2. Brahmapurohita	1 yojana
		1. Brahmakāyika	1/2 yojana
I. Kāmadhātu	5. Kāmadeva	6. Paranirmitavaśavartin	1-1/2 krośa
		5. Nirmāṇaratī	1-1/4 krośa
		4. Tuṣita	1 krośa
		3. Yāma	3/4 krośa
		2. Trāyastriṃśa (Meru)	1/2 krośa
		1. Caturmahārājakāyika (Meru)	1/4 krośa
	4. Manuṣya	(Kuru-28 hasta; Godānīya-14 hasta; Videha-7 hasta; Jambudvīpa-3-1/2 hasta)	
	3. Preta		
	2. Tiryagyoni		
	1. Naraka		

Kāñcanamayībhūmi
Ābmaṇḍala
Vāyumaṇḍala
Ākāśa

Fig. 7.—The Height of Beings[1]

1. Ibid., pp. 170-71.

Dhātu	Division	Abode	Height
III. Ārūpyadhātu		IV. Naivasañjñānāsañjñā	
		III. Ākiñcanya	
		II. Vijñānānantya	
		I. Ākāśānantya	
		No Abodes Above Akaniṣṭha	
II. Rūpadhātu	IVth Dhyāna	8. Akaniṣṭha	4,194,304 x 40,000 yojanas
		7. Sudarśana	2,099,152 x 40,000 yojanas
		6. Sudṛśa	1,048,576 x 40,000 yojanas
		5. Atapa	524,288 x 40,000 yojansa
		4. Avṛha	262,144 x 40,000 yojanas
		3. Bṛhatphala	131,072 x 40,000 yojanas
		2. Puṇyapraveśa	65,136 x 40,000 yojanas
		1. Anabhraka	32,768 x 40,000 yojanas
	IIIrd Dhyāna	3. Śubhakṛtsna	16384 x 40,000 yojanas
		2. Apramāṇaśubha	8192 x 40,000 yojanas
		1. Parīttaśubha	4096 x 40,000 yojanas
	IInd Dhyāna	3. Ābhāsvara	2048 x 40,000 yojanas
		2. Apramāṇābha	2024 x 40,000 yojanas
		1. Parīttābha	512 x 40,000 yojanas
	Ist Dhyāna	3. Mahābrahma	256 x 40,000 yojanas
		2. Brahmapurohita	128 x 40,000 yojanas
		1. Brahmakāyika	64 x 40,000 yojanas
I. Kāmadhātu	5. Kāmadeva	6. Paranirmitavaśavartin	32 x 40,000 yojanas
		5. Nirmāṇarati	16 x 40,000 yojanas
		4. Tuṣita	8 x 40,000 yojanas
		3. Yāma	4 x 40,000 yojanas
		2. Trāyastriṃśa (Meru)	2 x 40,000 yojanas
		1. Caturmahārājakāyika (Meru)	40,000 yojanas
	4. Manuṣya		
	3. Preta		
	2. Tiryagyoni		
	1. Naraka		

Kāñcanamayībhūmi	320,000	1,120,000 yojanas
Ābmaṇḍala	800,000	
Vāyumaṇḍala		1,600,000 yojanas
Ākāśa		

Fig. 8.—Vertical Dimensions[1]

1. Ibid., pp. 140, 167-68.

Basic Images

Most accounts of the *cakravāla* include these details with some variation. However, as noted in the Introduction, the details of the *cakravāla* provided by modern scholars are largely uninterpreted. And it is here that the problems begin with the *cakravāla* and indeed with all the Indian cosmologies. In the midst of this mass of names, measurements and descriptions, it is impossible to know where to focus. As stated in the Introduction, it has been the study of the mathematical cosmologies which has provided the major insights into the full spectrum of Buddhist cosmological speculation. Therefore, in order to grasp the general intention of the single world system, it is necessary to begin with certain assumptions which suggest themselves as a result of having worked with all the materials of this study.

As we have seen, the *cakravāla* is composed of a relatively limited number of images. Among these images we find : (1) islands, (2) mountains of various types—Meru, ring, *cakravāla* and the ant-hill mountains of Jambudvīpa, (3) jewels and precious substances, (4) various types of waters—circle of water (*ābmaṇḍala*), seas (*sītā*), great ocean (*mahāsamudra*), lakes and rivers, (5) wind and perhaps space and finally (6) trees and other plant life, notably lotuses and their corresponding fruit, e.g., Jambu tree and the fruit of the same name from which Jambudvīpa takes its name. This list of images substantially exhausts the cosmographic features of the *cakravāla*. Without going into detail we find that they constitute the basic images of the other Indian cosmographies as well. In some cases, we may add the countries, regions ór climes into which the land masses are sometimes divided. There is no doubt that each of these images has a precise significance as does the size, number, location and sequence of each of them. As we have already noted, ring islands in the Purāṇas are juxtaposed to ring mountains in the "*cakravāla*-cosmology." The Buddhist texts state that all the mountains except the *cakravāla* mountain are made of the golden earth while the Purāṇas stress that the *lokāloka* mountain which surrounds the Purāṇic cosmos is made of golden earth which only those with special powers may approach without danger. The islands of the *cakravāla* are regarded as floating. While Jambudvīpa is not a mountain, it nevertheless has some qualities of a mountain, e.g., only those with miraculous powers may pass to the region beyond Himavat. Whatever the full implications of this discussion involving floating islands, golden earth, mountains and magical powers, its traces appear as far away as P'eng-lai, the Taoist isle of immortality, which we are told, is a floating mountain.[1]

The jewels of the *cakravāla* are found in the heavens where we might expect to find them. We are also told that the gods reside in jewel-palaces. Jewels are not restricted to the heavens, however. Mountains are said to be filled with jewels.[2] Finally, we also find jewels in the great ocean (*mahāsamudra*), a substance which we would think totally devoid of celestial significance. The imagery of the jewels carries into the Mahāyāna in statements about the Sahā world which appears alternately pure (bejewelled/ornamented) and impure (unornamented). The image of the "jewel in the lotus" constitutes an important continuity with this symbolism.

The fact that there are so many types of waters which find their way into the "*cakravāla*-cosmology" is a clear indication of their importance. The rivers, particularly the Gaṅgā, are interpreted at some length in Chapter VI in the discussion of the eschatology of the "*asaṅkhyeya*-cosmology." The seas (*sītā*) and the lakes are situated either between mountains or in mountainous regions. They each possess the eight qualities.[3] The primordial waters (*ābmaṇḍala* ?) are possessed of unique potencies which when they evaporate after falling at the beginning of a world period, leave

1. For a discussion of P'eng-lai as a floating mountain, see Michael Soymié, "Le Lo-feou Chan; Étude de géographie religieuse," *Bulletin de 'école français d'Extrême-Orient* [hereafter cited as *BEFEO*] 48 (1956): 1-139, esp. pp. 51-68. An excellent discussion of the magical properties belonging to the "white isle" of the Purāṇas is found in Kasten Rönnow, "Some Remarks on Śvetadvīpa," *Bulletin of the School of Oriental Studies* (University of London) 5 (1929) : 253-84.

2. Przyluski has shown that the Babylonians associated a river, color, planet, precious substance and symbolical animal with each of the directions. It is possible that these mountain jewels exhibit some continuity with this symbolism of the planetary heavens. See Jean Przyluski, "La ville de cakravartin," *Rocznik Orientalistyczny* 5 (1927) : 165-86; idem, "Le symbolisme du pilier de Sarnath," in *Études d'orientalisme publiées par le Musée Guimet à la mémoire de Raymonde Linossier* (Paris : Libraire Ernest Leroux, 1932), pp. 481-98.

3. See above, p. 24, n. 1.

jewels in their place. Finally, there is the great ocean (*mahāsamudra*) which is said to flow about the seventh ring mountain to the *cakravāla* wall and to support the islands of the world disk. The term *mahāsamudra* is also used in a number of other contexts which are suggestive. For instance, we are told that the essential teaching of Mahāyāna Buddhism, the Prajñāpāramitā, is a great *mahāsamudra*.[1]

Finally, the images of trees and their fruits is suggestive of a whole range of agricultural imagery which is found in the Buddhist texts. Purāṇic texts inform us that Mt. Meru is shaped like the seed vessel of a lotus. The *Kośa* states that the winds which destroy the world (and lastly Mt. Meru) are the seeds (*bīja*) which result in the formation of the next world.[2] Transmigration is described as the "series of rice."[3] The *śrāvaka* follows the path which leads to the state of *arhat* taking possession at various stages of the "fruits" of the religious life.[4] The Sarvāstivādins are criticized by the Mahāyāna because in their teaching, the appearance of a Buddha is as rare as the blooming of an *udumbara* plant. On the other hand, the Mahāyānists encourage the faithful to plant their merits in the supreme field of merit (*paramapuṇyakṣetra*). Nothing could be more certain than that trees and all the agricultural images associated with the production of fruits and seeds are associated in one way or another with the process and manner of rebirth.

As a result of this hasty review of the images of the *cakravāla*, three facts are apparent. First, the Buddhist *cakravāla* is composed of a limited number of images. Second, these images have counterparts in other representations of the single world system as well as in other phases of Buddhist cosmological speculation. Third, the manner in which the various images are juxtaposed as in the case of the mountains and the islands, the

1. Lamotte, *Traité*, p. 3. Elsewhere we read that the law of the Buddha is a Great Ocean (ibid., p. 56), and that Kāśyapa's spirit is similar to an ocean "limpide et tranquil" (ibid., p. 91). Compare: ". . . .the *Aqua permanens* is divine gnosis, the *philosophia prima*. He who purifies himself therein and drinks of it will never taste the bitterness of death." Corbin, *Avicenna*, p. 160, also pp. 158, 321, n. 1, 324, n. 2.

2. La Vallée Poussin, *Kośa*, chap. iii, p. 210.

3. Ibid., p. 33.

4. See below, Chapter IV.

various types of waters, the mechanisms of rebirth, etc., suggests that each is chosen with great care. As a result, it is clear that these cosmologies are not simply vague metaphors about the universe. Neither do they represent some form of primitive or uninformed cartography. While it is not possible to explain all the detail of the *cakravāla*, it should not be dismissed as confused or vague. It is nothing if not precise. The extent to which this is the case will become more apparent in the examination of the mathematical cosmologies.

A second suggestion has to do with the general nature of the cosmos that is represented. As noted, what appears should not be construed as a primitive or uninformed cartography. It actually represents a serious attempt to account for appearances. While it is generally understood that the *cakravala* is a representation of the cosmos, it is important to stress the fact that it is precisely the entire cosmos that is represented and not simply what we call the earth. What we might call the earth is represented by Jambudvīpa which apparently represents the "known world" and is surrounded by water on every side. It should also be emphasized that Mt. Meru does not lie at the center of the earth in the sense that we understand the term earth. Nor is it at the center of the known world. Meru is clearly at the center of the world disk, i.e., at the center of the universe. As such, it is literally the axis or axle of the universe. Throughout the Classical world, the sun, moon, planets and fixed stars are represented as circulating about the Cosmic Mountain whose summit is directly in line with the polar star; the Cosmic North. This line through the top of the Cosmic Mountain and the polar star is in fact the motionless axle of the wheel of the universe. Because of the rotation of the earth, the wheel of the fixed stars describes a perfect, circular motion about this axis.[1] This basic structure of the cosmos is widespread throughout the Classical world and may be found in Plato and Aristotle as well as in the Abhidhamma.[2] But the appearance of the cosmos as represented by the *cakravāla* is an appearance from a certain point of view. In this case, that point of view is the theological evaluation of the cosmological sciences from the Buddhist perspective. In order

1. Kirfel, *Kosmographie*, p. 15.*
2. See above, p. 22, n. 2.

to illustrate what may seem a rather dubious point, I will cite three examples.

That the *cakravāla* is dominated by a series of measurements is clear from the exhibits which have been included. The significance of these measurements, however, is anything but obvious. Without providing an explanation of each one, it should be noted that most of them belong to various mathematical series. For instance, we are told that the mountain ranges are each one-half the height of the preceding range, thus forming a series, one, one-half, one-quarter, one-eighth, etc. The various heavens, on the other hand, are each twice as high as the preceding one, thus forming the series, 1, 2, 4, 8, 16; etc. The duration of life of various beings can be divided into four series : those belonging to the various islands (1,000 years; 500 years; 250 years; variable); those belonging to the various classes of the gods of desire (500 years consisting of 360 days each of which is equal to 50 years of human life, i.e., solar years; etc.); and those belonging to the 17 heavens of the Rūpadhātu which progressively double from one-quarter Kalpa to 16,000 Kalpas, concluding with a new series for the Ārūpyas. Finally, the height of beings forms a geometrical progression for the islands (three and one-half, 7, 14, 28) and for the beings of the second *dhyāna* (2, 4, 8, etc.) and above, but an arithmetical progression for the Kāmadevas and the beings of the first *dhyāna* (one-quarter, one-half, three-quarters, etc.). Clearly the thrust of all these measurements is to point up the fact that all measurement is measurement relative to something. Whatever is taken to be the unit is what determines all remaining measurement. On this insight is based an entire metaphysics of measurement. In the following chapters, it will become increasingly evident that this aspect of the Buddhist cosmos is a statement that all measurement is ultimately empty and similarly that all knowledge derived or associated with statements about measurement, e.g., the limited or unlimited nature of the universe, is ultimately empty as well.

Since the measurements of the *cakravāla* stress the importance of the manner in which the selection of the unit occurs, it is important to point out a second fact, namely that the cosmos as represented in the "*cakravāla*-cosmology" is ultimately a universe. This in turn has two implications. First, while from one perspective the *cakravāla* may be represented in terms of a series of measurements, from another point of view the *cakravāla* itself is a unit. The significance of this fact will become apparent in the discussion of the "*sāhasra*-cosmology." A second implication to be derived from the fact that the *cakravāla* is a universe is that it is a continuous, material mass in which the refined or subtle matter of the *dhyāna* realms is contiguous with the gross matter of the Kāmadhātu. The fact that it is a solid and continuous mass is another way of stating that it is without empty spaces, i.e., there are no voids. Later notions which regarded the universe as having gaps and empty spaces (*ākāśa*) appear to coincide with the development of the notion of emptiness (*śūnyatā*), i.e., the emptiness of the elements (*dharmaśūnyatā*) characteristic of the Mahāyāna. The focus of Hīnayānist philosophy, of course, is the emptiness of the self (*ātmaśūnyatā*).

The Starry Heavens and the Teaching of Brahmā

Throughout the Classical world, as in the Hindu Purāṇas, the single world system is not a static structure, but is dominated by a series of motions. The moon appears each night in a different residence (*nakṣatra*) and journeys through the night sky in that residence. The planets appear in a variety of conjunctions (*yuga*) which become the basis for measuring that aspect of cosmic time. The animals and heroes of the zodiac appear along the celestial equator and rise and fall with the ecliptic in the course of the solar year.

For the most part, these motions can only be imputed to the Buddhist cosmos. We may assume that the sun appears from behind the Yugandhara mountain in the East, journeys to the South and disappears behind the same mountain in the West. In all the Buddhist literature I am aware of, there is not a single explicit reference to the movements of the planets. A lone reference in the *Kośa* calls attention to the circular motion of the "fixed" stars which completes itself each night, appearing as a great wheel in the sky; a phenomenon we might reasonably expect to dominate such a cosmology. The *Kośa* remarks only that "the stars turn about Meru as though caught in a whirlpool." We will have occasion to return to this curious silence of the Buddhist texts concerning these great motions.

While the absence of any reference to the great motions remains a puzzle, it is not unreasonable to expect that the "*cakravāla*-cosmology" has made some provision for the planets and the stars. With this thought in mind, it is logical to assume that there is some relationship between the seven circular mountain rings and the seven spheres marked out by the "planets" of Antiquity, i.e., Sun, Moon, Mercury, Venus, Mars, Jupiter and Saturn. The precise manner in which these moving bodies are to be identified with the mountain rings is not clear. However, if we are permitted to make this identification, the seven ring mountains would serve the function of the crystalline spheres which, in Hellenistic speculation, were regarded as supporting the heavenly bodies and holding them in their paths.[1] The relative heights[2] and distances[3] of the mountain rings from each other would also correspond to the general effort to find simple mathematical relationships between the distances to the heavenly bodies.[4] Finally, variations in the order of the mountains can thus be understood as disagreement regarding the relative distance of the moving bodies.[5]

While the absence of information regarding the movements of the planetary bodies is one of the curiosities of the Buddhist texts, various scattered references tend to corroborate this association between the mountains and the "moving" bodies. These include references to the innermost mountain ring Yugandhara as the place where the chariots of the sun, moon and stars are kept[6] and again to Yugandhara as the place from which the seven suns issue at the end of the Kalpa.[7] Robert Spence Hardy has also observed a link between the mountains and the Purāṇic materials in which the valleys are taken to be ruts caused by the

1. An excellent introduction to the significance of the planetary heavens in Hellenistic thought is available in Corbin, *Avicenna*, passim, and idem, *Terre céleste*, esp. the chapter on "Le huitième climat," pp. 125-38. See also Duhem, *Système*, 1: 111 ff.

2. La Vallée Poussin, *Kośa*, chap. iii, p. 143.

3. Ibid., pp. 143-45.

4. Duhem, *Système*, 2: 15 ff.

5. See above, p. 23, n. 2.

6. "Half-way up Meru are the chariots of the sun (51 leagues), of the moon (a league further down), and of the stars." La Vallée Poussin, "Cosmogony," p. 134.

7. La Vallée Poussin, *Kośa*, chap. iii, p. 184, n. 2.

chariot driven by Priyavrata.[1] Other references appear to identify the planets with the so-called seven jewels to which various characteristics are attributed. In this context, it is important to remember that mountains are also regarded as being filled with jewels.[2] Finally, one of the results of exposure to the Hellenistic materials has been the discovery of structures which make clear identifications between the planets and circular land masses belonging to the cosmography. Plato's description of the Spindle of Necessity in the "Myth of Er" makes this association with particular clarity. The Spindle of Necessity, is made up of a series of whorls, each fitted inside the other.

> The first and outermost whorl had the broadest rim; next broadest was the sixth, next the fourth, next the eighth, next the seventh, next the fifth, next the third and last of all the second. And the rim of the largest and outermost was many-coloured, that of the seventh was the brightest, the eighth was illuminated by the seventh, from which it takes its colour, the second and the fifth were similar to each other and yellower than the others, the third was the whitest, the fourth reddish and the sixth second in whiteness. The whole spindle revolved with a single motion, but within the movement of the whole the seven inner circles revolved slowly in the opposite direction to that of the whole, and of them the eighth moved the fastest, and next fastest the seventh, sixth and fifth, which moved at the same speed, third in speed was the fourth, moving as it appeared to them with a counter-revolution; fourth was the third, and fifth the second.[3]

Next, it is necessary to make some statement about the place of the "fixed" stars within the "*cakravāla*-cosmology." It is tempting to identify the seventeen classes of the gods of the Brahmaloka with the "fixed" stars; perhaps as constellations

1. Robert Spence Hardy, *A Manual of Buddhism* (Delhi, Motilal Banarsidass 1974), p. 12, n.

2. Meru in particular is said to be filled with jewels: "le Meru a quatre aces qui sont respectivement, du nord a l'ouest, d'or, d'argent, de lapis et de cristal." (La Vallée Poussin, *Kośa*, chap. iii, p. 142.)

3. Plato, *The Republic*, trans. Sir Henry Desmond Pritchard Lee (Baltimore: Penguin Books, 1955), pp. 396-97.

within the firmament. The most obvious reason for making this assumption is that the Brahmaloka is situated where we expect to find the stars, namely above the earth. Another reason is the frequent association of the Brahmaloka with the realm of light, together with other statements concerning its luminous quality. We are told, for instance, that the gods of the Brahmaloka are luminous in appearance.[1] Other references draw a close parallel between the Akaniṣṭha and the realm of light.[2]

However, the automatic equation of the Brahmaloka with the realm of the "fixed" stars encounters some serious obstacles. Primary among these is the fact that while there are almost no specific references to the stars in the Buddhist literature, those few which do exist are at variance with such an idea. As noted, the *Kośa* regards the stars as turning about Meru.[3] But the tip of Meru is below the first *dhyāna*. The Purāṇic literature states that the stars are in the third of the seven Purāṇic heavens, the *svarloka*. This places the stars at the level of Mt. Meru and not in the four highest Purāṇic heavens. The Jains too seem to have placed all the heavenly bodies below the summit of Mt. Meru while nevertheless allowing the "heavens" to extend vertically in the manner of the "*cakravāla*-cosmology." The Jain texts consequently distinguish the following classes of gods :[4]

(4) *Vaimānika*-gods of the heavens residing in the palaces (*vimāna*) located in the various heavens;

(3) *Jyotiṣa*-gods of the heavenly bodies living in the region between the earth and heaven;

(2) *Vyantara*-gods of the underworld living in cities located in the layer which separates Ratnaprabhā from the earth; and

(1) *Bhavanavāsin*-gods of the underworld living in palaces (*bhavana*) and the hell Ratnaprabhā.

Thus, it is the clear, if limited, testimony of the Indian texts that the starry heavens are not identical with the seventeen heavens

1. La Vallée Poussin, *Kośa*, chap. iii., p. 173.
2. The Nishyanda-Buddha is said to have his abode in the Akaniṣṭha whence he emits rays of light. That the Akaniṣṭha is resplendent with light is mentioned in several places in the *Laṅkāvatāra Sūtra*. See Daisetz Teitaro Suzuki, *Studies in the Laṅkāvatāra Sūtra* (London: Routledge & Kegan Paul Ltd., 1930), p. 324.
3. La Vallée Poussin, *Kośa*, chap. iii, p. 156.
4. Kirfel, *Kosmographie*, pp. 261 ff.

and four *dhyāna* realms of the Brahmaloka. However, even if we accept the distinction between the starry realm and the four *dhyāna* realms of the Brahmaloka, there can be no doubt of a close relationship between the two. As a result of exposure to the Hellenistic materials, we know the significance of the perfect, circular motion of the stars appearing as a great wheel in the sky. We also know that these great motions are equated theologically with the "teaching". The Buddhist concept of the great wheel of the law or great wheel of the teaching (*dharmacakra*) seems to be a precise equivalent of these interpretations of the starry heavens. A clear association is drawn between the wheel of the law and Brahmā's realm by virtue of its seemingly interchangeable designation as the wheel of Brahmā (*brahmacakra*).[1] The *Kośa* informs us that the *brahmacakra* is a wheel (*cakra*) because it moves, that it has rays or spokes, and that it has twelve aspects.[2] The *Mppś* adds that like Brahmā's realm which is pure, the *brahmacakra* is also pure because it belongs to Brahmā.[3]

While the *Lotus Sūtra* states that it is the great accomplishment of the cosmic Buddha to have set in motion the wheel of the law, the *Buddhacarita* informs us that it is Brahmā who entreats the Buddha not to pass into the extinction of *nirvāṇa*, but to remain active in order to accomplish the teaching.[4] In short, it is Brahmā who is concerned with the teaching. One might even say that Brahmā is the teaching. Thus, a clear relationship is apparent between Brahmā's realm, the Rūpadhātu, and the starry heavens understood as the teaching and expressed in terms of the *dharmacakra/brahmacakra* apparently belonging to the Kāmadhātu, the realm of desire. Perhaps it is appropriate to regard the teaching as belonging to the realm of desire and not to the realm of Brahmā as such. To suggest an overall structure to this relationship, we might say that the soul/yogin must first gain access to or pass through Brahmā's teaching before gaining access to Brahmā's world.

Finally, it remains to be pointed out that the *cakravāla* is the stage for a drama of salvation. Moreover, it is only when

1. Lamotte, *Traité*, pp. 467, n. 2, 1598-1603; La Vallée Poussin, *Kośa*, chap. vi, pp. 244-50.
2. La Vallée Poussin, chap. vi, pp. 243-46.
3. Lamotte, *Traité*, p. 1598.
4. Materials relating to Brahmā's request can be found ibid., p. 246, n.2.

approached from this perspective that the various aspects of the "*cakravāla-* cosmology," and indeed of all the Buddhist cosmologies, can be integrated one with another.[1] The realm of purity, the Brahmaloka, is contiguous with the realm of desire. The *cakravāla* is a universe without gaps of empty space (*ākāśa*). The basic drama, then, is the passage of the Buddhist monk absorbed in trance, through the teaching whose relationship to Brahmā has been made clear, to the world of Brahmā, there to journey through the various meditation realms and finally to move beyond the cosmos into *nirvāṇa.* Clearly the cosmos represents the map of the path to enlightenment. Equally clear is the fact that the heavens are accessible to the meditations of the monk yogin.

However, it is not clear to what extent or in what manner the drama of the single world system is to be distinguished from the drama which characterizes the "*sāhasra*-cosmology" which, as we shall see, relies heavily on an understanding of the single world system, though with a somewhat different emphasis. To pursue this issue would require a comparison of the role of the single world system in the Pāli and Sanskrit traditions which would be interesting but which is not our immediate goal. Therefore, a more thorough examination of this elaborate drama is restricted to Chapter IV.

1. This statement applies equally to the Purāṇic cosmologies. Kirfel provides access to the variations in the names and measurements of Purāṇic cosmography, and the Purāṇic measurements of cosmic time are accurately described in a variety of secondary sources. However, the only discussion of Purāṇic cosmology which attempts to grasp it in its totality, i.e., as the basis for a drama of salvation, is that of Madeleine Biardeau, "Études de mythologie hindoue: Cosmogonies purāṇiques," Parts 1-3, *BEFEO* 54 (1968): 19-45; 55 (1969): 59-105; 58 (1971): 17-89; "Bhakti et avatāra," Part 4, *BEFEO* 63 (1976): 111-263.

CHAPTER III

THE "SĀHASRA-COSMOLOGY" OR "COSMOLOGY OF THOUSANDS" TO MULTIPLY WHAT IS UNIFIED AND UNIFY WHAT IS MULTIPLE

"Mother of Mountains"

Time and the Ever-Measuring World System

The name "*sāhasra*-cosmology" or "cosmology of thousands" suggests itself as a designation of the structures discussed in this Chapter because of the prominence of this particular numerology. There exist countless variations within this general heading, but the combinations of thousands of worlds and the superimposition of one cosmic level upon another is a fundamental characteristic of the "*sāhasra*-cosmology." Another basic characteristic of these cosmologies is that all the various combinations of worlds ultimately belong to the realm of a single Buddha, a single Buddha field (*buddhakṣetra*), or similarly unifying entity.

In general, the thousands of worlds are related to divisions within the Brahmaloka, the realm of the *dhyāna* heavens. The *Majjhimanikāya* (III, 101) provides a striking example of this division of the Brahmaloka into multiples of thousands of worlds. There we find a distinction between a *sahassobrahmā* governing a *sahassī lokadhātu*, and equivalent realms governed by a *dvisahasso-brahmā*, a *trisahasso-brahmā*, a *catussahasso-brahmā*, *pañcassahasso-brahmā* and a *saṭasahasso-brahmā*, gods which rule over 1,000 up to $(1{,}000)^{100}$ worlds.[1] We may anticipate some of our conclusions by stating that the idea seems to be that of ever-increasing circles described by the various heavenly bodies whose circular motion affords them dominion over ever-increasing realms measured in multiples of thousands of worlds.

In the *Mahāvastu*, we read that the *buddhakṣetra* is the equivalent of sixty-one triple chiliocosms, while an *upakṣetra* is four times as large. In the *Mppś*, we read that one million suns and moons, one million Sumerus and one million celestial spheres, etc. form

1. Kirfel, *Kosmographie*, p. 197; La Vallée Poussin, "Cosmogony," p. 137.

a triple chiliocosm, while an infinite number of the latter constitute a single *buddhakṣetra*. Elsewhere in the same text the *trisāhasra-mahāsāhasralokadhātu* is said to constitute a *lokadhātu*. These *lokadhātus*, existing in the ten regions in numbers equal to the sands of the Gaṅgā, form a *buddhalokadhātu*. These *buddhalokadhātus*, existing in the ten regions in numbers equal to the sands of the Gaṅgā form a sea (*samudra*) of *buddhalokadhātus*. These *samudras*, existing in the ten regions in numbers equal to the sands of the Gaṅgā, form a seed (*bīja*) of *buddhalokadhātusamudras*. These *bījas*, existing in the ten regions in numbers equal to the sands of the Gaṅgā, form a *buddhakṣetra*.[1]

Perhaps the most bizarre of these combinations of thousands of worlds is contained in the *Āvataṃsakasūtra* where we find a systematic arrangement of these chiliocosms.

> On whirlwinds rests the Fragrant Ocean, which carries an infinite number of world-germs (*lokabīja*); from it there issue lotuses infinite in number—very far removed, indeed, from each other. From each of these lotuses is born a universe (great chiliocosm), above which (separated by whirlwinds) there are three, then five, and so on up to the twentieth tier, where there are 39 great chiliocosms . . . The *Sahālokadhātu* forms part of the thirteenth stage, and constitutes the "field" of the Buddha Vairocana, and . . . ., on the same level at the same stage, in the extreme west, is the blessed universe of the Buddha Amitābha, the *Sukhāvatī*, where a *kalpa* of our universe is equal to a day and a night.[2]

For the most part, however, it is the *trisāhasramahāsāhasralokadhātu* which dominates the "*sāhasra*-cosmology" and which emerges as the cosmological equivalent of the *buddhakṣetra*.[3] Even Mahāyāna texts which recognize the existence of innumerable *buddhakṣetras* acknowledge the fact that each is a *trisāhasramahāsāhasralokadhātu*.[4] A frequently cited example of the

1. Lamotte, *Enseignement*, "Note I : Les buddhakṣetra," p. 396.
2. La Vallée Poussin, "Cosmogony," pp. 137-38.
3. According to La Vallée Poussin,the *trisāhasramahāsāhasralokadhātu* became the cosmological equivalent of the *buddhakṣetra*. Ibid., p. 137. Sources for the occurrence of the *trisāhasramahāsāhasralokadhātu* in the Buddhist literature can be found in Lamotte, *Enseignement*, p. 395.
4. According to Lamotte, "Les grands chiliocosmes sont répartis dans

trisāhasramahāsāhasralokadhātu is contained in *Aṅguttara*[1] I, 227. There the Buddha addresses Ānanda as follows :

> As far as moon and sun move in their course and light up all the quarters with their radiance, so far extends the thousand-fold world-system. Therein are a thousand moons, a thousand suns, a thousand Sumerus, lords of mountains : a thousand Rose-Apple Lands, a thousand Western Ox-Wains, a thousand Northern Kurus, a thousand Eastern Videhas; four thousand mighty Oceans, four thousand Mighty Rulers, a thousand Four Great Rulers, a thousand heavens of the Devas of Delight, a thousand heavens of the Devas that delight in creation, the same of those Devas that delight in others' creations, and a thousand Brahma worlds. This, Ānanda, is called "The system of the thousand lesser worlds." A system, a thousandfold the size of this, is called "The Twice-a-thousand Middling Thousand-fold World-system." A system, a thousandfold the size of this, is called "The Thrice-a-thousand World-system." Now, Ānanda, if he wished it, the Tathāgata could make his voice heard throughout this last-named world-system, or, even further, if he chose...In this connexion, Ānanda, the Tathāgata suffuses with radiance the Thrice-a-thousand Mighty Thousand-fold World-system. When its inhabitants perceive this, then the Tathāgata would give utterance and make the sound heard. That is how he would do it.

Thus the *Aṅguttara-nikāya* presents us with (1) a system of a thousand universes or a "small chiliocosm" (*sahassī chūḷanikā lokadhātu* or *sahassadhā loka*), (2) a system of a thousand "small

les dix regions." Lamotte, *Enseignement*, p. 345. Also see idem, "Mañjuśrī," *T'oung Pao* 47 (1960): 14-17. The fact that the fields in the regions are *trisāhasramahāsāhasralokadhātus* is recognized throughout the literature, but the significance of this fact is elusive. Moreover, it is not certain that all the fields are *trisāhasramahāsāhasralokadhātus*. La Vallée Poussin notes that while *Sahālokadhātu* seems to denote a great chiliocosm, "it is certain that its natural meaning should be the small universe the chakravāla in which; we live." La Vallée Poussin, "Cosmogony," p. 138, n. 1. In at least one instance, it is possible that *Sukhāvatī* is not a great chiliocosm, but rather a privileged *cakravāla* with no hell and no cosmic mountains. Ibid., p. 138, n. 2.

1. *The Book of Gradual Sayings or More-Numbered Suttas* (*Aṅguttara-nikāya*), trans. Frank Lee Woodward, 5 vols. (London: Oxford University Press, 1932-1936): 1, 221-222.

chiliocosms" or a "middle chiliocosm" (*dvisahassī majjimikā lokadhātu*), and (3) a system of a thousand "middle chiliocosms" or a "great chiliocosm" or "triple chiliocosm" (*tisahassī mahāsahassī lokadhātu*). From this it appears that a *trisāhasramahāsāhasralokadhātu* (*tisahassī mahasahassī lokadhātu*) is 1,000,000,000 universes such as the one in which we live; each consisting of four islands, a *cakravāla* wall, seven concentric ring mountains, a sun and a moon and a Mt. Meru.

For reasons which will become apparent, the *trisāhasramahāsāhasralokadhātu* appears to be closely associated with the Sarvāstivādins. The *trisāhasramahāsāhasralokadhātu* is clearly the cosmology of the *Kośa*, and the *Mppś* provides important additional details. While the reference in *Aṅguttara*, I, 227 is emphatic about restricting the *trisāhasramahāsāhasralokadhātu* to $(1{,}000)^3$ worlds the *Kośa* is indecisive. Although recognizing the structure of the *trisāhasramahāsāhasralokadhātu* as described above and as graphically represented in cphapter II,[1] the *Kośa* allows for another possibility in which the fourth *dhyāna* embraces an unlimited number of worlds.[2] Since the number of *dhyāna* heavens are inversely related to the number of worlds they embrace, the second description of the *trisāhasramahāsāhasralokadhātu* provided by the *Kośa* may be outlined as follows : (1) a *trisāhasramahāsāhasralokadhātu* or 1,000,000,000 *cakravālas* consisting of 4,000,000,000 land masses, 1,000,000,000 Mt. Merus etc., together with 1,000,000,000 first meditation realms; (2) *dvisāhasramahāsāhasralokadhātu* consisting of 1,000,000 second meditation realms; (3) a *cūḍika* consisting of 1,000 third medtiation realms; and (4) a single fourth meditation realm which is without measure.[3] This hierarchical structuring of chiliocosms and meditation realms is indirectly supported by the *Mppś* which states that a *trisāhasramahāsāhasralokadhātu* is 1,000,000,000 suns, moons, etc. up to a million Mahābrahmās, i.e., the highest of the first meditation realms.[4] Presumably there are less of the higher realms.[5]

1. See Chapter II, Fig. 4, "The Universe in Lateral Expanse (A).
2. See Chapter II, Fig. 5, "The Universe in Lateral Expanse (B).
3. La Vallée Poussin, *Kośa*, chap. iii, p. 169.
4. Lamotte, *Traité*, p. 448.
5. In at least one place the notion that there is only a single fourth dhyāna and therefore a single Akaniṣṭha is contested. The *Śūraṃgamasamādhisūtra*' explicitly states that there are 1,000,000,000 Akaniṣṭhas as well. See Lamotte, "Marche," p. 223.

The possibility that the *trisāhasramahāsāhasralokadhātu* is in some sense an unlimited world system is supported by other passages which state that the number of worlds is infinite like space.[1] The doctrinal significance of this fact is that even though there is no creation of new beings and even though innumerable Buddhas lead innumerable beings to *nirvāṇa*, the beings of the innumerable worlds are never exhausted.[2] The discrepancy between these two representations of the *trisāhasramahāsāhasraloka-dhātu* as limited on the one hand and unlimited on the other appears as a striking incongruity. However, this discrepancy is one of the facts which will cause us to focus with some care on the meaning of the *trisāhasramahāsāhasralokadhātu* and on the intention behind this concept.

Clearly there is an association between the number of worlds and the various meditation realms. While some texts regard the various worlds as arrayed vertically in the manner of the meditation realms, the *Kośa* is emphatic regarding the horizontal arrangement of these worlds. If they were arranged vertically, it would mean that there would be a Kāmadhātu above the Akaniṣṭha. This would appear to violate the rule that one detached from the Kāmadhātu is detached from the Kāmadhātus of all the universes.[3] In some sources, the horizontal grouping of the *cakravālas* leads to combinations of three tangent circles resulting in the formation of a region of intramundane darkness (*lokāntarika niraya*).[4] Moreover, we are told that all worlds in a *trisāhasramahāsāhasralokadhātu* perish at once.[5] Buddhaghosa's *Visuddhimagga* asserts that "in lateral expansion the world cycle always perishes to the extent of a Buddha's domain," which domain is the equivalent of the Buddha's authority realm.[6]

1. Buddhaghosa' *Atthasālinī* (sec. 160) states that four things are infinite: space, the number of universes, the number of living beings and the wisdom of a Buddha. Maung Tin, *The Expositor*, 1: 213-14.

2. La Vallée Poussin, *Kośa*, chap. iii, p. 10.

3. Ibid., pp. 10-11.

4. La Vallée Poussin, "Cosmogony," p. 132.

5. La Vallée Poussin, *Kośa*, chap. iii. p. 170, n. 2.

6. The "authority domain" is further defined as 100,000 x 10,000,000 worlds in contrast to the infinite "domain of wisdom." See Henry Clark Warren, *Buddhism in Translations* (New York: Atheneum, 1968), p. 321 and Buddhaghosa's *Visuddhimagga* (sec. 414). *The Path of Purification*,

As we shall see, the authority realm is equivalent to the cube of the 10,000 world system with which Buddhaghosa begins his speculations, while the *trisāhasramahāsāhasralokadhātu* is obviously the cube of a 1,000 world system. Thus, the various destructions by fire, water and wind each destroy the same number of worlds even though they reach to different *dhyāna* heavens. Clearly the worlds and the *dhyāna* heavens of the *trisāhasramahāsāhasralokadhātu* are all on corresponding horizontal planes. If we continue to follow the *Kośa*'s second definition of a *trisāhasramahāsāhasralokadhātu*, it appears that we may readily identify it with one of the speculative positions rejected in the *Brahmajālasutta*, namely that the universe is unlimited in lateral expanse, but limited upwards and downwards.[1]

One final example of the "*sāhasra*-cosmology" must occupy us momentarily, namely the 10,000 world system. The 10,000 world system is apparently embraced by the Pāli tradition in preference to the system of thousands we are examining in conjunction with the Sarvāstivādins. References to the 10,000 world system occur both in Pāli canon and in Buddhaghosa. The Pāli texts, in particular the *Jātakas* present a vague outline of the 10,000 world system which trembles when a Buddha is born :

> Now at the moment when the future Buddha made himself incarnate in his mother's womb, the constituent elements of the ten thousand world-system quaked, and trembled, and were shaken violently.[2]

Buddhaghosa presents what is either a more complete or a substantially more evolved picture of the 10,000 world system. In the *Visuddhimagga* (*Path of Purification*), reference is made to the three "fields" or "domains" (*khetta*) of a Buddha :

> Birth-domain (*jāti-khetta*) comprises 10,000 worlds; all tremble at different moments in the life of a Buddha. Authority-domain (*āṇā-khetta*) comprises a hundred thousand times ten millions of worlds; over all extends the protecting power of the "formulae of protection" (the so-called parittas) given by

trans. Bhikku Ñāṇamoli (Kandy: Buddhist Publication Society, 1975), pp. 455-56.

1. See above, Chapter II, p. 24, n. 2.
2. Rowell, "Background," 6:236. Other references in Rowell to the 10,000 world-system are to be found on 6:217, 246; 7:133.

the Buddha. Knowledge-domain (*visaya-khetta*) is without limit.[1]

While it is premature to offer an explanation, it is of more than casual interest to note that the "authority-domain" is characterized as constituting the numerical cube of the "birth-domain," i.e., $10{,}000^3$. This representation of the 10,000 world system is a clear counterpart to the *trisāhasramahāsāhasralokadhātu.*

Before attempting to find an equivalent which adequately conveys the meaning of the term *trisāhasramahāsāhasralokadhātu*, it is important to understand the use of the single world system in the context of the "*sāhasra*-cosmology." What we find is that the single world system of the *cakravāla* becomes the cosmological unit of measurement par excellence. Nowhere is this more evident than in the multiples of single world systems which make up the *trisāhasramahāsāhasralokadhātu.* The single world system is not only the unit of spatial measurement, it is the basic unit of temporal measurement as well. A *mahākalpa* is the duration of time from the formation of one world to the formation of the next, and as such is the basic unit of cosmic time.

The basic idea behind the term Kalpa is that of discrimination or measurement; a meaning preserved in the term *vikalpa*, generally understood as "false discrimination." The Kalpa measures the temporal limits of the world just as the *cakravāla* wall measures its spatial limits. In Islamic cosmology, a similar world system is surrounded by Mt. Qaf. Mt. Qaf is the *barzakh*, the boundary of the world. As such, it is the basis of all discrimination, all multiplicity and all particularity. In a word, it is the "mother of mountains."[2]

1. This outline of the 10,000 world system appears in the cosmological section of Buddhaghosa's *Visuddhimaggu* (sec. 414). See La Vallée Poussin, "Cosmogony," p. 137; Warren, *Buddhism*, p. 321; Rowell, "Background," 6:216; Ñāṇamoli, *Path of Purification*, pp. 455-64. It is the approach of the only monograph on the subject of the *buddhakṣetra* that the idea of an infinite field of knowledge is one which is clearly rooted in the Hīnayāna. As such, it is another expression of the Buddha as *dharmakāya*. What is foreign, it is thought, is the spatially limited realms of authority and birth. Rowell, "Background." This point of view is apparently adopted by Conze as well in capsule summary of Buddhist cosmological speculation. Edward Conze, *Buddhism: Its Essence and Development* (New York: Harper & Row, Publishers, 1959), pp. 154-55.

2. Corbin, *Terre célèste*, p. 126.

The *cakravāla* is not only the unit of measurement, but it is also the means or the instrument by which the measurement is made. This fact emerges with particular clarity when we examine the relationship between the spatial configuration of the islands of the *cakravāla* and the measurements of time already familiar to us. To begin with, we observe that the *cakravāla* is arranged with four inhabited islands at the points of the compass. It is by means of these islands and these directions that the conjunctions (*yuga*) are determined. Conjunctions of the planets can only occur as the result of viewing their motions from certain positions and by measuring their movement with the aid of the directions, i.e., their position relative to some other point. That the islands are associated with a process similar to the computation of the *yugas* which occupy such a prominent place in the Purāṇic texts is suggested further by the nature of life found in each. Beginning with Uttarakuru where the duration of life is 1,000 years, we find a steady decline in the duration of life in the other *dvīpas*. These variances in the duration of life are one of the primary characteristics of the four yugas (*kṛta*, *tretā*, *dvāpara* and *kali*).[1] Moreover, each *yuga* in the Purāṇic texts is said to be preceded by a dawn and followed by a twilight, a structure which is perfectly reflected by the two lesser islands located to either side of the four major *dvīpas*.

A second fact which we know about the computation of the *yugas* is that the most prominent system places them in a ratio of 4:3:2:1 in their relative duration.[2] The islands of the *cakravāla*

1. See above, Chapter II, p. 26,n. 2.

2. A partial list of useful and for the most part recent works on the "ages of the world" and the "Great Year" include the following: Duhem, *Système*, 1:65-85, 275-96; John Faithfull Fleet, "The Kaliyuga era of B.C. 3102," *Journal of the Royal Asiatic Society* (1911), pp. 479-96, 675-98; Hermann Jacobi, "Ages of the World (Indian)," *ERE* 1:200-202; Edward Stewart Kennedy, "Ramifications of the World Year Concept in Islamic Astrology," *Ithaca. Actes du Dixième Congrès Internationale d'Histoire des Sciences* 1 (1964): 23-43; La Vallée Poussin, "Ages"; David Pingree, *The Thousands of Abū Ma'shar* (Leiden : E. J. Brill, 1968), esp. pp. 28-30; idem, "Astronomy and Astrology in India and Iran," *Isis* 54 (1968): 229-46; Bartel Leenderx van der Waerden, "The World-Year of the Persians," *Journal of the American Oriental Society* 83 (1963): 315-27; idem, "Das Grosse Jahr und Die ewige Wiederkehr," *Hermes* 80 (1952): 129-55; Heinrich Zimmer,

are linked to this aspect of the *yugas* by virtue of their relation to the *cakravartins* which dominate the *cakravāla*. The *Kośa* states that there are four types of *cakravartins* which appear:

> . . . those possessing a wheel of gold who reign over four continents, those whose wheel is silver ruling over three continents, those whose wheel is copper ruling over two continents and and those whose wheel is iron whose dominion is limited to a single continent.[1]

Since it appears that the islands essentially spatialize the Purāṇic understanding of the *yugas*, it is reasonable to assume that the *cakravāla* or *caturdvīpaka* is a Buddhist equivalent of a *caturyuga*. The parallels do not end here. Clearly, the thousands of *cakravālas* which make up the *trisāhasramahāsāhasralokadhātu* must be seen as the equivalent of the thousands of *caturyugas* which make up the Kalpas of Purāṇic chronometry.

> The Kalpa is the daytime of the god Brahman; and his night is of the same length. At the end of the daytime of a day of Brahman everything is destroyed: during his night a state of chaos prevails: and then creation is renewed by him. The process of creation and destruction alternates during the whole life of Brahman which is known as the Mahakalpa and lasts for 100 years, each composed of 360 such days and nights.

Myths and Symbols in Indian Art and Civilization, ed. Joseph Campbell (Princeton: Princeton University Press, 1946), pp. 15-19. Relevant Judaeo-Christian materials can be found in David Syme Russell, *The Method and Message of Jewish Apocalyptic* (Philadelphia: Westminster Press, 1964) and Oscar Cullmann, *Christ and Time* (Philadelphia: Westminster Press, 1964). Specifically religious themes associated with these apprehensions of time are discussed in Henry Corbin, "Cyclical Time in Mazdaism and Ismailism" in Joseph Campbell ed., *Man and Time* (New York: Pantheon Books, 1957), pp. 115-54 and Eliade, "Time and Eternity in Indian Thought," ibid., pp. 173-200, also published in *Images and Symbols*, pp. 57-91.

1. La Vallée Poussin, *Kośa*, chap. iii, pp. 196-98. Just as we are suggesting that the *trisāhasramahāsāhasralokadhātu* spatializes the "thousands" of Purāṇic chronometry, we must wonder if the 10,000 world system does not in some way serve the same function. In this context, al-Biruni makes an observation which is suggestive. He refers to "an Indian idol, cut out of stone, the neck of which is surrounded by numerous iron collars (recall the *cakravāla* ring is made of iron), which represent the Indian eras of 10,000 years, and, if counted, would amount to an enormous sum of years." Sachau, *Chronology*, p. 96.

Then everything is overwhelmed by a final destruction and resolution into ultimate sources, and apparently remains so until another Brahman comes spontaneously into existence.[1]

The connection between the thousands of worlds of the *trisāhasramahāsāhasralokadhātu* and the days and nights of Brahmā becomes even clearer when we see that it is precisely in the Brahmaloka that the thousands of worlds of Buddhist speculation come into play. Thus, the first *dhyāna* of the Brahmaloka extends over 1,000 *cakravālas*, the second over 1,000 x 1,000, the third over 1,000 x 1,000 x 1,000 while the fourth is without measure.

In addition to these links with Purāṇic chronometry, the numerology of thousands points to an undeniable relationship between the structure of the *trisāhasramahāsāhasralokadhātu* and the measurements of cosmic time so characteristic of the Classical cosmologies. In their efforts to calculate the duration of a Great Year, i.e., the time required for the planets with their apogees and nodes to make a complete revolution without remainder,[2] the astronomers constantly arrived at fractional measurements. The means of determining a complete cycle thus depended on multiplying all the empirical results by various orders of thousands to arrive at a full cycle without remainder. The extent to which the numerology of thousands was associated with efforts to measure the movements of the heavenly bodies is indicated by the very title of Abū Ma'sur's astronomical treatise, "The Book of Thousands" (*Kitāb al-ulūf.*)[3]

One of the examples of this type of reckoning is found in the writings of al-Biruni. For purposes of brevity, only a fragment of this system is cited.

a. The mighty *quisma* (division) moves 1° along the equator every 1,000 years or 365,259 days; therefore, it makes one revolution in one "world-year" or 360,000 solar years. . . .

b. The big *qisma* (division) moves 1° along the equator every 100 solar years or 36,525;54 days; therefore it makes 10 revolutions in a "world-year.". . .

1. Fleet, "Kaliyuga Era," p. 482-83.
2. Al-Biruni, *The Book of Instruction in the Elements of the Art of Astrology*, trans. R. Ramsay Wright (London: Luzac & Co., 1934), sec. 204, p. 113.
3. Pingree, *Thousands.*

c. The middle *qisma* (division) moves 1° along the equator every 10 solar years, and makes 100 revolutions in a "world-year"; therefore, each revolution takes 3,600 solar years or 1,314,932;5,26 days. . . .

d. The small *qisma* (division) moves 1° along the equator every 1 solar year, and makes 1,000 revolutions in a "world-year."[1]

The significance of the numerology of thousands, then, appears to be inextricably related to those systems which sought to measure the limits of the universe, particularly in its temporal duration. Beyond the evidence here adduced, there can be no doubt that the *trisāhasramahāsāhasralokadhātu* is closely associated with speculations on the nature of cosmic time. As we shall see in Chapter IV, the drama associated with the *trisāhasramahāsāhasralokadhātu* is framed by the passage of the *mahākalpas* which are the units of cosmic time for the Buddhists. Keeping in mind that it is as an instrument of measurement or discrimination that the single world system is related to the *trisāhasramahāsāhasralokadhātu*, we may now attempt to understand the meaning of this term which has proven so opaque to Western scholarship.

Following the representation of the *trisāhasramahāsāhasralokadhātu* in *Aṅguttara*, 1:227, La Vallée Poussin has emphasized that this term must be understood to mean $1{,}000^3$ or 1,000,000,000 universes such as the one in which we live.[2] Apparently understanding 3,000 (*trisāhasra*) to be multiplied by 1,000 (*mahāsāhasra*), Max Müller has interpreted this term to mean 3,000,000 worlds in his translations of the Pure Land Sūtras.[3] While there is considerable textual authority for regarding the *trisāhasramahāsāhasralokadhātu* as 1,000,000,000 worlds distributed among the four-tiered structure of *dhyāna* heavens, we have already seen an alternative interpretation in the *Kośa* which describes the fourth *dhyāna* as unlimited in extent.[4] La Vallée Poussin specifically stresses the erroneous nature of the translation of *trisāhasramahāsāhasralokadhātu* as 3,000 worlds.[5] However,

1. Ibid., p. 59.
2. La Vallée Poussin, "Cosmogony," p. 137.
3. Cowell, *Buddhist Mahāyāna Texts*, pp. 14, 72.
4. La Vallée Poussin, *Kośa*, chap. iii, p. 169.
5. La Vallée Poussin, "Cosmogony," p. 137.

no less an authority than Chih-I, the founder of Chinese T'ien-t'ai Buddhism, has understood this term in precisely this sense. As a result, the *trisāhasramahāsāhasralokadhātu* is the basis for the 3,000 Great Worlds of the T'ien-t'ai.[1]

These striking discrepancies in translation and interpretation are heightened when we examine a number of related examples outside the Buddhist tradition. There we find scattered instances of formulae placing the numbers three and 1,000 in various combinations which are of interest. In Orphism and in Plato's "Myth of Er," we are told that it is the lot of each soul to transmigrate three periods of 1,000 years each.[2] In Persia, Āṭṭar's mystical epic about the birds ("Language of the Birds"; *Manṭig al-Ṭayr*) tells a story in which thousands of birds set out in a flight to the center of the earth. Most of them are killed by fire, wind, etc. Finally, only thirty (*Sī-murgh*) arrive.[3] In the *Śūramgamasūtra* (2 B 11), we are confronted with a cluster of 3,000 islands.[4] Ājīvika chronometry tells us that it takes 300,000 *saras* or "lakes" to make a *mahākappa*.[5] The Bundahisn divides the total duration of cosmic time which is held to be 12,000 years, into a series of four tri-millenia, each of which is associated with a particular metal or quality (gold, silver, steel and iron).[6] Finally, the numerology of thousands appears

1. Leon Hurvitz, "Chih-I," *Mélanges chinois et bouddhiques* 12 (1960-62): 318.

2. "The whole (Orphic) process of the 'weary circle' was something like this. A soul dies and is judged and according to its deserts is assigned to a place of punishment or happiness. Whichever it is, the sojourn there is temporary. After a lapse of time which together with its previous earthly life completes a period of a thousand years, it is prepared for another earthly life.....For the ordinary mortal it seems to have been necessary to complete the circle ten times before salvation could be hoped for. He who chose a righteous....life three times in succession probably had a special dispensation whereby he could escape without further trial." Guthrie, *Greeks*, p. 323.

3. Corbin, *Avicenna*, pp. 199-200.

4. La Vallée Poussin, *Kośa*, chap. iii, p. 146, n. 3.

5. Basham, *Ājīvikas*, p. 254.

6. See Robert Charles Zaehner, *Zurvan: A Zoroastrian Dilemma* (Oxford: Clarendon Press, 1955), esp. pp. 80-104; Nathan Söderblom, "Ages of the World (Zoroastrian)," *ERE*, 1:205-10.

to have become associated even with the Taoist quest for immortality with 3,000 years being taken as an equivalent of immortality.[1]

Because of the dispersion of this numerology and because of the variations we encounter, it is necessary to attempt to find a meaning which suggests the intention behind the term *trisāhasramahāsāhasralokadhātu* as well as to account for the value assigned to it in a specific text. A widely used translation as "three-thousandth-great-thousandth universe" does not provide any particular sense of meaning and must therefore be disregarded except for its apparent literalness. The term "chiliocosm" or "triple chiliocosm" was invented by Rémusat.[2] While it does convey the importance of the thousands of worlds which dominate this cosmology in a variety of combinations, it still does not provide a real sense that the number and spatial arrangement of worlds is only one aspect of the "*sāhasra*-cosmologies."

In my opinion, the *trisāhasramahāsāhasralokadhātu* most logically suggests a two-fold structure, i.e., an aggregation whose dimension is 1,000 units and whose circumference is therefore 3 x 1,000. Three in this instance is an approximation of pi, a value we cannot doubt since the *Kośa* is specific in stating that the circumference is the triple of the diameter.[3] *Mahāsāhasra* is then to be understood as a multiplier; a factor of 1,000 by means of which the limits of the universe could be multiplied in an unlimited manner.

Scholastic debate either disguised the intention behind this kind of mathematical measurement of the universe, or found that it must affirm some kind of limited cosmic nexus. The limited manner in which the *trisāhasramahāsāhasralokadhātu* was conceived took a variety of forms. The Sarvāstivādins apparently took this limited cosmic nexus to mean the square and the cube of one thousand. Chih-I, while accepting the term *trisāhasramahāsāhasralokadhātu* as designating the universe,

1. The name of one of the drugs allegedly used by the Taoists for the purpose of obtaining immortality was the "peches-de-la-Si-wang-mou-qui-poussent-tous-les-trois-millesans." Kenneth Schipper, *L'empereur Wou des Han dans la légende taoiste, Han Wou-ti Nei-tchouan* (Paris: Publications de l'école française d'Extrême-Orient, 1965), p. 23.

2. La Vallée Poussin, *Kośa*, chap. iii, p. 170, n. 1.

3. Ibid., p. 141; 141, n. 1.

obviously did not accept this solution and preferred 3,000 worlds as a more appropriate designation of the cosmos in its limited value. We must therefore conclude that there is either an original or esoteric meaning of *trisāhasramahāsāhasraloka-dhātu* as a circular system of "3,000 worlds whose diameter is ever increasing by thousands." The *trisāhasramahāsāhasralo-kadhātu*, then, is an "ever-expanding world system" or an "ever-millenializing world system" or perhaps simply an "ever-measuring world system." Moreover, because of the close relationship between the *trisāhasramahāsāhasralokadhātu* and the *mahā-kalpas* of Buddhist speculation, we must conclude that this "ever-measuring world system" is closely tied to the measurements of cosmic time.

Buddhas of Multiplication

The significance of the *trisāhasramahāsāhasralokadhātu* cannot be understood without an awareness that the structure of the "ever-measuring world system" is ultimately a statement about the nature of the Buddha whose field it is. In order to understand the relationship between the Buddha and the *trisāhasramahāsāhasralokadhātu*, it is necessary to examine the structure of the *nirmāṇabuddhas* or magically created Buddhas which are associated with this "ever-measuring world system." The *nirmāṇabuddhas* find no mention in the *Kośa*, a curiosity which need not detain us. However, they occupy a prominent place in the *Mppś* where they are closely associated with the teaching of the Buddha in a *trisāhasramahāsāhasralokadhātu*. The *Kośa* on the other hand does provide an elaborate account of the miraculous powers (*siddhis*, *ṛddhis*, *iddhis*) and superknowledges (*abhijñā*) which underlie the speculations centering on the *nirmāṇabuddha*, and it is with a description of these miraculous powers that we must begin.

It is likely that from the beginning the Buddhists acknowledged the acquisition of miraculous powers by the great saints and the great magicians.

This multiplication or projection of images is ascribed to the Buddha during his lifetime. It is reported that he sometimes projected a radiant or refulgent image of himself with the aim of helping someone in a crisis.[1] While the significance of such

1. Edward Conze, *Buddhist Meditation* (New York: Harper & Row Publishers, Inc., 1969), p. 61.

practices was minimized in the Pāli tradition, examples are by no means lacking. Magical powers of the adept such as the *adhiṭṭhāna iddhi*, referring generally to powers of self-multiplication and the *vikubbanā iddhi*, referring to powers of self-transformation are mentioned both in the Pāli Canon and in Buddhaghosa.[1] The Sanskrit term *adhiṣṭhāna* is prominent in the *Kośa* and in a number of Mahāyāna texts.[2] In the *Lotus Sūtra* for instance, we read that the Buddha creates myriads of Tathāgatas (and presumably their *buddhakṣetras* as well) throughout the ten regions by means of his power of *adhiṣṭhāna* or self-multiplication. These Tathāgatas or Tathāgata-frames (tathāgatavigraha) are understood to be illusory.[3] While the Pāli texts reveal only traces of such phenomena, the Sarvāstivādin texts are replete with examples. The Sarvāstivādins, in fact, are recognized as having established an exhaustive theory about *nirmāṇa* and other associated supernatural powers,[4] and it is the outlines of just such a system which we will attempt to reconstruct insofar as it appears as an integral part of the "*sāhasra*-cosmology."

The development of the techniques of yoga in India has always carried with it the acquisition of certain miraculous powers (*siddhi*). In Buddhism, the *siddhis* are one of the five classes of *abhijñās* or "superknowledges" which include: (1) magical powers or *siddhis* including the powers of multiplication (*nirmāṇa*) and displacement (*gamana*); (2) divine eye (*divyacakṣus*); (3) divine hearing (*divyaśrotra*); (4) knowledge of another's thought (*paracittajñāna*); and (5) recollection of previous existences (*pūrvanirvāsānusmṛti*). As mentioned, the ability to multiply one's image and become one again is listed among the *siddhis*. Specifically, it is listed under the *siddhi* of creation (*nirmāṇa*). It is further described as the ability to multiply what is unique, to unify what is multiple and to create all species

1. Rowell, "Background," 7:135-40; "Appendix C," 7:154-63.

2. Ibid., "Appendix C," 7:154-63; Suzuki, *Studies*, pp. 202-5. Extensive but confusing notes on the term *adhiṣṭhāna* can be found in La Vallée Poussin, *Kośa*, chap. iv, p. 241; chap. vii, pp. 119-20; *La Siddhi de Hiuan-tsang* (*Vijñaptimātratāsiddhi*), trans. and ann. Louis de La Vallée Poussin, 2 vols. (Paris: Librarie Orientaliste Paul Geuthner, 1928), pp. 771-73.

3. Rowell, "Background," 7:135.

4. *Siddhi*, p. 770.

of things. The *Mppś* adds that the creations of the heretics (*tīrthika*) never last more than seven days, while those of the Buddha and the disciples have unlimited duration.[1]

Despite the prominence of the miraculous powers among the Sarvāstivādins and their systematic attempts to structure a theory of *nirmāṇa*, the importance of these powers does not originate with the Sarvāstivādins or even with Buddhism, but rather is an integral part of the yogic experience as such. The development of the techniques of yoga in India has always carried with it the acquisition of certain miraculous powers. The lists of these powers is for the most part stereotyped and occurs in all the ascetic and mystical literature of India.[2] As a result, we must assume that the powers of *nirmāṇa* and *adhiṣṭhāna* were originally related to the experience of the yogin absorbed in meditation. The connection between the concentrations (*samādhi*) and the magical powers (*ṛddhi*) and superknowledges (*abhijñā*) is firmly established in several places. In the *Majjimanikāya* it is clearly stated that the *abhijñās* are the fruit of the *vimokṣas* or liberating *samādhis*.[3] In the *Kośa*, we read that

1. Lamotte, *Traité*, p. 330. The *Kośa* provides the following list of six *abhijñās*: (1) Abhijñā de pouvoir magique, *ṛddhiviṣayajñānasākṣātkriyābhijñā*, l'Abhijñā, qui consiste dans la réalisation du savoir portant sur l'objet de la *ṛddhi* (c'est-à-dire *gamana* et *nirmāṇa*, déplacement et création); (2) ouïe divine, *divyaśrotrajñānasākṣātkriyābhijñā*; (3) connaissance de de le pensée d'autrui, *cetaḥparyāyajñānasākṣātkriyābhijñā*; (4) souvenir des anciennes existences, *pūrvanivāsānusmṛtijñānasakṣātkārābhijñā*; (5) vue divine, *cyutyupapādajñānasākṣātkārābhijñā*, and (6) destruction des "vices," *āsravakṣayajñānasākṣātkārābhijñā*. La Vallée Poussin, *Kośa*, chap. vii, pp. 97-100. Those who were not Buddhist saints could master the first five *abhijñās*, but only the Buddhists could master the sixth. Lamotte, "Marche," p. 25; La Vallée Poussin, *Kośa*, chap. vii, p. 100. For striking parallels between the first five *abhijñās* and the five sciences which are the core of the education of the philosopher-king (arithmetic, plane geometry, solid geometry, astronomy and harmonics), see Plato, *The Republic*, pp. 291-300.

2. Mircea Eliade, *Yoga : Immortality and Freedom* (Princeton: Princeton University Press, 1970), p. 179. According to La Vallée Poussin, "La bibliographie des Abhijñās est infinie." La Vallée Poussin, *Kośa*, chap. vii, p. 97, n. 5. Lamotte provides additional bibliography in *Traité*, p. 128, n. 3, together with an exhaustive discussion on pp. 1809-27. For the relationship between *vidyā* and *abhijñās*, see Lamotte, *Traité*, p. 129; 129, n. 3.

3. Lamotte, *Enseignement*, p. 32 n.

the *ṛddhi* is identical with the concentrations,[1] and also that the *nirmāṇacitta* or thoughts of transformation proceed from the *dhyānas* or meditations.[2] As a result of the close relationship between the meditations and the *abhijñās*, it is not surprising that it is the Buddha and the *arhat* who confront us with the great feats of *nirmāṇa* which are integral to the "*sāhasra*-cosmology." The relationship between the *arhat* and the powers of *nirmāṇa* after gaining access to *nirvāṇa* are explored in the next Chapter.

Whatever the experiential basis for these miraculous powers, we now find the creation of elaborate speculative systems employing these magical creations or fictional bodies as intermediaries relating the Buddha in his cosmic form to the drama of salvation. We are told that the Buddha is able to produce magical creations even after his *parinirvāṇa*.[3] This fact and others suggest that the *nirmāṇa-buddhas* emanate from the Buddha absorbed in a state of trance. Clearly this statement touches on the relationship between the absorption of the Buddha into *nirvāṇa* and the acquisitions of the *abhijñās* which is an integral expression of the negative relationship between the Buddha and the world.

The fact that the *nirmāṇabuddhas* are products of the power of magical multiplication also suggests that they are in some way subordinate to the Buddha-nature itself. In at least one image, the *nirmāṇabuddhas* are represented as multiplying in the manner of leaves from the stem of a plant. According to the *Mppś*, the Buddha, in practicing the "Concentration of the Rising of the Sun " (*sūryodayasamādhi*) is able to multiply images for the purpose of saving all beings. The Bhagavat issues a lotus from his navel. This lotus multiplies leaves on which are seated other Buddhas who in turn issue lotuses from their navels, etc. When these *nirmāṇabuddhas* have completed their work of salvation they return to their point of departure and re-enter the navel of the Buddha.[4] Not only are the *nirmāṇa-buddhas*

1. La Vallée Poussin, *Kośa*, chap. vii, p. 112.
2. "Du *dhyāna* est produit son fruit, le *nirmāṇacitta*, pensée de creation." Ibid., p. 117.
3. Ibid., pp. 119-20.
4. Lamotte, *Traité*, pp. 532-35.

products of multiplication, but they are also able to multiply themselves. Clearly the relationship of the *nirmāṇabuddhas* to the Buddha, like that of the leaves to a plant, does not violate the unity or integrity of the Buddha-nature.

While the *Kośa* makes no mention of the *nirmāṇabuddhas* or "fictional" Buddhas, they occupy a prominent place in the *Mppś*, and it is clear from what we read there that the *nirmāṇabuddhas* are closely associated with the "*sāhasra*-cosmology" in general and the *trisāhasramahāsāhasralokadhātu* in particular. The *trisāhasramahāsāhasralokadhātu*, in fact, is the power of multiplication par excellence. In addition to this the *nirmāṇabuddhas* and the *trisāhasramahāsāhasralokadhātu* exhibit a number of common characteristics. First, it is implied that the *nirmāṇabuddhas* are restricted to a *trisāhasramahāsāhasralokadhātu*.[1] We may infer this from the fact that the *nirmāṇabuddhas* assist the Buddha in preaching within a *trisāhasramahāsāhasralokadhātu*. Moreover, the *nirmāṇabuddhas* are self-multiplying in the same way that the *trisāhasramahāsāhasralokadhātu* represents the "ever-expanding" or "self-multiplying" universe of thousands. As we have also seen, those who sought to calculate the values of cosmic time relied on multiplying their measurements by thousands in order to eliminate the fractions which prevented the accurate calculation of a full cycle for a Great Year, a multiplication whose intention is captured in the numerology of thousands and, we may suspect, in the self-multiplying nature of the *nirmāṇabuddhas*. Finally, the self-multiplying nature of the *nirmāṇabuddhas* and the *trisāhasramahāsāhasralokadhātu* is much like the body of Nārāyaṇa which is said to expand by multiples of ten.[2]

1. "Actuellement les Buddha des dix régions prêchent toujours la loi et délèguent toujours des Buddha fictifs dans les univers des dix régions pour prêcher les six Pāramitā. . . ." Ibid., p. 471. "Dans les dix régions, ces Trisāhasramahāsāhasralokadhātu sont aussi nombreux que les sables du Gange et chacun d'eux constitute l'univers d'un Buddha (*ekabuddhalokadhātu*); on n'y rencontre qu'un seul Buddha, jamais deux. Dans un de ces univers de Buddha, le seul Buddha Śakyamuni crée sans cesse des Buddha fictifs (*nirmāṇabuddha*) qui recourent à des predications (*dharma-paryāya*), à des corps (*kāya*) fictifs, à des causes (*nidāna*) et à des artifices (*upāya*) des toutes sortes pour sauver les êtres." Ibid., pp. 540-41.

2. For a discussion of the self-multiplying body of Nārāyaṇa, see ibid., p. 269, n. 2. For the so-called "*nārāyaṇabala*" see La Vallée Poussin,

Another fact about the "*sāhasra*-cosmology" which cannot fail to strike us, is the manner in which the cosmos is made to correspond to various parts of the Buddha's body. The passage cited from the *Visuddhimagga* shows various portions of the cosmos associated with the thought of the Buddha, his authority and the realm of the Buddha's birth. The description of the *trisāhasramahāsāhasralokadhātu* in *Aṅguttara* 1:227 concludes with the statement that the Buddha's voice can be heard throughout. We may provisionally associate the realm of the Buddha's authority with that of his voice. The full significance of this fact, together with the implications for the dharma or the teaching of the Buddha will become evident in the course of this work.

The birth realm of the Buddha impresses us as being a statement about the body of the Buddha and is almost certainly an attempt to define the relationship between the physical universe and the body of the Buddha. Other references throughout the Buddhist literature tend to support this association. In the *Mppś*, for instance, we find a threefold division of the universe similar to that in the *Visuddhimagga*. There we read that in the Buddha there are three secrets: that of his body, that of his voice and that of his thought. The secret of the Buddha's body is that it may appear being any size: "haute d'une brasse et de six pieds," 1 li, 10 li, 100, 1,000, 10,000 or 100,000 li; sometimes it is infinite (*ananta*), immense (*apramāṇa*), like space (*ākāśa*). Similarly, the secret of the Buddha's voice is that the assemblies are able to hear it at a distance of 1 li, 10 li, 100, 1,000, 10,000 or 100,000 li as well as at a distance which is incalculable (*asaṅkhyeya*) and immense (*apramāṇa*) like space. Finally, it appears that the secret of the Buddha's thought is to know the true nature of all things without having created them, as is claimed by Viṣṇu and others.[1]

A thorough discussion of the relationship between the Buddha and the universe would require a full survey of the history of

Siddhi, pp. 769, 786. "Nārāyaṇa dispose dans son corps, ou dans chacune de ses articulations, d'une force constituant le septième terme d'une série qui commence par l'éléphant et dont chaque terme vaut dix fois le précédent." Lamotte, *Enseignement*, p. 287, n. 8. See also La Vallée Poussin, *Kośa*, chap. vii, p. 72.

1. Lamotte, *Traité*, pp. 560-62.

Buddhist ontology. Suffice it to say that it is not exhausted by these examples from the "*sāhasra*-cosmology" but is implicit in those of the "*asaṅkhyeya*-cosmology" as well, and, we may suspect, in all Buddhist cosmological speculations. The *Śūraṃgamgasamādhisūtra* defines the relationship between the world and the bodhisattva practicing this particular concentration (whom we may regard as a Buddha) in a particularly striking manner: "The nature of things (*dharmasvabhāva*) makes up the body of the bodhisattva; things constitute his domain (*vihāra*)."[1]

As a result of these considerations, it is not unreasonable to conclude that the "realm of thousands which is ever increasing by thousands" and the Buddha are coterminus. Arguments which restrict the domain of a Buddha to a *trisāhasramahāsāhasralokadhātu* understand the *trisāhasramahāsāhasralokadhātu* as a limited cosmic nexus rather than as encompassing the entire cosmos as we have suggested for its original meaning.[2] Because the *nirmāṇabuddhas* are related to the Buddha as leaves to the stem of a plant, or even better as a plant to the seed, they do not violate the integrity of the Buddha-nature. Similarly, the existence or appearance of the *nirmāṇabuddhas* does not violate the contention of the Sarvāstivādins, and of the Hīnayāna in general, that there is only one Buddha and a single *buddhakṣetra*. The significance of this fact will be explored more completely in the next Chapter. For the time being it will suffice to note that the *Mppś* clearly juxtaposes the *nirmāṇabuddhas* to the *daśadigbuddhas* or Buddhas of the ten regions. The *daśadigbuddhas* are said to be equally real and to reside in innumerable *buddhakṣetras* distributed throughout the ten regions of space.

An additional attribute of the *nirmāṇabuddhas* is that they are clearly linked to the teaching of the *dharma*. Within a *trisāhasramahāsāhasralokadhātu* the Buddha utilizes the *nirmāṇabuddhas* for the preaching of the law.[3] As such, they are the

1. Lamotte, "Marche," p. 152.

2. La Vallée Pousin, *Kośa*, chap. iii, p. 199, n. 1.; Lamotte, *Traité*, pp. 302, n. 1; 535, 536 ff.

3. "Actuellement les Buddha des dix régions prêchent toujours la loi et délèguent toujours des Buddha fictifs dans les univers des dix régions pour prêcher les six Pāramitā. . . ." Lamotte, *Traité*, p. 471. "Dans les dix régions, ces Trisāhasramanāsāhasralokadhātu sont aussi nombreux que

"voice" of the Buddha, a fact which is the focus of a full range of speculations concerning the relationship between the Buddha and the *nirmāṇabuddhas*. Certain doctors argued that the *nirmāṇabuddhas* could only speak when the Buddha spoke. Others maintained that they could speak only when the Buddha was silent, both apparently stressing the phantom-like character of the *nirmāṇabuddhas*. However, La Vallée Poussin, in summarizing this discussion, concludes that "Les 'êtres crées' ne sont pas plus seulement des fantômes qui parlent quand parle leur 'créateur' et se taisent quant il se tait. Le Bouddha fait converser deux bouddhas fictifs."[1] The *Mppś* resolves this relationship by stating that the Buddha remains constantly in *samādhi*, but due to merits, answers in other ways.[2] Again, these speculations appear to examine the relationship between the meditations of the Buddha and the acquisition of the powers of *nirmāṇa*. If the *nirmāṇabuddhas* speak when the Buddha is silent, this means that they are related to his absorption or extinction in *nirvāṇa*. If they speak when the Buddha speaks, the Buddha is not fully extinct, etc. This discussion parallels that of the extinction of the Tathāgata which belongs to the fourteen difficult questions[3] and, like them, every possible position appears to have been argued.

Because the *nirmāṇabuddhas* are so closely associated with the teaching of the *dharma*, the voice of the Buddha, and are probably coterminus with what Buddhaghosa has referred to as the "authority realm" (*āṇākhetta*) of the Buddha, it is important to understand the precise manner in which the teaching is manifest. Stated briefly, the thrust of our research leads to the conclusion that the *nirmāṇabuddhas* find their cosmological expression in the wheel of the "fixed" stars. As noted in the Introduction, the perfect, circular motion of the stars was

les sables du Gange et chacun d'eux constitue l'univers d'un Buddha (*ekabuddhalokadhātu*); on n'y rencontre qu'un seul Buddha, jamais deux. Dans un de ces univers de Buddha, le seul Buddha Śakyamuni crée sans cesse des Buddha fictifs (*nirmāṇabuddha*) qui recourent à des predications (*dharmaparyāya*), à des corps (*kāya*) fictifs, à des causes (*nidāna*) et à des artifices (*upāya*) de toutes sortes pour sauver les êtres." Ibid., pp. 540-41.

1. La Vallée Poussin, *Siddhi*, p. 770.
2. Lamotte, *Traité*, pp. 559-60.
3. See above, Chapter I.

regarded as an indication of divinity. Because the motion of the stars is eternal, the beings who inhabited these realms are immortal; they are gods. As a result, the pure motion of the luminous bodies was further regarded as the manifestation of an eternal divine law, a teaching of the immortality of the soul. As revealer of the law, the wheel of the stars is the teacher of mankind; an activity which exactly parallels the teaching function of the *nirmāṇabuddhas*.

The wheel of the stars, while it is the wheel of immortality, is also the wheel of time. It is by virtue of the motion of the heavenly bodies that time is reckoned. We have already postulated a relationship between the wheel of the stars and the wheel of the *dharma*; the wheel of the law; the teaching. Moreover, the thrust of this Chapter has been to point out the close relationship between the "ever-multiplying" or "ever-measuring" universe, the *trisāhasramahāsāhasralokadhātu*, and the self-multiplying *nirmāṇabuddhas*. It should also be noted that in at least one of its meanings, the idea of *nirmāṇa* is closely associated with the idea of "measurement" of "discrimination." Thus, while both the *trisāhasramahāsāhasralokadhātu* and the *nirmāṇabuddhas* are "ever-multiplying" or "ever-measuring," both affirm an underlying unity; a single universe and a single Buddha. Finally, because the primary function of the *nirmāṇabuddhas* is the teaching, the teaching of the *nirmāṇabuddhas* and the setting for the cosmic drama of salvation provided by the *trisāhasramahāsāhasralokadhātu*, appears to be inextricably related to the passage and measurement of time.

CHAPTER IV

THE DRAMA OF THE "*SĀHASRA* COSMOLOGY" AND THE "PATH"

The appearance of a Buddha is as rare as the blooming of an *udumbara* plant.

Intervals of Cosmic Time

The manner in which salvation occurs within the structures of the *trisāhasramahāsāhasralokadhātu* is inextricably related to the passage of cosmic time. The development of doctrines concerning cosmic time is a topic of enormous scope and exceeds the boundaries of both Buddhism and India. The fundamental idea which underlies the measurement of cosmic time eventuating in the doctrines of world cycles derives from the observation of the planetary motions and their conjunctions. Since the planets follow basically circular paths, albeit irregular in appearance, it is logical to conclude that there was a time when all planets were in conjunction, a configuration to which they will again return at some future time, thus marking the end of a world cycle. A world cycle then is the period in which the planets with their apogees and nodes make a complete revolution without remainder.[1] By observing the motions of the heavenly bodies, the astronomers sought to mathematically compute the duration of time between the beginning and the end of the world cycle. While it is not the concern of the Buddhist texts to calculate the length of time which constitutes the duration of a Kalpa, there can be little doubt that the "*sāhasra*-cosmologies" are inspired by the theologies of time and eternity associated with these speculations. Therefore, we must begin this examination of the drama of salvation belonging to the *trisāhasramahāsāhasralokadhātu* by reviewing the structures of cosmic time which dominate this drama.

The divisions of cosmic time outlined in the *Kośa* are predictably elaborate. A *mahākalpa* consists of four moments (*kalpa*)

1. Al-Biruni, *Astrology*, p. 113.

each of which contains twenty *antarakalpas*. Thus, the *mahākalpa* consists of (1) a *kalpa* of creation (*vivartakalpa*) which extends from the primordial wind to the production of the first being which inhabits the hells; (2) a *kalpa* which consists of the duration of the creation (*vivartasthāyikalpa*) which begins with the appearance of the first being in the hells;[1] (3) a *kalpa* of dissolution (*saṃvartakalpa*) commencing with the moment when beings cease to be reborn in the hells to the moment when the receptacle world is destroyed;[2] and (4) a *kalpa* during which the world remains dissolved (*saṃvartasthāyikalpa*) and during which nothing remains but space (*ākāśa*) where the world was.[3]

Each of the four *kalpas* are sometimes designated as *asaṅkhyeyakalpas*, a fact for which I have no explanation,[4] particularly in light of the other uses of the *asaṅkhyeyakalpas* discussed in conjunction with the career of the bodhisattva. As noted, each of these four *kalpas* further consists of twenty small or "intermediate" *kalpas* (*antarakalpas*). In a period of creation, the receptacle world (*bhājanaloka*) is created during the first *antarakalpa* while beings appear during the remaining nineteen. A reverse process occurs during a period of destruction. At the end of a period of creation, humans have a life which is infinite in duration. During the first *antarakalpa* of the duration of the creation, it diminishes (*apakarṣa*) down to ten years. Each of the next eighteen *antarakalpas* consists of an augmentation (*utkarṣa*) of life from ten years up to 80,000 years and a subsequent diminution back down to ten years again. The twentieth *antarakalpa* consists solely of augmentation up to 80,000 years. The time required for the augmentation and diminution which constitute the middle eighteen *antarakalpas* is equivalent to the total time required for the diminution of the first *antarakalpa* and the augmentation of the last.[5] We may simply note in passing that the full duration of the twenty *antarakalpas* then is equivalent to thirty-six *antarakalpas* of the middle variety. There is no augmentation or diminution of human life during

1. La Vallee Poussin, *Kośa*, chap. iii, p. 186.
2. Ibid., p. 182.
3. Ibid., p. 185.
4. Ibid., p. 181, n. 2.
5. Ibid., p. 187.

the other three *kalpas* although each is equal in duration to the twenty *antarakalpas* which constitute the period of the duration of the creation.[1] The "intermediate" *kalpa* ends by means of the sword (*śastra*), disease (*roga*) and poverty (*durbhikṣa*) which have a duration respectively of seven days, seven months and seven years.[2] The continents of Videha and Godānīya are not familiar with the three calamities. However, wickedness, discoloration and weakness, hunger and thirst reign in these realms when Jambudvīpa is overcome by the sword, disease and poverty.[3]

When all beings have disappeared from the inferior realms and are reunited (*saṃvart*) in a *dhyāna* heaven, the destructions (*saṃvartānis*) take place.[4] The destructions are of three kinds: those by fire, those by water and those by wind.[5] The second *dhyāna* is the limit (*sīmā*) of the destruction by fire; everything which is lower is burned and scorched. The third *dhyāna* is the limit of the destruction by water; everything which is lower is decomposed or dissolved.[6] The fourth *dhyāna* is the limit of the destruction by wind; everything which is lower is scattered. The destructions succeed one another in the following sequence: seven by fire followed by a destruction by water. This cycle of eight destructions is repeated a total of seven times. This is then followed by seven more destructions by fire, followed by a final by wind. Thus there are 7 x 8 or 56 destructions by fire; 7 by water and a final 64th destruction by wind.[7] The various

1. Ibid.
2. Ibid., pp. 207; 207, n. 1; Lamotte, *Traité*, p. 449. Compare: "In any quarter where all the planets together either appear of set helically, will be danger from the raging of the sword, from famine and calamities." *The Bṛhat-Saṃhitā or Complete System of Natural Astrology of Varāha-Mihira*, trans. Hendrik Kern (London: Paternoster Row, 1869), p. 112.
3. La Vallée Poussin, *Kośa*, chap. iii, p. 209. A summary of this structure of the *mahākalpa*, *asaṅkhyeyakalpas* and *antarakalpas* is also provided in Lamotte, *Enseignement*, p. 296, n. 37.
4. La Vallée Poussin, *Kośa*, chap. iii, p. 210.
5. Ibid. For the relationship between the destructions and the atomic nature of matter, see ibid., pp. 184, n. 4; 210-14. There is no destruction by earth because that which is known as the "receptable" (i.e., that which is destroyed) is made of earth. Ibid., p. 216.
6. Ibid., p. 184, n. 4.
7. Ibid., pp. 216-17.

receptacles exist as a result of the duration of the gods who are born there as a result of their meditation.[1]

The Path and the Wheel of Brahmā

While the drama of salvation within the *trisāhasramahāsāhasra-lokadhātu* is framed by the elaborate speculations on cosmic time, speculations which are at the very heart of the "*sāhasra*-cosmology," the drama proper may be said to divide itself into four apparently discrete moments. The first is that of the progress of the *śrāvaka* or one who has taken up the religious vocation toward the state of *arhat*. Second is the exercise of the miraculous powers, and particularly that of *nirmāṇa* by the *arhat*. Third is the career of the bodhisattva; the *arhat* who makes a vow in the presence of a Buddha to pursue Buddhahood rather than pass into the extinction of *nirvāṇa*. The fourth moment in the drama is the appearance of a Buddha. Each of these moments in the drama of salvation is so complex and the witness of every text belies so many layers of speculation that more than a cursory review would embroil us in a history of Buddhist doctrine which we are totally unprepared to undertake. However, since this area is extremely suggestive for future research, my intention is to indicate some of the detail which confronts us together with some of the bibliographical resources at our disposal.

The progress of the *śrāvaka* toward the state of *arhat* consists of a series of practices, teachings and meditations designated in a general way as "the path".[2] Properly speaking, the path

1. Ibid., p. 217.

2. For discussions of the complex and detailed career of the *Śrāvaka* toward the state of *arhat*, several excellent summaries are available. Among these are La Vallée Poussin, *Kośa*, "Avant-Propos: Note sommaire sur le Chemin," chap. iv, pp. iv-xi which calls attention to the role of the *brahma-cakra/dharmacakra* without attempting to interpret its significance; Lamotte, "Marche," pp. 14-16, 246, n. 299 emphasizing the role of *prajñā* in the pursuit of *nirvāṇa*; idem, *Histoire*, pp. 677-86 and Eugen Obermiller, "The Path of the Śrāvaka," in "The Doctrine of Prajñā-pāramitā as exposed in the Abhisamayālaṃkāra of Maitreya," *Acta Orientalia* 11 (1932): 18-26. In keeping with our overall thesis, it is important to emphasize that the career of the *śrāvaka* should not be regarded in isolation from other "journeys of the soul" found in other traditons, both non-Buddhist and non-Indian. The journey

is made up of the abandonment of the *kleśas* or defilements. However, this is preceded by a series of practices which are regarded as preparatory or as part of an extended path (*prayogamārga*). These preparatory acts constitute the First Five steps of the overall path to liberation which may be summarized as follows:

(1) Acquisition of the "roots of good which are productive of deliverance" (*mokṣabhāgīya kuśalamūla*). These include the thought and acts inspired by the desire for deliverance in an existence prior to the one in which those acts immediately preparatory to the path occur.

(2) Acquisition of the *āryavaṃśas* or moral qualities of the monk. These consist of the qualities of the monk (*upāsaka*) who has mastered the *Prātimokṣa* or monastic code of conduct.

(3) Practice of the meditation on the horrible and the application of memory to respiration. In this manner, one masters desire and distraction, thus becoming able to enter into concentration (*bhāvanā* or *samādhi*).

(4) "Applications of memory" or "applications of *prajñā* as a result of memory" (*smṛtyupasthāna*) which allow an understanding of the special and general characteristics of the body, sensation and thought, i.e., the dharmas in general.

(5) Acquisition of the four "roots of good" (*kuśalamūla*) which are *smṛtyupasthānas* of a superior nature, the highest of

of the soul in Ājīvika doctrine provides a particularly interesting contrast to Buddhist teaching. The nature of *nirvāṇa* and the subsequent role of the bodhisattva (see Chapter I, p. 2, n.1) is of particular interest in its Ājīvika setting. For an exceptionally coherent account of the relevant materials, see Basham, *Ājīvikas*, esp. pp. 258 ff. The journey of the soul in the Purāṇas and its relationship to the various *pralayas* is discussed in Biardeau, "Mythologie," esp. Pt. III. Concluding the *Mahābhārata* is a detailed account of the journey of the Pāṇḍavas through all the abodes of heaven and hell, a theme which we have not emphasized, but which is present in Buddhism (see La Vallée Poussin, *Kośa*, chap. vii, pp. 95-96; Warren, *Buddhism*, pp. 109-10), in the Ājīvika tradition (see Basham, *Ājīvikas*, pp. 245-46) and in Orphism (see Plato, *The Republic*, pp. 393-401). The 12,000 year journey of the soul caught in a cosmic struggle between good and evil in the *Bundahisn* is outlined in Zaehner, *Zurvan*, esp. pp. 80-104. Orphic materials are summarized in Guthrie, *Greeks*, esp. pp. 318-26. An exceptionally rich interpretation of the symbolism associated with numerous mystical journeys in the Persian Sufi and Shi'ite traditions is found in Corbin, *Avicenna*. Cumont provides access to comparable Hellenistic materials in *Astrology*, esp. pp. 92-110 and idem, *After Life*, esp. pp. 91-109.

which, the *laukikāgradharmas* or "the highest meditation on the mundane order" leads directly to a pure view of the truths, the *abhisamaya*. The completion of this stage constitutes the completion of the preliminary path (*prayogamārga*).

(6) The *abhisamaya* or the *satyābhisamaya*, the "comprehension of the truths" is the beginning of the path proper. Each truth, i.e., the Four Holy Truths identified with the sermon at Benares, has four aspects (*ākāras*), and their comprehension is gradual (*anupūrva*). Because there are four truths, each composed of four aspects, the *abhisamaya* consists of sixteen thoughts, each of which consists of two moments; a patience (*kṣānti*) and a knowledge (*jñāna*). The first moment makes the ascetic an *Ārya* or candidate for the first fruit of the path.

(7) The first fifteen moments of the *abhisamaya* constitute the "path of vision" (*satyadarśanamārga* or *darśanamārga*) because they constitute the first pure view of the truths. The "path of vision" is identified with the *dharmacakra* or wheel of the law which we are told moves with such rapidity that it is difficult for a saint able to know the thoughts of others to follow the progress of an ascetic entered upon the *darśanamārga*. We have already seen that the *dharmacakra* finds its cosmological expression in the wheel of the "fixed" stars. The fact that it is here identified with the four holy truths confirms our earlier insight that the *dharmacakra* is the manifestation of the teaching par excellence.

At the sixteenth moment of the *darśanamārga*, which coincides with the first moment of the "path of meditation" (*bhāvanāmārga*), the ascetic takes possession of the first fruit of the path, that of *srotāpanna* or "Stream-winner." At this point, his deliverance is certain and it is rapid. He will obtain *nirvāṇa* after seven (or after fourteen) rebirths at the most. The fact that deliverance is a certainty is tantamount to a notion of becoming "fixed" in the path of enlightenment.[1] Gosāla associates this event with the passage of time. The Mahāyāna apparently associates it with the copious displays of light exhibited by the Buddha. In any event, it is clear that as a result of having completed the sixteenth moment of the *darśanamārga*, the ascetic has mastered the teaching and has become "oriented."

1. See below, Chapter V, p. 98, n. 1, 2.

He has entered the stream of *nirvāṇa*. As a result, his deliverance is now a certainty.

The "path of vision," however, only liberates one from the false views (*dṛṣṭis*), e.g., the idea of "self," etc. The *kleśas* can be abandoned only by means of the path of meditation (*bhāvanāmārga*). The path of meditation may be pure (*anāsrava*) and supermundane (*lokottara*) or impure (*sāsrava* or *samala*) and mundane (*laukika*). If the ascetic has not extricated himself from the *kleśas* by means of the mundane path of meditation, he leaves the "path of vision" encumbered with countless *kleśas*.

(8) An ascetic who is still encumbered by all the bonds which must be discarded through meditation, exits the path of vision and enters upon the pure path of meditation. The pure path may not be practiced except by one who has travelled the "path of vision." It consists in the repeated contemplation of the truths. In this manner, the ascetic abandons the nine categories of *kleśas* associated with each of the nine stages of existence (i.e., Kāmadhātu, four Dhyānas and four Ārūpyas). The abandonment of each of the nine categories of *kleśas* at each of the nine stages of existence constitutes a moment of abandonment or expulsion (*prahāṇa* or *ānantaryamārga*) and a moment of deliverance (*vimuktimārga*) at which moment the ascetic takes possession of the destruction of that category, thus making a total of 162 moments in the path of meditation.

The ascetic who abandons the sixth category of *kleśas* of the Kāmadhātu becomes *sakṛdāgāmin* or a "once-returner." He will not be reborn in the Kāmadhātu more than one more time. The individual who abandons the ninth category of the Kāmadhātu becomes *anāgāmin* or a "never-returner." He is liberated from further rebirth in the Kāmadhātu altogether.[1] The path

1. It is generally recognized that the goal of the Hīnayāna is to reach a plane beyond the three dhātus (Kāmadhātu, Rūpadhātu and Ārūpyadhātu). This is clear in the *Visuddhimagga*, for instance, where the four fruits of the path are found "above" the Ārūpyadhātu. See Ñāṇamoli, *Path of Purification*, p. 881. To the best of my knowledge, the *Kośa* makes no specific statement regarding the "location" of the fruits of the path. Moreover, it is not clear whether or not the distinction of the *Kośa* between *lokottara* and *laukika* is intended as a statement that the possession of the "fruits" is possible within the three dhātus. The emphatic manner in which the *Kośa* denies that the Ārūpyas are in any way "above" the meditation realms may suggest a tendency to restrict the path and its fruits to these realms.

of abandonment (*ānantaryamārga*) by means of which the ascetic abandons the ninth category of *kleśas* of the ninth sphere (the 4th Ārūpya; the *bhavāgra*) is known as the *vajropamasamādhi*. It is followed by the "path of deliverance" (*vimuktimārga*) in which the ascetic takes possession of the destruotion of all the *kleśas* or *āsravas*. The ascetic has become *arhat* or *aśaikṣa*. He is unshakable/indestructible ("inébranlable") (*akopya*.)[1]

It is normal for an ascetic to have practiced the mundane path of meditation before entering the path of the pure view of the truths. This includes all those beings who are reborn in the *dhyānas* during certain periods of chaos.[2] An individual who has pursued the mundane path of meditation does not become a *srotāpanna* in following the path of vision but only a *sakṛdāgāmin* or *anāgāmin* as the case may be. The Buddha is an example of this method. He was a *pṛthagjana* when he went under the Bodhi tree, but a *pṛthagjana* who had practiced the mundane path of meditation to its limit. He had no attachment except to the fourth Ārūpya, the *bhavāgra*. At the same time he obtained the quality of *arhat*, which for him was the quality of *samyaksambuddha*,[3] in thirty-four moments of thought. These consisted of the sixteen moments of the "comprehension of the truths" (*abhisamaya*) corresponding to the "path of vision" or the *dharmacakra*. This made him an *anāgāmin* detached from all existence except the *bhavāgra*. The sixteen moments of the *abhisamaya* were followed by nine moments of deliverance which destroyed the *kleśas* of the *bhavāgra*.

Once having attained the state of *arhat*, a number of events occur. First, the *arhat* orients his thought in such a way as to produce from his body another body which has form but which is spiritual in nature.[4] These creations of the *arhat* are

1. La Vallée Poussin, *Kośa*, chap. vi, p. 250. I have included the French "inébranlable" since La Vallée Poussin's conclusion that *nirvāṇa* constitutes "un séjour inébranlable" has been followed by a number of scholars. See Lamotte, *Histoire*, p. 676; Guy Welbon, *The Buddhist Nirvāṇa and Its Western Interpreters* (Chicago : University of Chicago Press, 1967), p. 299.

2. La Vallée Poussin, *Kośa*, chap. viii, p. 217.

3. According to Lamotte, Śākyamuni became an *arhat* as a result of his concentrations under the Bo-Tree. He became a Buddha as a result of meritorious acts performed in previous existences. "Marche," p. 20.

4. Ibid., pp. 23-24.

related to the powers of *nirmāṇa* or magical creation which he acquires. We are told that the *śrāvakas* who are *aśaikṣa* attain enlightenment (*sambodhi*) not with a birth body (*janmakāya*) which is subject to karmic retribution (*karmavipākakāya*), but with a *nirmāṇakāya* which is not created by the retribution of acts.[1] We read further that the non-arhat, being born in a time when there is no Buddha, practices the meditations in order to obtain a *nirmāṇa*-existence.[2] In fact, as we shall see, the power of *nirmāṇa* appears to be closely related to the non-appearance of a Buddha.

It is my opinion that in order to come to terms with the role of the magical creations of the *arhat*, it is necessary to examine the structure of the *antarakalpas*. We may simply recall that each of the *antarakalpas* except the last presents us with a picture of a steady diminution in the duration of human life. This fact has several corollaries which provide clues in helping to unravel the drama of the *antarakalpas*. First, a steady decline in the duration of human life from endless down to ten years suggests that all beings born in the same *antarakalpa*, regardless of the moment of their birth, are destined to live to the end of the *antarakalpa*. A person born at the beginning would be infinitely remote from the end of the *antarakalpa*, but the duration of his life would be commensurately infinite. Similarly, the time during which human life is only ten years, is right at the end of the *antarakalpa*, so that those individuals would also be destined to witness or experience the end of the *antarakalpa*.

A second feature of life in the *antarakalpas* is what the *Kośa* terms *antarāmṛtyu*,[3] interrupted life or intermediate death, i.e., death which is prior to the exhaustion of one's allotted destiny. The phenomenon of *antarāmṛtyu* is found in all of the *dvīpas* except Uttarakuru.[4] Placing the phenomenon of *antarāmṛtyu* together with the idea that all beings are destined to live to the end of the *kalpa* means that everything we might term observable or physical death is really an interruption of a destined order. The very fact of transmigration suggests this in

1. *Siddhi*, p. 507.
2. Ibid., p. 508.
3. La Vallée Poussin, *Kośa*, chap. iii, p. 176.
4. Ibid.

itself. It is in this context that we begin to understand the powers of *nirmāṇa* which belong to the *arhat*.

The power of *nirmāṇa* as employed by the *arhat* is generally related to the creation of a body which exists after death. In the *Abhidhamma-Piṭaka* we find arguments refuting the power of the *arhat* to extend his life,[1] although the ability of the *arhat* to produce magical creations is not challenged and in some cases is affirmed.[2] However, in other places the issue centers about the question of the duration of these creations. The creations of the heretics last only seven days while those of the Buddha and the disciples have unlimited duration.[3] According to some, the prolonged life of the *arhat* is the fruit of previous existences.[4] Elsewhere, it is clear that the central issue is whether the *arhat* can create a magical body which will endure until the end of the Kalpa,[5] or more than a Kalpa.[6] Because of the declining nature of life in the *antarakalpa* and because of the phenomenon of *antarāmṛtyu* which the *Kośa* informs us occurs everywhere except Kuru, it is my opinion that the question of the "end of the Kalpa" in this case may mean the end of the *antarakalpa*. The power of *nirmāṇa*, then, would effectively permit the *arhat* to live out his full destiny without regard to any "intermediate death."

In a sense, the *arhat* is one who has experienced the final death of *nirvāṇa* in a premature sense, i.e., before the end of the *antarakalpa*. Since he cannot be reborn in a transmigrating body or birth body, he must continue to exist to the end of the *antarakalpa* (the apparent destiny of all beings) in a different mode. While we are not in a position to elaborate on the full drama

1. Bhikku Nyanatiloka, *Guide Through the Abhidhamma-Piṭaka* (London : Luzac & Co., 1938), pp. 53, 59.
2. See Conze, *Meditation*, p. 61 and Rowell, "Background," 7:154-63.
3. Lamotte, *Traité*, p. 330.
4. La Vallée Poussin, *Kośa*, chap. ii, p. 121.
5. The issue is taken up in Question No. 109 of the *Kathā-Vatthu* : "May one endowed with magical power live on for a world period (*kappa*) ?—This erroneous view of the Mahās (āṃghikas), is based on the wrong understanding of the word *kappa* in the famous passage of the Mahāparinibbāna-Sutta where it has not the usual meaning of 'world period,' but of 'life-time.' Magical power....may only prevent untimely death." Nyanatiloka, *Guide*, p. 53.
6. La Vallée Poussin, *Kośa*, chap. ii. p. 124, n. 3.

of the *antarakalpa*, it appears that the *antarakalpas* provide a a kind of *terminus ad quem* for the *nirmāṇa* bodies; an intermediate point where the *arhats* may cease transmigrating until the destructions occur in earnest. Conceivably, the passages which speculate as to whether the *arhat* can extend his life more than Kalpa are speculating on the possibility that he extends it beyond the *antarakalpa* all the way to the full destruction at the end of a *mahākalpa*.[1]

The importance of reaching the end of the *mahākalpa* can only be understood in terms of the special prerogatives which are afforded beings at this eschatological moment. The end of the *mahākalpa* is a time when all beings are elevated into the *dhyāna* heavens as a result of the destruction of the Kāmadhātu. They are elevated to the second, third or fourth *dhyānas* depending on the moment in the cycle of sixty-four destructions. Coincident with being elevated to the *dhyānas* and probably as a result of this elevation, all beings obtain what amount to the the "super-knowledges" (*abhijñā*).[2]

Finally, we read in a particularly striking passage that the *parinirvāṇa* of the *arhat* coincides with the *nirvāṇa* of the Buddha.[3] If we allow ourselves to equate the Buddha's *nirvāṇa* with the destruction of the *mahākalpa*, we may read that the *parinirvāṇa* of the *arhat* occurs at the end of the *mahākalpa*. This interpretation is facilitated by the efforts to make the universe correspond to parts of the Buddha's body, the multivalence of the term *pralaya* to mean the destruction of the world at the end of an age, the spiritual extinction of *nirvāṇa* and the

1. The power of the *arhat* in this regard appears to be analogous to a more general phenomenon of which we are aware, namely the special destiny reserved for those individuals subject to premature death, especially children and warriors. In both cases, the interruption of the natural destiny of these individuals is compensated for by the formation of a shadow existence, an *eidolon* or mental body, which continues until the original destiny has been completed. See especially Franz Cumont, "Virgile et les morts prématurée," in *Conférences* (Paris : Librarie E. Droz, 1945), pp. 121-52, and idem, *After Life*, especially the chapter on "Untimely Death," pp. 128-47.

2. According to the *Mppś*, "at the end of a Kalpa, at the moment of combustion, all beings obtain the concentration (of wisdom) (*prajñāsaṃbodhi*), the divine eye (*divyacakṣus*) and the divine ear (*divyaśrotra*)...." See Lamotte, *Traité*, p. 527.

3. Ibid., p. 89; 89, n. 2.

physical extinction of death and finally by the fact that we are constantly reminded of the non-appearance of a Buddha in a *trisāhasramahāsāhasralokadhātu*. The implication of this final fact in this context is that the void established by the Buddha's *nirvāṇa* is only manifest when the world passes into extinction. The Buddha never appears in a *trisāhasramahāsāhasralokadhātu* because it is the destruction of the *trisāhasramahāsāhasraloka-dhātu* which results in the Buddha's appearance.

Finally, we must recall that an *arhat* can only become a Buddha if he makes a vow in the presence of a Buddha. In this context, it would seem that only the *arhats* pass into *parinirvāṇa* at the end of the *mahākalpa*. All the other beings will be reborn when the retribution of their acts causes the *trisāhasramahāsā-hasralokadhātu* to form again after twenty *antarakalpas* of extinction.

A second event of considerable importance which may occur after attaining the state of *arhat* has to do with whether the *arhat* takes possession of *nirvāṇa* or not. Having achieved the state of *arhat* means that this is the last birth for the *arhat*. Upon dying he will no longer be reborn, but will pass into extinction. However, an individual who achieves the state of *arhat* in an era in which a Buddha appears has another option. He may renounce immediate *nirvāṇa* by virtue of a vow (*praṇidhāna*) to himself become a Buddha, from that moment becoming a bodhisattva. The Buddha of that era then makes a prophecy or prediction (*vyākaraṇa*) as to when and where this bodhisattva will become a Buddha.[1]

1. The activities, appearances, perfections and career of the bodhisattva represent one of the most technical and arduous products of Buddhist scholasticism. The available secondary literature is sufficient to reveal the complexities of the subject, but not to synthesize it into a meaningful whole. Examples include Har Dayal, *The Bodhisattva Doctrine in the Buddhist Sanskrit Literature* (Motilal Banarsidass, Delhi, Reprint, 1976); Louis de La Vallée Poussin, "Bodhisattva," ERE 2:739-53; idem, *Siddhi*, pp. 721-42. For the role of the *buddhakṣetra* in the career of the bodhisattva, see Rowell, "Background," 6:379-405. The problem of the celestial bodhisattvas or bodhisattvas of the tenth stage is introduced in Richard H. Robinson, *The Buddhist Religion* (Belmont, Calif. : Dickenson Publishing Co., Inc., 1970), pp. 58-63. The problem is developed more fully in Étienne Lamotte, "Manjusri," *T'oung Pao* 48 (1960) : 1-96 and to a certain extent in

The bodhisattva then perfects the various virtues (*pāramitā*) during three *asaṅkhyeyas* of *mahākalpas*.[1] During the first *asaṅkhyeyakalpa*, he honors 75,000 Buddhas, 76,000 during the second and 77,000 during the third.[2] The last Buddha of the first *asaṅkhyeyakalpa* is Ratnaśikhin. Dīpaṅkara completes the second and Vipaśyin the third.[3] After countless rebirths among the excellent destinies,[4] the bodhisattva is born in the Tuṣita heaven, during which time he apparently develops the acts which are productive of the 32 marks of a *mahāpuruṣa*.[5]

"Marche." Lamotte summarizes the ten stages of the career of the bodhisattva as understood in the *Śūramgamasamādhisūtra* in "Marche," p. 155, n. 112.

Western scholars generally characterize the bodhisattva as an "enlightenment-being" whose compassion prevents the taking possession of *nirvāṇa* in order to work instead for the salvation of all beings. But the bodhisattva doctrine has been bent to too many purposes to allow even this characterization to go unqualified. A striking exception is the close relationship between the bodhisattvas and the doctrine of *nirvāṇa* as non-abiding (*apratiṣṭhita nirvāṇa*), see Lamotte, *Histoire*, p. 90; idem, "Marche," p. 235; idem, *Enseignement*, p. 144, n. 8. Holmes Welch observes : "..there is not the absolute difference between buddhas and bodhisattvas that we read about in Western books on Buddhism, I have read—and written—that buddhas are withdrawn in nirvana and take no active part in the saving of others; whereas bodhisattvas have postponed entering nirvana themselves until they can help all sentient beings to enter it before them. But according to the monks I have talked to, buddhas exert themselves to save all sentient beings...Furthermore, on their missions of salvation, all of them, like Vimalakirti, may take the form of bodhisattvas or of laymen." Holmes Welch, *The Practice of Chinese Buddhism*, 1900-1950 (Cambridge: Harvard University Press, 1967), p. 85. Clearly what is at stake is a disagreement regarding the relationship of the bodhisattva to *nirvāṇa*. This issue is further complicated by the observation of Leon Hurvitz that the boshisattva of the Pāli texts appears as the Buddha before he attains the state of Buddhahood while the best known bodhisattvas of the Sanskrit tradition are destined to be bodhisattvas forever. See Hurvitz, "Chih-I," p. 255.

1. La Vallée Poussin, "Bodhisattva," p. 739.
2. Idem, *Kośa*, chap. iv, p. 227.
3. Ibid., p. 228.
4. Ibid., p. 222.
5. Lamotte, *Traité*, pp. 249-55, 271-81, 294-96, 1905-19; La Vallée Poussin, *Kośa*, chap. iv, pp. 220-27; Lamotte, *Histoire*, p. 738. Long discussions of the 32 *lakṣaṇas* are found in Eugène Burnouf, *Le lotus de la bonne loi*, 2 vols. (Paris : Maisonneuve frères, 1925), 2 : 553-647; and Émile Senart,

During the course of 100 supplementary cosmic ages (*kalpaśate śeṣe*),[1] he projects in Jambudvīpa those acts which have the marks as retribution. He projects them being a male and he projects them only in the presence of a Buddha.[2] The *Śāstra* informs us that the duration of life in the Tuṣita coincides with the epochs in which the Buddhas appear.[3] As a result of the purification of his energy, Śākyamuni was able to skip 9 of the 100 ages, projecting the acts productive of the marks during the course of 91 cosmic ages (*ekanavatyāṃ kalpeṣu*).[4] Although the *Kośa* does not elaborate, we must assume that the career of the bodhisattva culminates with a journey to the center of Jambudvīpa for the purpose of assuming his position on the "adamantine throne" (*vajrāsana*). It is on this throne and nowhere else that the bodhisattva realizes the *vajropamasamādhi*, thus becoming at once *arhat* and Buddha.[5]

The final stage of the drama of the *trisāhasramahāsāhasra-lokadhātu* has to do with the appearance of a Buddha. Despite the importance of a Buddha's appearance, there is little agreement as to when or where this occurs. Indeed, it is a major focus of doctrinal disagreement. It is generally agreed that a Buddha only appears during a period when the length of human life is declining and when it is between 80,000 and 100 years. More than this and human beings live too long to be aware of the impermanent nature of things; less than this and life is too short and the five corruptions (*kaṣāyas*) are too strong.[6] However, there are a wide range of opinions with regard to when the Buddhas appear, what era we are currently in and the length

Essai sur la légende du Buddha (Paris : Imprimerie Nationale, 1975), pp. 106-91. See also Hurvitz, "Chih-I," pp. 353-61; and Edward Conze, "The Buddha's lakṣaṇas in the Prajñāpāramitā," *Journal of the Oriental Institute* (Baroda) 14 (1965) : 225-29.

1. Lamotte, *Traité*, p. 252; 252, n. 1; La Vallée Poussin, *Kośa*, chap. iv, pp. 223; 223, n. 2; 224, n. 1.
2. La Vallée Poussin, *Kośa*, chap iv, p. 223.
3. Lamotte, *Traité*, p. 268; 268, n. 7.
4. La Vallée Poussin, *Kośa*, chap iv, p. 225; 225, n. 1. See also La Vallée Poussin, "Les neuf kalpas qu'a franchis Śakyamuni pour devancer Maitreya," *T'oung Pao*, 2d series 26 (1929) : 17-24.
5. La Vallée Poussin, *Kośa*, chap. iii, p. 145.
6. Ibid., p. 193.

of life at the time of appearance.[1] The question of the appearance of a Buddha in a *trisāhasramahāsāhasralokadhātu* is further complicated when we recall the relation which we observed between the Buddha and the *nirmāṇabuddha*. There, we concluded that the *nirmāṇabuddhas* were the product of the *abhijñās* of a Buddha absorbed in trance—fully extinct. If this is the case, then a Buddha would never appear in a *trisāhasramahāsāhasralokadhātu*. In point of fact, this position corresponds exactly to that of the Sarvâstivâdins who maintained that one who has achieved *nirvāṇa* no longer exists.[2]

If we are to understand the question of the Buddha's appearance in the sense of the final product of an infinitely long apprenticeship—the preliminary path (*prayoga*), the 16 moments of the *abhisamaya*, the 182 moments of the *bhāvanāmārga*, followed by the 3 *asaṅkhyeyakalpas* of the bodhisattva's career—we must agree that the cultivation of the qualities of a Buddha is an arduous and lengthy process. It is the expression par excellence of the gradualist approach which characterizes the Hīnayâna.[3] Moreover, there could be no clearer statement of the meaning of "self-power" as the path to salvation.[4] Whether

1. Excellent summaries of the variations which confront us regarding the appearances of the Buddhas can be found ibid., p. 192, n. 3; Lamotte, *Traité*, pp. 269, n. 1; 299-302; Lamotte, *Enseignement*, p. 385, n. 29; idem, "Marche," p. 190, n. 180.

2. Lamotte, *Histoire*, p. 676; 676, n. 49. The Sarvâstivâdin position thus appears to coincide with question ten among the fourteen questions which the Buddha is said to have refused to answer, i.e., does the Tathâgata not exist after death ? See above, Chapter I.

3. "Tel qu'il était conçu par les Sarvâstivâdins, le Chemin bouddhique représente un admirable monument de scholastique. Il respose sur le conviction que la compréhension des vérités (*abhisamaya*), et partante la marche dans la voie du salut, est progressive ou graduelle (*anupūrva*)." Lamotte, *Histoire*, p. 685.

4. The characterization of the path or drama of the "*sāhasra*-cosmology" as an expression of "self-power" is intended as an important point of contrast with the "other-power" which characterizes the "*asaṅkhyeya*-cosmology." For a discussion of these terms as they play a role in the theologies of Pure Land Buddhism, see Bloom, *Shinran's Gospel;* Paul O. Ingram, "Honen's and Shinran's Justification for Their Doctrine of Salvation by Faith Through 'Other Power,' " *Contemporary Religions in Japan* 9 (1968) : 233-51

we take the appearance of the Buddha to mean the outcome of this arduous gradualism, or whether in the sense of the Buddha being fully extinct with only the *nirmāṇabuddha* appearing, we must accept the judgment of the *Mppś* that the appearance of a Buddha in a *trisāhasramahāsāhasralokaahātu* is a rare event. To borrow the phrase which occurs throughout the Buddhist literature, the appearance of a Buddha is as rare as the blooming of an *udumbara* plant.[1]

In summary, this hasty review of the drama associated with the *trisāhasramahāsāhasralokadhātu* has uncovered two important points. First, the great wheel of the "fixed" stars, the cosmic expression of the teaching in all its forms, whether as the voice of the Buddha, the four holy truths, the *nirmāṇabuddha*, or the *dharmacakra/brahmacakra*, plays a decisive role in the progress of the *śrāvaka*. He must pass through the teaching to gain access to the realms of liberation, the four *dhyāna* heavens of the world of Brahmā. Having fully comprehended the teaching in all its aspects, i.e., having realized the sixteenth moment of the *darśanamārga*, salvation is assured. The ascetic is "fixed" in the path of enlightenment. He is a "Streamwinner," having entered the stream of *nirvāṇa*.[2] Having mastered the teaching, the meditation realms are now accessible to the meditations of the ascetic. He enters the *bhāvanāmārga*. Seven births remain.

Second, it is clear that the overall drama of the *trisāhasramahāsāhasralokadhātu* is cast in the framework of temporal speculations, a fact which further encourages us to see the *trisāhasramahāsāhasralokadhātu* as a Buddhist alternative in expressing the duration of the *mahākalpa* which constitutes the life of Brahmā. If the *Purāṇas* maintain that Brahmā is a creator and that there is a single life of Brahmā which endures for one *mahākalpa*, the Buddhists clearly affirm that it is the acts of beings which

1. Occurrences of this phrase in Mahāyāna texts are cited in Lamotte, *Traité*, p. 304, n. 2. For a parable on whether the Tathāgatas are as numerous as the sands of the Gaṅgā, or as rare as the blooming of an *udumbara* plant, see Daisetz Teitero Suzuki, *Studies*, pp. 148-53. The general conclusion of the *Mppś* seems to be that the appearance of a Buddha in a *trisāhasramahāsāhasralokadhātu* is in fact rare, but this is why it affirms the reality of the Buddhas in the ten regions. See Lamotte, *Traité* pp. 531-80.

2. La Vallée Poussin, *Kośa*, chap. vi, p. 200.

create the world, that there are countless *mahākalpas* and that transmigration has no beginning and no end.

This cursory review of the Hīnayānist drama of salvation has been intended simply to give an indication of a clearly discrete drama associated with the *trisāhasramahāsāhasralokadhātu.* Against the background of this arduous gradualism dominated by the temporal categories of the *mahākalpas* and *antarakalpas*, the drama of the "*asaṅkhyeya*-cosmology" stands out in sharp relief. Despite the tentative nature of our conclusions with regard to the details of this drama of the Hīnayāna, there can be no doubt with regard to the overall thrust.

Further analysis of the career of the *arhat*, bodhisattva and Buddha must be along the lines of drawing a closer relationship between the various moments of the drama and the particulars of the cosmography. It is in conjunction with such an interpretation that we would expect the events associated with an "orientation" to take on a profound significance. We have already seen the outlines of a journey which takes the *śrāvaka* from Jambudvīpa through Brahmā's teaching into the *dhyāna* heavens. From there, a series of seven births await the *srotāpanna.* Then, as bodhisattva, he journeys to the Tuṣita heaven and from there to Jambudvīpa where he travels to the northern region beyond the three sets of ant-shaped mountains to assume his possition on the *vajrāsana.* The details of these careers must be examined in terms of a cosmic journey which is closely associated with them and apparently underlies them. One area in which this approach may yield particular benefits is in connection with the seven births which remain after completing the sixteenth moment of the *darśanamārga.* Where do these births occur and what is their significance? We will offer a suggestion in the form of a quote describing an important moment in the Hellenistic "sidereal mysticism" studied by Cumont:

> . . . our soul descends from the height of heaven to this sublunary world, passing through the gates of the planetary spheres, and thus at its birth the soul acquires the dispositions and the qualities peculiar to each of these stars. After death it regains its celestial home by the same path. Then, as it traverses the zones of the sky, which are placed one above another, it divests itself of the passions and faculties which it has acquired during its descent to earth, as it were of garments. To

the moon it surrenders its vital and alimentary energy, to Mercury its cupidity, to Venus its amorous desires, to the sun its intellectual capacities, to Mars its warlike ardour, to Jupiter its ambitious dreams, to Saturn its slothful tendencies. It is naked, disencumbered of all sensibility when it reaches the eighth heaven, there to enjoy, as a sublime essence, in the eternal light where live the gods, bliss without end.[1]

1. Cumont, *Astrology*, p. 108. The following additional observation is suggestive with regard to understanding the cosmological expression of the "path of the ancestors" (*pitṛyāna*) and the "path of the gods" (*devayāna*) which are prominent in the Brāhmaṇic materials. According to Cumont : "The Milky Way, originally regarded as the path of the sun, remained, according to an opinion which persisted until the end of antiquity, the road by which the gods and heroes rose to the zenith. It was said to cut the zodiac in the tropical signs of Cancer and Capricorn, and it was there that those gates opened by which souls went down from heaven to earth and rose from earth to heaven. The former of these gates was called the Gate of Men, the other the Gate of Gods." Cumont, *After Life*, pp. 152-53.

Chapter V

THE "*ASAṄKHYEYA*-COSMOLOGY" OR "COSMOLOGY OF INNUMERABLES" AND THE TEACHING OF LIGHT

Plant your merits
in this supreme field of merit.

While the "*asaṅkhyeya*-cosmology" preserves the notion that a *buddhakṣetra* is in fact a *trisāhasramahāsāhasralokadhātu*, the numerology of thousands is no longer prominent. Rather, it is the numbers of Buddhas and *buddhakṣetras* distributed throughout the ten regions of space which are important and which are designated in terms of the numerology of the *asaṅkhyeya*. The term *asaṅkhyeya* (*asaṅkhya*; *asaṅkheyya*) is literally an "innumerable" or an "incalculable," and the primary characteristic of the "*asaṅkhyeya*-cosmology" is that of the "innumerables" of Buddhas and *buddhakṣetras* so prominent in the Mahāyāna. Moreover, the powers of the Buddha in the context of the "*asaṅkhyeya*-cosmology" are repeatedly described as being immense (*apramāṇa*), incalculable (*asaṅkhyeya*) and inconceivable (*acintya*).

As with the thousands of the "*sāhasra*-cosmology," these "innumerables" are related to speculations regarding the dimensions or limits of the universe. In the last analysis, these speculations constitute statements about the relation of the Buddha to the world. The primary focus of this relationship is the question of the omniscience of the Buddha. Clearly, the understanding of this relationship in the "*asaṅkhyeya*-cosmology" departs in the most spectacular manner from all those systems which see the cosmos as the domain of a single Buddha. To express the difference most simply, it is that the Buddha whose domain or residence is a single *trisāhasramahāsāhasralokadhātu* is not the same as the Buddha who provides access to all the *buddhakṣetras* in the ten regions of space.

As we have seen, the "*sāhasra*-cosmology" is associated with the schools of the Hīnayāna, in particular the Sarvāstivādin. A number of references in the *Mppś* confirm this association of the "*sāhasra*-cosmology" with the Hīnayāna and the "*asaṅkhyeya*-cosmology" with the Mahāyāna. First, where we find the emphasis on the *buddhakṣetra* as *trisāhasramahāsāhasralokadhātu*, it is understood that there exists a single *buddhakṣetra* consisting of 1,000,000,000 worlds such as the one in which we live. This single *buddhakṣetra* is the *Dharmadhātu* of the Hīnayāna. This, in any event, is the implication in the assertion of the *Śāstra* that in the Hīnayāna there is no question of Buddhas in the ten directions (*daśadigbuddhas*), but only of the one-hundred past Buddhas and five-hundred future Buddhas.[1] Second, another reference suggests that the ability to view the *trisāhasramahāsāhasralokadhātu* is a power of the *arhat*, the saint of the Hīnayāna, and not of the bodhisattva, the saint of the Mahāyāna.[2] Third, a distinction is made between Hīnayānist and Mahāyānist forms of the *buddhānusmṛtisamādhi* or "Concentration Which Recalls the Buddhas." The Hīnayāna is said to regard it as seeing with the eye of thought a single Buddha filling the regions. The bodhisattva, on the other hand, honors all the Buddhas of the ten regions and three times present in the innumerable *buddhakṣetras*.[3] Finally, we read that the Hīnayāna questions the reality of the regions and that for the Hīnayāna, only the "Dharma" region is real.[4] Clearly a single *buddhakṣetra* is juxtaposed to innumerable *buddhakṣetras*.

Just as the "*sāhasra*-cosmology" was dominated by the temporal categories of the Kalpa, the "*asaṅkhyeya*-cosmology" is dominated by spatial categories whose focus is the ten regions. The importance of this spatial imagery is underscored by the reminder of the *Mppś* that according to the Mahāyāna, time does not exist.[5] Just as the appearance of the Buddhas in the "*sāhasra*-cosmology" was linked to the passage of time, the Buddhas which appear in the "*asaṅkhyeya*-cosmology" are associated with the directions or points of space and are referred to as the Buddhas of the ten regions (*daśadigbuddhas*). The *daśadigbuddhas* are all regarded as equally real, and are specifically

1. Lamotte, *Traité*, p. 300, 300, n. 1.
2. Ibid., pp. 331, 332, n. 1.
3. Ibid., p. 409.
4. Ibid., p. 595.
5. Ibid., pp. 1694-96.

juxtaposed to the illusory *nirmāṇabuddhas* of the "*sāhasra*-cosmology." As a result, the appearance of the Buddha is no longer a rare event. Instead, it is repeatedly stated that the Buddhas are as numerous as the sands of the Gaṅgā.

The Basic Mytheme

Commensurate with this new cosmic setting is a drama characterized by a sense of the miraculous and spectacular which cannot be overstated. It is a drama which is variously described from text to text. The Pure Land sūtras of course depict the drama in terms of rebirth in Sukhāvatī as a result of repetition of the name of Amitābha.[1] Other related techniques more closely associated with the Tendai involve the visualization of Buddhas and of the Pure Land.[2] In texts such as the *Śūraṅgamasamādhisūtra*, the drama centers about the concentrations of the *bodhisattvas* of the tenth stage (*bhūmi*).[3]

In the Prajñāpāramitā literature, we find the drama expressed in a mytheme which describes the Great Concentrations of the Buddha Śākyamuni in his cosmic form, and the manner in which the concentrations provide access to the Buddhas and their fields in the ten regions. Because the Great Concentrations are fundamental to the drama of the "*asaṅkhyeya*-cosmology" in all

1. For an excellent discussion of the varieties of techniques associated with the repetition of Amitābha's name (*nembutsu*), see Andrews, *Teachings*, passim.

2. Various techniques of visualization are discussed in Andrews, *Teachings* and Conze, *Miditation*, p. 60. The Greater and Lesser *Sukhāvatī-Vyūha* provide descriptions of the Pure Land Sukhāvatī and the *Amitāyur-dhyāna-Sūtra* describes a series of meditations which have as their goal the visualization of Sukhāvatī. See Cowell, *Buddhist Mahāyāna Texts*. Shan-tao's commentary on the latter text further amplifies the techniques involved in visualizing this paradise. See Julian F. Pas, "Shan-tao's Interpretation of the Meditative vision of Buddha Amitāyus," *History of Religions* 14, No. 2 (November, 1974) : 96-116. Descriptions of the imagery of Sukhāvatī are provided in de Lubac, *Amida*.

3. Lamotte,,"Marche," esp. pp. 31-43. The so-called "Great Concentrations" are a topic of particular interest in Mahāyānist Buddhology. They seem indistinguishable from the concentrations of Śākyamuni described in the *Mppś*, in particular, the *samādhirājasamādhi*. This latter concentration is described as embracing all other concentrations. The Great Concentrations and the *samādhirājasamādhi* are further discussed in Lamotte, *Traité*, p. 1492, n. 1.

its forms, and because the access to the regions afforded by these concentrations pre-figures themes of rebirth in other worlds, we will discuss this mytheme of the Prajñāpāramitā in some detail.

The mytheme in question receives ample comment in a series of ten Acts in Chapters XIV and XV of the *Mppś*. What confronts us is an eschatology uniquely associated with the "*asaṅkhyeya*-cosmology"; what has elsewhere been referred to as the "apocalypses of the *buddhakṣetra*."[1] A summary of the various Acts of the mytheme follows:[2]

Act. I. The Bhagavat enters into the "Concentration which is the King of Concentrations" (*samādhirājasamādhi*) and in which are contained all the concentrations. It is supreme among the *samādhis* and is situated in the fourth *dhyāna*. It is easy for the Buddha to enter the *samādhirājasamādhi*, and it can be obtained by him in an instant. In addition, in the *samādhirājasamādhi*, the Buddha is able to penetrate the ten directions without obstacle or limit and to manifest his great miraculous powers (*ṛddhibala*) through all manner of metamorphosis (*nirmāṇa*) without people mistaking him for a god instead of a man.

Having peacefully departed from the *samādhi*, the Buddha contemplates the universe with his "divine eye" and sees all the beings searching for happiness (*sukha*) but finding only suffering (*duḥkha*). The Buddha then laughs with his entire body, issuing rays of light from a grosser portion of his body (*sthūlabhāga*). Six hundred thousand *prabhedakoṭis* of rays then issue from the thousand-spoked wheels imprinted on the soles of his feet, filling the *trisāhasramahāsāhasralokadhātu* and the ten regions with light and causing countless beings to be intent upon supreme and perfect enlightenment (*anuttarasamyaksambodhi*).

Act II. The Buddha laughs for a second time with all the pores of his skin (*sarvaromakūpa*) and issues rays of light which illuminate the *trisāhasramahāsāhasralokadhātu* and extend to the universes of the ten regions. This time the Buddha laughs with a subtle portion of his body (*sūkṣmabhāga*), causing additional countless beings to be intent upon supreme and perfect enlightenment (*anuttarasamyaksambodhi*).

1. Rowell, "Background," 7:131-45.
2. Lamotte, *Traité*, pp. 431-616; Conze, *Large Sūtra*, pp. 2-9.

Act III. The Buddha emits or projects yet another kind of light; that of his natural or ordinary splendor (*prakṛtiprabhā*) which is that of an aurora or halo extending for a fathom on all four sides of the Buddha. Beings touched by this splendor are again caused to become intent upon enlightenment.

Act IV. The Buddha engulfs the *trisāhasramahāsāhasralokadhātu* with his tongue and begins to laugh for the third time. Hundreds of thousands of *prabhedakoṭis* of rays are emitted from his tongue.[1] Magical Buddhas then appear which begin preaching the six virtues. The beings hearing this demonstration of dharma are caused to become intent upon enlightenment.

Act V. The Buddha enters the *siṃhavikrīḍitasamādhi*, the "Concentration known as the Play of the Lion," and the *trisāhasramahāsāhasralokadhātu* trembles in six directions. In the ten regions, all the hells, animal births and worlds of Yāma are abolished. The beings deceased in these destinies are reborn among men and among the gods of the Kāmadhātu.

Act VI. The Buddha, seated on the Lion's Throne, manifests his light, his splendor, his color and his eminent form.

Act VII. The Buddha shows his natural or ordinary body (*prakṛtyātmabhāva*) to all the beings of the *trisāhasramahāsāhasralokadhātu*, and those who had doubts obtain deliverance through faith (*śraddhāvimukti*). The natural or ordinary body of the Buddha in this context is the body of the thirty-two primary marks and eighty minor marks.

Act VIII. The Buddha laughs with his entire body for a fourth time, illuminating the *trisāhasramahāsāhasralokadhātu* and the ten regions with innumerable rays of light. The effect of this final illumination is to enable the assemblies in the ten regions to view each other. It is only after this has been done that the transformation of Sahā into a "pure" land commences.

Act IX. Having witnessed the rays of light emitted by the Buddha Śākyamuni, the reaction of the Buddhas in the ten regions (*daśadigbuddhas*) is exemplified by that of Ratnākara in the field Ratnāvatī. Ratnākara dispatches the bodhisattva Samantaraśmi to Sahā to honor Śākyamuni with thousand-petaled lotuses. In doing this, he cautions Samantaraśmi

1. For another description of the "langue de lumière," see Corbin, *Lumière*, p. 126, n. 97.

regarding the cleverness of the bodhisattvas of Sahā and the sharpness of their *prajñā* and *upāya*. Before departing for Sahā, Samantaraśmi honors the innumerable Buddhas of the Eastern region. He does this by entering into concentration and extracting all manner of cultic object (*pūjādravya*) from his body. He honors the *daśadigbuddhas* in this manner because they constitute a supreme field of merit (*paramapuṇyakṣetra*).

Act X. Samantaraśmi is then transported to Sahā by means of the rays of Śākyamuni. When he arrives in Sahā, together with the bodhisattvas from the other regions, he honors Śākyamuni with the thousand-petaled lotuses. All the other bodhisattvas make similar offerings, and the sky is filled with flowers. Śākyamuni accepts the offerings which Samantaraśmi has brought and multiplies them to fill the regions, honoring in return the *daśadigbuddhas*. He does this because he too is aware that the *daśadigbuddhas* constitute a supreme field of merit (*paramapuṇyakṣetra*). Following this extravaganza, Sahā appears ornate and bejeweled, i.e., as a "pure" land.

Clearly, there are four discrete moments to this mytheme: (1) the entrance of Śākyamuni into concentration (*samādhi*), (2) the exercise of the miraculous powers, particularly that of illumination, (3) the honoring of Śākyamuni by the Buddhas of the ten regions (*daśadigbuddhas*), and (4) the transformation of Sahā into a "pure" land.[1] Several other significant relationships are apparent within these four broad structures. First, the exercise of the miraculous powers is contingent upon the entrance of Śākyamuni into *samādhi*. Second, the transformation of Sahā takes place only after the *pūjā* performed by the *daśadigbuddhas* for the purpose of honoring Śākyamuni. Finally, it should be noted that this cosmic *pūjā* can only take place as a result of Śākyamuni's having illuminated the regions, permitting the assemblies to view one another. Thus, it would seem that the eschatological drama of the "*asaṅkhyeya*-cosmology" is possible only because of a series of vital interplays between Śākyamuni and the Buddhas of the ten regions (*daśadigbuddhas*).

1. In some cases, the transformation of Sahā into a pure land apparently coincides with its appearance as thousands of worlds. Is this intended to equate the apprehension of Sahā as a *trisāhasramahāsāhasralokadhāta* with an understanding of its pure nature ? Examples in Kern, *Lotus*, pp. 194, 284.

In commenting upon the *pūjā* performed by the *daśadigbuddhas*, the *Mppś* distinguishes three kinds of *pūjā:* superior (*agrā*), middle (*madhyā*) and inferior (*avarā*). Inferior *pūjā* consists of honoring someone beneath oneself. Superior *pūjā* consists in honoring someone above oneself. Middle *pūjā*, on the other hand, consists in honoring one's equal.[1] Clearly the *pūjā* practiced by Śākyamuni and the *daśadigbuddhas* in this instance is one between equals. As if this were not apparent, the *Mppś* makes a number of specific references to the equality of the Buddhas. With regard to morality, concentration, wisdom and salvific activity, the Buddhas are all the same.[2] The Buddhas are of equal force (*samabala*) and no longer seek to acquire merit.[3] Where apparent differences do exist between Buddhas, the *Mppś* affirms their essential sameness. For instance, although Ratnākara is larger in body and superior in the color of his body and rays to Śākyamuni, and although his *buddhakṣetra* is superior as well, he is absolutely identical to Śākyamuni with regard to wisdom (*prajñā*) and miraculous powers (*ṛddhibala*).[4]

Pūjā, of course, is a form of gift (*dāna*) and as such belongs to the first perfection (*dānapāramitā*). In this regard, it is important to note that the *Mppś* distinguishes four types of gifts: (1) the donor is pure and the beneficiary impure; (2) the donor is impure and the beneficiary pure; (3) both donor and beneficiary are pure; and (4) both donor and beneficiary are impure[5] The gifts, then, are exchanged and the *pūjā* performed, not simply between equals, but between exemplary equals. Because both are Buddhas, both donor and beneficiary are pure. Moreover,

1. Lamotte, *Traité*, p. 587.
2. Ibid., p. 562.
3. Ibid., p. 568.
4. Ibid., p. 583; "Pour le *saṃbhāra*, le *dharmakāya*, et le service des êtres, les Bouddhas sont pareils; non pas pour la durée de la vie, la caste, la taille, etc." La Vallée Poussin, *Kośa*, chap. vii, p. 79.
5. Lamotte, *Traité*, p. 590. The *Kośā* has an extensive discussion of the intricacies of the gift in chap. iv, pp. 231-55. One conclusion of particular interest: morality, which includes the gift, has as its result the sky (heaven); meditation has as its result disconnection or liberation (chap. iv, p. 249). Other discussions of the *dānapāramitā* can be found in Lamotte, *Traité*, pp. 650-769 and Dayal, *Bodhisattva*, pp. 173-93.

the Buddha is the greatest among beings.[1] Among those who are omniscient, the Buddha is the first.[2] As a result, the merit resulting from this exchange is infinite (*apramāṇa*). Moreover, there is no recompense (*vipāka*) as a result of this merit because a Buddha is not reborn.[3] With this stroke of mytho-philosophic genius, a fundamental problem is overcome. Merit is acquired which is outside the karmic laws of retribution, i.e. it does not result in rebirth and is not productive of further conditioned existence.

The exchange of a gift or offering in this setting may also be understood in terms of the *buddhakṣetra* as a field of merit (*puṇyakṣetra*). Generally speaking, the merit (*puṇya*) deriving from a gift varies according to the excellence of the giver (*dāyaka*), the thing given (*deya*) and the beneficiary (*pratigrāhaka*). It is the latter who brings to fruition the alm or gift deposited in him and who is known as the field of merit.[4] The field of merit is apparently understood in primarily agricultural terms, i.e., gifts are brought to fruition or grow in such a field. In much the same way, beings residing in a *buddhakṣetra* are brought to maturity or ripeness. The *Mppś* repeatedly refers to the *daśadigbuddha* as a supreme field of merit (*paramapuṇyakṣetra*), and the faithful are exhorted to plant their merits in this field.[5] The merits of the faithful are then brought to maturity, apparently free from the recompense normally associated with the acquisition of merit. It would appear that the *daśadigbuddhas* play a central role in obviating the karmic laws of retribution.

1. Lamotte, *Traité*, p. 537.
2. Ibid., p. 539.
3. Ibid., p. 590. According to the *Kośa*, the best of gifts is that of one who is delivered to another who is also delivered. Immediately following this statement, however, is one which extols the gift of the bodhisattva. The gift of the bodhisattva which is given for the good of all beings, given by one who is not detached to others who are not detached, this is the best of gifts. La Vallée Poussin, *Kośa*, chap. iv, pp. 238-39.
4. Lamotte, "Marche," p. 231, n. 266. "Le don est excellent par l'excellence du donneur, de l'objet donné, du champ." La Vallée Poussin, *Kośa*, chap. iv, p. 234.
5. Lamotte, *Traité*, pp. 591-92. The agricultural imagery is unmistakable in passages such as the following : "Even when planted in a bad field, the gift produces good fruits because there is no opposition between the fruit and the grain." La Vallée Poussin, *Kośa*, chap. iv, p. 246.

Buddhas of the Ten Regions

Thus, it is clear that the "*asaṅkhyeya*-cosmology" involves more than just a new set of numbers. Its most consistent and ubiquitous characteristic is the drama which centers about the significance of the ten regions (*daśadiś*) and of the Buddhas of the ten regions (*daśadigbuddhas*). Strictly speaking there are four regions (*diś*), i.e., East (*pūrvā*), South (*dakṣiṇā*), West (*paścimā*) and North (*uttarā*); four intermediate regions (*vidiś*), i.e., Northeast (*uttarapūrvā*), Southeast (*pūrvadakṣiṇā*), Southwest (*dakṣiṇapaścimā*) and Northwest (*paścimottarā*); as well as Zenith (*ūrdhvam*) and Nadir (*adhaḥ*).

While the ten regions frequently refer to all of space in a general sense, there are a number of indications that in certain contexts at least, the term "regions" is employed in a technical sense. For instance, the Vaiśeṣikas maintained that determinism (*niyati*) emerges from *diś* or the regulators of position in space. Time, in turn, emerges from *niyati*.[1] The Sāṅkhya, on the other hand, maintains what appears to be almost the opposite position.[2]

A second technical meaning associated with the regions is one which suggests the idea of a provisional limit in an otherwise unlimited universe. This is particularly the case in the discussions about the *buddhakṣetras* which exist at the limits of the worlds in such and such a direction. For instance, we read that Abhirati lies at the limit of the universes to the East. Similarly, Sukhāvatī is at the limit of the worlds to the West.[3] The *Mppś* assures us that this is not the absolute limit, but only a practical limit.[4] In the *Lotus Sūtra*, we find reference to the "limit of the existing world"[5] as well as to a list of sixteen Buddhas residing in the various directions presumably at the limits of the universe.[6]

As indicated above, the regions refer to all of space in a general sense. Space (*ākāśa*), however, is also a term which is used

1. Basham, *Ājīvikas*, p. 281.
2. According to the Sāṅkhya, space is caused while time is not. See M. Hiriyanna, *Outlines of Indian Philosophy* (London : George Allen & Unwin Ltd., 1975), pp. 367-68.
3. Lamotte, *Traité*, p. 594.
4. Ibid., p. 595.
5. Kern, *Lotus*, p. 240.
6. Ibid., pp. 177-79.

with considerable precision and occupies a central place in scholastic debate and which takes on increased significance in the Mahāyāna. First, as we have seen, the world is regarded as resting on *ākāśa*, understood as a kind of ether. This ether is itself unsupported by anything, but it supports all the other primary elements, i.e., air, water, earth and fire.[1] Second, while four "great elements" (*mahābhūta*) are recognized throughout the literature, the status of *ākāśa* in this regard was a source of controversy. The Vaibhāṣikas viewed *ākāśa* as a fifth "great element." For the Sautrāntikas and Mādhyamikas, however, *ākāśa* was simply "space," the absence of anything tangible, that which gives place to things.[2] Third, *nirvāṇa* and *ākāśa* were frequently regarded as similar if not identical. Among the sects, the Sarvāstivādins, Mahāsaṅghikas, Mahīśāsakas, Uttarāpathakas, Sautrāntikas, Satyasiddhi and later also the Yogācārins included *ākāśa*, together with *nirvāṇa*, among the unconditioned (*asaṃskṛta*) dharmas.[3] The Theravādins, Vātsīputrīya and Śāriputrābhidharma do not. Finally, in the Mahāyāna, with the identification of all things with *nirvāṇa*, their properties are said to be the same as those of space (*ākāśasama*).[4]

1. Edward Conze, *Buddhist Thought in India* (Ann Arbor : University of Michigan Press, 1967), p. 164.

2. La Vallée Poussin, "Cosmogony," p. 131; also Conze, *Buddhist Thought*, pp. 161-69. For a discussion of *ākāśa* as a comparison (*upamāna*) or metaphor for the reality of the dharmas, see Lamotte, *Traité*, pp. 364-68.

3. For a list of the 72 conditioned dharmas and three unconditioned dharmas of the Sarvāstivādins, see Junjiro Takakusu, *Essentials of Buddhist Philosophy* (Bombay : Asia Publishing House, 1956), p. 72a. Lamotte discusses the Theravādin and Sarvāstivādin classifications of the dharmas in *Histoire*, pp. 658-64. For a discussion of the dharma theory as a technique of meditation, see Conze, *Buddhist Thought*, esp. pp. 97-106, 244-48.

4. Conze, *Buddhist Thought*, p. 166. For other discussions of the use of *ākāśa* in the Upaniṣads and early Buddhism, see Ananda K. Coomaraswamy, "Kha and Other Words Denoting 'Zero' in Connection with the Metaphysics of Space," *Bulletin of the School of Oriental Studies* (University of London) 7 (1933-35) : 487-97; Paul Deussen, *The Philosophy of the Upanishads* (New York : Dover Publications, Inc., 1966), pp. 111 ff.; Etienne Lamotte and Jean Przyluski, "Bouddhisme et Upaniṣad," *Bulletin de l'école français de l'Extrême-Orient* 32 (1932): 141-69; Lilian Silburn, *Instant et cause, le discontenu dans la pensée philosophique de l'Inde* (Paris : Libraire philosophique J. Vrin, 1955), pp. 110-14. For spatial representations of "World." "self" and "deity," see Gonda, *Loka*; idem, *Dhāman*.

Another context in which we encounter the use of the term "regions" is in the repeated reference to the ability of the Buddha to move throughout the ten regions "without obstacle." This power to move without obstacle and to view the regions is apparently related to powers acquired as a result of certain techniques of meditation. In the early Upanisads, for instance, one who has realized the nonduality between the *ātman* and the *Brahman* is said to be able to move freely in all the worlds (*lokas*). In this sense, then, access to all the worlds or to the regions is the power of one who has attained a stage of enlightenment.[1] Certainly we must regard access to all the *buddhakṣetras* in the ten regions as involving similar imagery. Because of the cosmic drama provided by the illuminating rays of Śākyamuni, the assemblies are also provided access to the regions. They are permitted to see each other and to hear the *dharma* being preached.

Finally, it is important to note that the unique status of the *daśadigbuddha* is the result of a complex scholasticism. The central consideration is the frequency of the appearance of the Buddha. The importance of this fact in the "*sāhasra*-cosmology" has to do with the fact that one who has achieved the status of *arhat* can only take a vow to become a Buddha in the presence of a Buddha. The *Mppś* adds that a *bodhisattva* must achieve the thirty-two marks in the presence of a Buddha.[2] Unfortunately, it is the judgment of the *Śāstra* that the appearance of a Buddha in a *trisāhasramahāsāhasralokadhātu*, a cosmology dominated by the temporal categories of the Kalpa, is as rare as the blooming of an *udumbara* plant.[3]

A number of systems emerged attempting to explain in which Kalpas a Buddha or Buddhas appeared. It was commonly maintained that a total of six Buddhas including Śākyamuni had appeared in only three of ninety-one Kalpas.[4]

In the "*asaṅkhyeya*-cosmology" by contrast, there is not a series of *buddhakṣetras* successively destroyed by the passage of *kalpa* upon *kalpa*. Rather, there are innumerable worlds presently distributed throughout the ten regions. Similarly,

1. Gonda, *Loka*, pp. 41; 51, n. 53; 52; 104 f.; 106; 144 f.
2. Lamotte, *Traité*, p. 249. Also, see above, Chapter IV.
3. See above, Chapter IV, p. 87, n. 1.
4. Lamotte, *Traité*, pp. 532, n. 2; 541 f. Also, see above, Chapter IV, p. 85, n. 4; p. 86, n. 1.

there are innumerable Buddhas presently distributed throughout the ten regions of space: "... s'il y eu, dans le passé, d'innombrables Buddha, s'il y aura, dans le futur, d'innombrables Buddha, il doit aussi avoir, dans le présent, d' innombrables Buddha."[1]

As a result, the *Śāstra* argues that while the claim of the *Sutta* is correct that two Buddhas do not appear in the same world at the same time, we must understand world in this context to mean the same *trisāhasramahāsāhasralokadhātu.* The quantity of *trisāhasramahāsāhasralokadhātus* is innumerable. Consequently, there is never a Kalpa without a Buddha; in one world perhaps, but not in the *asaṅkhyeyas* of worlds which fill the ten regions of space.[2] Clearly, the plenitude of the *daśadigbuddhas* of the "*asaṅkhyeya*-cosmology" is juxtaposed to the rare appearance of a Buddha in the "*sāhasra*-cosmology." Moreover, the reality of the *asaṅkhyeyas* of *daśadigbuddhas* is in sharp contrast to the magical or phantom-like quality of the *nirmāṇabuddhas* associated with the "*sāhasra*-cosmology," whose existence, as we saw, does not violate or in any way compromise the unitary nature of the Buddha.

Having seen the significance of the regions for the "*asaṅkhyeya*-cosmology," we must turn our attention to the exercise of the miraculous powers in this new context. Of particular interest is the power of illumination which enables the assemblies in the ten regions to view one another and permits a series of ritual activities to take place.

Throughout the literature of the Mahāyāna, miraculous feats are repeatedly ascribed to the celestial Buddhas and bodhisattvas.[3] The facility of the bodhisattva to play at will with the

1. Lamotte, *Traité*, p. 544.
2. Ibid., p. 542.
3. Cf. Benoytosh Bhattacharyya, *An Introduction to Buddhist Esoterism* (Rep. Motilal Banarsidass, Delhi, 1980), in which he discusses the Buddha as *vidyārāja.* See also Jean Przyluski, "Les vidyārāja," *BEFEO* 23 (1923): 301-18. Mircea Eliade discusses the *siddhis* and *abhijñās* in *Yoga*, esp. pp. 79-85, 173-77. For a discussion of the "thaumaturgie" of the Mahāyāna see Lamotte, *Enseignement*, pp. 250-58. La Vallée Poussin discusses the assimilation of the miraculous powers and the image of the Buddha, particularly in the Mahāyāna in "Le Bouddha et les Abhijñās," *Le muséon* (Louvain) 44 (1931) : 335-42. The term *vidyācara* as an epithet of the Buddha is discussed in Lamotte, *Traité*, pp. 128 ff. For sources regarding the heretical

supernatural powers is one of the primary characteristics of the Mahāyāna, and it underscores a fundamental distinction between the bodhisattva and the arhat.

> La différence essentielle entre le Chemin des Śrāvaka et le Chemin des Bodhisattvas est que le premier tend au perfectionne-ent individuel de l'ascète tandis que le second vise uniquement au bien d'autrui .... Il en resulte que le Samādhi des Bodhisattva n'est pas seulement un exercice visant à purifier la pensée; c'est encore et avant tout une oeuvre d'édification, L'accent est mis, non plus sur la technique de la concentration, mais sur la force magique (*ṛddhibala*) qui en découle pour le plus grand bien des êtres.[1]

Over and over one encounters prodigious acts such as the multiplication of Buddhas; the manifestation of a glorious body; the transformation of assemblies; the capture and liberation of Māra; the creation of fictional bodhisattvas; changes of place without displacement; simultaneous manifestations of Buddhas and bodhisattvas in several places at one time; apparitions of the Buddhas of the ten regions and the transformation of an "impure" land into a "pure" land.[2]

Other displays of miraculous power are even less restrained. These include placing Mt. Sumeru in a grain of mustard; pouring the waters of the four oceans from a single pore of skin and tossing the *trisāhasramahāsāhasralokadhātu* to one side of the universes as numerous as the sands of the Gaṅgā and then returning it to its proper place. Elsewhere, the bodhisattvas place all the beings in the palms of their hands and circulate throughout all the universes but without displacing themselves; introduce the cosmic fires into their stomachs; diminish or expand time at will; etc.[3]

Rays of Light : Magical Power of the Extinct Buddha

Of all the spectacular displays which fill the Mahāyānist texts, the issuance of the rays of light is perhaps the most ubiquitous

view that the Buddha was a magician, see Lamotte, *Traité*, p. 15, n. 2. See also, La Vallée Poussin, "Magic (Buddhist)," ERE, 8: 255-57.

1. Lamotte, "Marche," pp. 30-31.
2. Ibid., p. 32.
3. Ibid., pp. 58-59; Lamotte, *Enseignement*, pp. 250-58.

and is indisputably the most striking. As we have seen, it is the magical power of illumination (*raśmirddhibala*) which is at the heart of the mytheme of the *Mppś*. The rays of light which issue from the Buddha after entering the *samādhirājasamādhi* permit access to the regions and enable visualization of the Buddhas of the ten regions (*daśadigbuddhas*). As such, they occasion a drama which in a variety of forms is at the heart of the "*asaṅkhyeya*-cosmology." The importance of the ability to perceive a multiplicity of presumably real Buddhas in the ten regions and to otherwise have access to the *daśadigbuddhas* leads us to a closer examination of the rays of light which issue from Śākyamuni.[1]

The primary attribute of the rays is that they are efficacious. The consequences resulting from the emission of the rays are manifold. In the first instance, the various types of rays, or the various modes of their emission, are related to the differing sensibilities of beings. Those rays issued from the grosser portion of

1. The displays of light in Buddhism are so striking and so prominent that a few miscellaneous examples seem appropriate. A description of the displays of light associated with the Akaniṣṭha is provided in Suzuki, *Studies*, p. 324. In the Sukhāvatī-Vyūha, we are told that the issuance of the rays of light is due to the perfection of austerities by Amitābha; see Müller, *Texts*, pp. 28-30. In the *Kośa*, the Buddha Puṣya enters into a concentration known as the *tejodhātu* which results in an extraordinary display of light. See La Vallée Poussin, *Kośa*, chap. iv, p. 229, n. 3. Alfred Bloom characterizes Shinran's theology as a "theology of Light since it is in the embrace of Light that passion-ridden beings are granted the status of salvation realized in the awakening of faith," *Shinran's Gospel*, p. 57. A Mahāyāna ritual characterized as "The March Toward the Light" is described in Paul Levy, *Buddhism: A Mystery Religion?* (New York: Schocken Books, 1968), pp. 38-60, a title which Louis Finot has given to his translation of the *Bodhicaryāvatāra* as well. *La marche à la lumière*, trans. Louis Finot (Paris : Classiques de l'Orient, No. II, 1920). For a further discussion of the mystic significance of light in Buddhism, see Mircea Eliade, *The Two and the One* (New York: Harper & Row, Publishers, 1969), pp. 33-43, and idem, "Spirit, Light and Seed," *History of Religions* 11 (1971): 1-30. For the self-illuminating quality of *ākāśa*, see Conze, *Buddhist Thought*, p. 164, and for the self-luminous nature of Thought, see Conze, *Essence*, pp. 162-63; and David Seyfort Ruegg, *La theorie du tathāgatagarbha et du gotra; études sur la sotériologie et la gnoséologie du Bouddhisme* (Paris : Publications de l'école français d'Extrême-Orient, 1969), pp. 409-54. The association between mystical insight and luminosity, of course, greatly exceeds the boundaries of Buddhism and of India. In addition to the works of Eliade on this subject, see Corbin, *Lumière*.

the Buddha's anatomy[1] fix certain beings in supreme and perfect enlightenment. Those rays issued from the subtle portion of the Buddha's anatomy have the same effect on beings possessed of other sensibilities. Finally, the natural or ordinary splendor of the Buddha erases the doubt in the minds of still other beings and facilitates their faith. Moreover, in the discussion of the *abhijñās*, the *Mppś* states that the *divyacakṣus* is obtained by reflection of all manner of light.[2] This display by Śākyamuni certainly is intended for that purpose. The effect, then, of this miraculous display of power is to install beings into a new condition, i.e., supreme and perfect enlightenment, freedom from doubt, or the possession of the *divyacakṣus* and the other *abhijñās*.

A second point must be noted in connection with the miraculous powers of the Buddha which are described repeatedly as immense (*apramāṇa*), incalculable (*asaṅkhyeya*) and inconceivable (*acintya*). The point has to do precisely with the enormity of these powers. The extent of the powers of the Buddha in this regard is so vast that the *Mppś* likens them to that of the force of the Kalpa at the moment of combustion, i.e., of cosmic dissolution.[3] In a number of places we read that the rays of the Buddha are similar in effect to the dissolution of the world. When the rays of the Buddha make it possible for the assemblies of the different universes to view each other, we read:

> Just as at the end of a Kalpa, at the moment of combustion, all beings obtain the concentration (of wisdom) (*prajñāsamādhi*), the divine eye (*divyacakṣus*) and the divine ear (*divyaśrotra*), so also the Buddha, by means of his miraculous power (*ṛddhibala*), enables all beings to see distantly.[4]

The most common example of the Buddha's "kalpic" power is that of the elevation of one class of beings to the level or abode of another class. For instance, it is mentioned that when the Buddha attains the state of Buddhahood, the gods of the lowest Brahma-heavens are transported to the Śuddhāvāsika realm. The gods of the Śuddhāvāsika are the chiefs of the Rūpadhātu, i.e., they reside in the five highest heavens of the Brahmaloka.[5]

1. Lamotte, *Traité*, p. 446.
2. Ibid., p. 330.
3. Ibid., p. 518.
4. Ibid., p. 527.
5. Ibid.

Again, the trembling of the earth caused by Śākyamuni's entrance into the *siṃhavikrīḍitasamādhi* is said to cause those in the three lower destinies (*durgati*) as well as those in the eight difficult conditions (*akṣaṇa*) to be liberated and to be reborn as men among the Cāturmahārājika and the Paranirmitavaśavartin.[1] Elsewhere, as a result of the Buddha's shaking of the earth in six directions, the deaf are made to hear, the blind to see and the lame to walk.[2] These singular and extraordinary powers also belong to the Kalpa at the moment of combustion. At the end of the Kalpa, all creatures possessing sufficient merit attain reincarnation in higher realms, i.e., in spheres which will not be overtaken by the destruction.[3] The similarities between the powers of the Buddha and those of the Kalpa are further enhanced by a curious passage which informs us that the Buddha manifests his *ṛddhibala* seven times in all.[4] It would appear that this passage is intended to draw a close parallel between the Buddha and the Kalpa by associating the *ṛddhibala* with the seven destructions of the world by fire.

We must conclude that since the rays of light bring beings to a state of enlightenment and provide them with the *abhijñās* which are a sign of enlightenment, they are tantamount to the teaching.[5] We are also told that it is by emitting rays of light that the *daśadigbuddhas* prevented Śākyamuni from passing into *nirvāṇa* as a *bodhisattva* of the seventh *bhūmi*.[6] While the reason given for this in the *Śāstra* is that this was to enable him to develop the 32 marks and 80 minor marks, we must recall that Brahmā prevented Śākyamuni from passing into *nirvāṇa* in order to preserve the teaching. Therefore, we may take this as a further indication that the rays are associated with the teaching.[7] The

1. Ibid., p. 479, n. 1.
2. Ibid., p. 479.
3. La Vallée Poussin, "Ages," p. 188. "When all beings, reunited (*saṃvart*) in a *dhyāna*-heaven, have disappeared from the lower receptacles, the destructions (*saṃvartanīs*) take place." La Vallée Poussin, *Kośa*, chap. iii, p. 210.
4. Lamotte, *Traité*, p. 604.
5. "The ray itself performs the teaching." Rowell, "Background," 7:133n.
6. Lamotte, *Traité*, p. 589.
7. It is by emitting rays of light that the *daśadigbuddhas* prevented Śākyamuni from passing into nirvāṇa as a bodhisattva of the seventh bhūmi.

rays of course, also permit the assemblies to see each other. The *Śāstra* is quite specific: "until now, the grand assemblies were unable to see each other"[1] "When the Tathāgata ceases his miraculous action, Akṣobhya is no longer visible."[2] As a result of the rays, it is now possible to see and hear the dharma being preached in the pure lands, a feat which again is tantamount to the teaching.

It is a curious attribute of the rays that they also provide the power which enables the bodhisattvas to travel to Sahā from their various fields.[3] This power is analagous to that of *gamana* or displacement. It is perhaps the most graphic manner in which the meditation of the Buddha provides access to the regions.

In conjunction with the "*sāhasra*-cosmology," we discussed the miraculous powers of multiplication, i.e., the creation or projection of illusory or fictional Buddha-images (*nirmāṇabuddha*), generally for the purpose of preaching the dharma. However, other practices of meditation carry with them powers similar to that of the multiplication of images, but with an important difference. Instead of multiplying and projecting Buddha-images, the goal of the adept is often to "visualize" them. Particularly in bhaktic Buddhism, the adherents were trained in visions of the Buddhas and bodhisattvas and of their paradises. Kumārajīva distinguishes three ways in which the Buddha can be seen.

This was to enable him to develop the thirty-two marks and eighty minor marks, Lamotte, *Traité*, p. 589. According to La Vallée Poussin the *Lalitavistara* states that the bodhisattva has to be "excited" by the *daśadigbuddhas* in order to make his vow. See Louis de La Vallée Poussin, "Adibuddha," ERE 1:96 n. According to Suzuki, the seventh vow of Samantabhadra is that the Buddhas do not enter into *nirvaṇa*, *Studies*, p. 234.

1. Lamotte, *Traité*, p. 527.
2. Ibid., p. 464, n. 1.
3. Ibid., p. 577. The power of the rays of light to transport beings to other realms is of critical importance and is widely documented in non-Buddhist sources as well. In the *Chāndogya Upaniṣad* VIII, 6,5 we read that the soul rises upwards on the rays of the Sun at the moment of death. See Eliade, *The Two and the One*, p. 27. According to the Pythagoreans, souls descended upon the earth, and reascended after death toward the sky, thanks to the rays of the sun, which served as the means of transport. Cumont, *Astrology*, p. 108.

First, those endowed with supernatural psychic powers may see him with the "divine eye," hear him with the "divine ear," and they may fly into the presence of all the Buddhas in all the ten directions.

Second, even those who have no supernatural powers can concentrate their minds on Amida in his Western Paradise, or on other Buddhas.

Third, the "mindfulness of the Buddha-body," apparently a *samādhi*, concentrates on the body of the Buddha as it is shown in images. Starting with the devout contemplation of an image, the beginner must fix his mind on his forehead. One or more images of the Buddha will then appear on it, depart and then return again. Alternatively, the mind may be fixed on the heart : Buddhas are then seen to issue from it. They hold sceptres of lapis-lazuli, from which rays of light shine forth; departing first and then returning. In some cases, they issue afterwards by the pores of the skin and illuminate the entire universe.[1]

An extensive literature is devoted to various techniques of visualization. To a large extent, these techniques are associated with the Tendai tradition in both its Chinese and Japanese forms. Shan-tao's commentary on the *Amitāyurdhyāna Sūtra* explains the manner in which the adept should concentrate on visualizing the pure land Sukhâvatī in all its detail.[2] Genshin's *Ōjōyōshū* which begins with a lengthy description of the heavens and hells belonging to a single world system, contains several sections devoted to the visualization of the marks of the Buddha.[3] According to Chih-I, the tenth part of *samādhi* involves envisioning the Buddha with all the marks in the mind's eye.[4] However, it is clear from our discussion of this mytheme which appears in the Prajñāpāramitā literature that these techniques of visualization are already important in India. This is further apparent from the fact that the Tendai draws to a great extent on Indian texts such as the *Seeing All Buddhas Samādhi Sūtra*[5] and the

1. Conze, *Meditation*, p. 60.
2. Pas, "Shan-tao's Interpretation."
3. Andrews, *Teachings*, p. 57.
4. Hurvitz, "Chih-I", p. 324.
5. *Pratyutpanna buddha sammukhāvasthita samādhi sūtra.* Ibid., pp. 12, 21-22.

Buddha Contemplation Samādhi Ocean Sūtra.[1] In the *Seeing All Buddhas Samādhi Sūtra*, there are three reasons given as to why all Buddhas appear before us : (1) because of the Buddha-power, (2) because of *samādhi*-power, and (3) because of the power of the practicer's stock of merit.

> Since we are thus able to see all the Buddhas of the present age of all the ten regions of the universe, just as a sharp-eyed person can see the stars in a clear night sky, it is called the *samādhi* of all Buddhas appearing before us.[2]

We have begun our approach to the problem of the Buddha's miraculous powers with a discussion of the *siddhis* and *abhijñās* in Chapter IV. However, it is clear that while the emission of rays (*raśmirddhibala*) bears many similarities to certain terms discussed in this regard, it is not identical with either the power of *adhiṣṭhāna* or that of *nirmāṇa*. Rather, what appears is an elegant symmetry. The rays of light do not create Buddhas or Buddha-images (*nirmāṇabuddha*) as such, but rather illuminate already existing Buddhas, the Buddhas of the ten regions (*daśadigbuddhas*). The efficacy of the *raśmirddhibala*, then, is due primarily to the fact that it permits the assemblies to view each other, i.e., because it is the central feature in the interplay between Śākyamuni and the *daśadigbuddhas*. In this sense, the *raśmirddhibala* is closely related to the power of the "divine eye" (*divyacakṣus*) in that it permits the assemblies to view each other. By extension of the fact that the assemblies are able to see each other, they are also able to hear the dharma being preached in the other universes by means of the "divine ear" (*divyaśrotra*) and to know the purity of the thoughts of the other assemblies (*paracittajñāna*). As a result, the rays serve as an agent of salvation which bestows the *abhijñās* upon the assemblies.

As we have already seen, the *daśadigbuddhas* are explicitly distinguished from the *nirmāṇabuddhas*. Similarly, there exists a fundamental opposition between the powers of multiplication (*adhiṣṭhāna; nirmāṇa*) and those of illumination (*raśmirddhibala*). Clearly, these powers represent parallel strategies for the salvation of beings. The position of the Sarvāstivādins is that this is accom-

1. *Buddha dhyāna samādhi sāgara sūtra.* Ibid., p. 19.
2. Ibid., p. 7.

plished by a single Buddha multiplying images. The position of the *Śāstra*, on the other hand, is that this is accomplished by the *daśadigbuddhas* to whom the assemblies are permitted access as a result of the miraculous powers of the Buddha, most notably that of illumination.

Finally, we must consider the implications of the "*asaṅkhyeya*-cosmology" for a question which more than any other preoccupied Buddhism from the earliest periods, namely the extinction of the Tathāgata. The mytheme of the *Mppś* begins with the entrance of Śākyamuni into *samādhi*. As a result of this concentration, he is able to exercise his miraculous powers. However, it is precisely the entrance into *samādhi* which makes one a Buddha and results in his extinction. In our summary of the "*sāhasra*-cosmology," we concluded that the appearance of a Buddha was a rare event precisely because the Buddha is extinct. As Lamotte has phrased it: "Le nirvāṇé n'existe pas."[1]

In the context of the "*asaṅkhyeya*-cosmology" however, the emphasis is not placed on the extinction of the Buddha as a result of his mastery of the *samādhis*, but rather on the facility with the miraculous powers which results from this mastery. The exercise of the miraculous powers is the strategy of salvation of the "*asaṅkhyeya*-cosmology." The combustion of the world at the end of the Kalpa has a similar salvific valence, precisely because it is this combustion which establishes the Void. While the "receptacle world" (*bhājanaloka*) is destroyed, the beings in it (*sattvaloka*) are saved, albeit only those possessing sufficient merit.

It should be noted that the attainment of *nirvāṇa* no longer belongs to the province of the individual. It is no longer the "self-power" of the individual expressed in the temporal categories of an extended number of rebirths which results in the attainment of the state of *arhat* and the possible state of Buddhahood. Rather, it is the "other-power" of the Buddha expressed in terms of the displays associated with the Great Concentrations which results in rebirth in other worlds. To borrow the phrase of the *Lotus Sūtra* :

> . . . he does not teach a particular Nirvāṇa for each being; he causes all beings to reach complete Nirvāṇa by means of the complete Nirvāṇa of the Tathāgata.[2]

1. Lamotte, *Histoire*, p. 676. Also, see above, Chapter IV, p. 86, n.2.
2. Kern, *Lotus*, p. 81.

The entrance of the Buddha into *samādhi* establishes the Void in a manner similar to the end of the Kalpa, and it is this that gives rise to the "kalpic" powers of the Buddha. The association of these events is facilitated by the multivalence of the term *pralaya*. On the one hand, *pralaya* is used to designate the destruction of the world at the end of the age. However, the passage of an individual into *nirvāṇa* is also characterized as a *pralaya*.[1] But the Buddha/bodhisattva of the Mahāyāna does not pass into *nirvāṇa* as such. Rather." . . . plus exactement, (il) s'installe dans le Nirvāṇa 'comme s'il n'y residait point' (*apratiṣṭhita nirvāṇa*) pour continuer son oeuvre salvatrice."[2] Because the Buddha/bodhisattva is "installed" in *nirvāṇa*, he is extinct. However, precisely because he is extinct,[3] he possesses miraculous powers which he uses for the edification of beings and which conduct countless beings to salvation. Therefore, all beings and the "world" are saved because it is the Buddha who is extinct and whose extinction establishes the world in its "pure" state, i.e., as Void.

1. Biardeau, "Mythologie," esp. Part III. Compare the orthodox position that the world will continue until the last being has attained emancipation. This moment will probably never come. But in each individual "the end of the world" (*lokasya anta*) may be achieved by the emancipation. La Vallée Poussin, "Agnosticism," p. 224, n. 2.

2. See above, Chapter IV, p. 83, n. 1. The "non-residing" of the bodhisattva is highly reminiscent of the Angel whose profession is to be "forever journeying," cited by Corbin as a personification of the Platonic doctrine of Space. According to Corbin, "forever journeying" suggests the "etymological" definition given by Plato and Aristotle to the Ether (*Aither*) as element of the divinity : *Aei thein* "incessant motion." Corbin, *Avicenna*, p. 294, n. 4. See also Suhrawahrdi's City of "Nonwhere." Ibid., pp. 24, 194, 335n., 342n.

3. The displays of light which issue from Śākyamuni are clearly contingent upon the entrance of the Buddha into *samādhi* which is equivalent to a *pralaya* or extinction. That the Buddha does become extinct is underscored by the fact that the *daśadigbuddhas* immediately perform a cosmic *pūjā*, showering all manner of cultic object upon him. Presumably it is just this imagery which is pursued in *Lotus* XI with its description of the extinct Buddha Prabhūtaratna emerging from a stūpa in the sky. The powers derived therefrom are directly analogous to those events which ensue at the combustion of the world at the end of the Kalpa. The basic idea behind the valorization of the field of merit (*puṇyakṣetra*) as a cosmic event draws on the significance of the gift and particularly the offering of gifts (*pūjā*) to a shrine believed to contain the relics of the extinct Buddha.

CHAPTER VI

THE ESCHATOLOGY OF THE "*ASAṄKHYEYA*-COSMOLOGY" BUDDHAS NUMEROUS AS THE SANDS OF THE GAṄGĀ

> There is never a Kalpa without a Buddha; in a single world perhaps, but that is why we affirm the Buddhas in the ten regions.

The Infinite and the Infinitesimal

It is one of the curiosities of the Buddhist literature that a wide range of attempts exists to assign a value to that which is termed an "innumerable" (*asaṅkhyeya*). It is logical for us to examine this problem which has so thoroughly frustrated Western scholarship.[1] By way of prologue, it is useful to understand that one of the common themes found in the Indian materials relating to the nature of the cosmos and in particular to the measurement of cosmic time, is the idea of conveying that which is essentially infinite by means of that which is essentially infinitesimal. A discourse in *Saṃyutta Nikāya* (xv. 5, 6) on the length of a Kalpa reads as follows:

> It is as if, O priest, there were a mountain consisting of a great rock, a league in height, without break, cleft, or hollow, and every hundred years a man were to come and rub it once with a silken garment; that mountain consisting of a great rock, O priest, would more quickly wear away and come to an end than a world-cycle.[2]

1. Efforts to ascertain the exact value designated by *asaṅkhyeya* are summarized in Burnouf, *Lotus*, 2 :551; Lamotte, *Traité*, p. 247, n. 1; La Vallée Poussin, "Ages," p. 188; idem, *Kośa*, chap. iii, p. 188, n. 1; p. 189, n. 2; chap. iv, p. 224, n. 1; idem, *Siddhi*, p. 731; Dayal, *Bodhisattva*, pp. 76-79.

2. Warren, *Buddhism*, p. 315n. Similar examples involving the wearing away of a rock as well as the removal of grains of mustard are found in Lamotte, *Traité*, pp. 352; 352, nn. 1, 2.

Ājīvika chronometry confronts us with two additional examples. In Buddhaghosa's *Sumaṅgala Vilāsinī* it is reported that the Ājīvikas understood a *mahākappa* to be the time taken to exhaust a great lake (*sara*) seven times, by removing one drop every hundred years.[1] In the *Bhagavatī Sūtra*, Gosāla expounds a system in which the bed of the Gaṅgā was 250 *yojanas* in length, half a *yojana* in width and 500 *dhanus* in depth.

> Seven *gaṅgās* equal one *mahāgaṅgā*; seven *mahāgaṅgās* equal one *sādīnagaṅgā*; seven *sādīnagaṅgās*, one *maccugaṅgā*; seven *maccugaṅgās*, one *lohiyagaṅgā*; seven *lohiyagaṅgās*, one *āvatīgaṅgā*; and seven *āvatīgaṅgās* equal one *paramāvatī*. The latter therefore equals seven to the seventh power or 117,649 *gaṅgās*. If one grain of sand were removed every hundred years from the bed of this imaginary river the total time required for the removal of all the sand would be one *sara*. 300,000 *saras* of this duration equal one *mahākappa*. . . .[2]

The idea of the sands of the Gaṅgā not only provides a readily understandable infinitesimal with which to contrast the infinite, it also represents a felicitous blend of acquatic images centering around the various waters of which the *saras* are one example and tellurian images centering around the mountain or at least Meru cosmology. In other words, the sands of the Gaṅgā are very close to being both drops of water and particles of dust.[3]

This concern with infinitesimals is not restricted to Buddhism, or even to India, but is a phenomenon which has a wide dispersion in the Hellenistic world. The basic idea is that the dust atoms in a mountain or even in a world system, the drops of

1. Basham, *Ājīvikas*, p. 254.
2. Ibid., p. 253.
3. Drops of water and particles of dust or grains of sand were in fact used as actual physical techniques of chronometry. For an account of the clocktower of Su Sung which relied on the dripping of water, see Derek John de Solla Price, *Science Since Babylon* (New Haven : Yale University Press, 1961), pp. 33-35. The use of "water-instruments" and "stringed sand-receptacles" in the measurement of time are described in the *Sūrya Siddhānta*. *Sūrya Siddhānta, A Text-Book of Hindu Astronomy*, trans. Ebenezer Burgess (New Haven : American Oriental Society and Yale University, 1860), pp. 261-64. Keeping in mind the chronometric significance of these images, we may wonder if the "sands of the Gaṅgā" do not in some sense constitute a "river of time."

water in a lake and the grains of sand in the river Gaṅgā, however large in number, are nevertheless finite and knowable. The mind, aided by the divine science of mathematics is able to analyze the universe, dissect it into its smallest particles and to "know" it in its totality. This approach to knowing the universe seems to have been carried to its extreme by Archimedes in his treatise "The Sand Reckoner" where he undertakes the curious task of computing the number of grains of sand which may be contained in a volume of the size of the universe. It is illuminating for our research to outline this treatise at some length.

Archimedes (d. 212 B.C.) begins by considering the theory of Aristarchus of Samos (d. c. 230 B.C.) which postulates a heliocentric view of the universe in contrast to the commonly held view which was equivalent to that of the single world system outlined above. Addressing his remarks to king Gelon, Archimedes summarizes Aristarchus' position as follows:

> Now you are aware that "universe" is the name given by most astronomers to the sphere whose centre is the earth and whose radius is equal to the straight line between the centre of the sun and the centre of the earth. This is the common account, as you have heard from astronomers. But Aristarchus of Samos brought out a book consisting of some hypotheses, in which the premises lead to the result that the universe is many times greater than that now so called. His hypotheses are that the fixed stars and the sun remain unmoved, that the earth revolves about the sun in the circumference of a circle, the sun lying in the middle of the orbit, and that the sphere of the fixed stars, situated about the same centre as the sun, is so great that the circle in which he supposes the earth to revolve bears such a proportion to the distance of the fixed stars as the centre of the sphere bears to its surface.[1]

Archimedes reasons that since the centre of a sphere occupies no space whatever and therefore bears no ratio whatever to the surface of a sphere, this cannot be what Aristarchus intended. Of course, we might equally say that the ratio tends toward infinity. In any event, Archimedes concludes that what Aristarchus must have said was as follows:

1. Heath, *Archimedes*, pp. 221-22.

Since we conceive the earth to be, as it were, the centre of the universe, the ratio which the earth bears to what we describe as the "universe" is the same as the ratio which the sphere containing the circle in which he supposes the earth to revolve bears to the sphere of the fixed stars.[1]

Having thus summarized Aristarchus' theory, Archimedes sets out to prove that even if the sphere of the fixed stars is as great as maintained by Aristarchus, it is possible to determine the number of grains of sand which it would contain. Archimedes begins his calculations by allowing that the circumference of the "earth" may be as great as 3,000,000 stadia, even though most recognize it to be only 300,000 stadia. The very measurement which Archimedes chooses for the dimensions of the earth is highly reminiscent of the meaning which we arrived at for the term *trisāhasramahāsāhasralokadhātu* in Chapter III as the "ever-expanding universe of thousands." The fact that the circumference is given alternately as 300,000 and 3,000,000 units recalls not only the statement of the *Kośa* that the circumference is the triple of the diameter, but also our analysis that the *trisāhasramahāsāhasralokadhātu* is a "universe" whose circumference is 3,000 units and whose diameter is ever expanding by thousands.

Relying on some simple observations of the arc of the horizon subtended by the sphere of the sun together with some principles on measuring the circumference of a circle previously demonstrated, Archimedes proves that the diameter of the universe—understood as the distance from one side of the circle of the earth to the other—is not greater than 10,000 times the diameter of the earth. Since the diameter of the earth is taken as not greater than 1,000,000 stadia, the diameter of the universe so defined is not greater than 10,000 × 1,000,000 or 10,000,000,000 stadia.[2]

Archimedes continues as follows: First, suppose that a quantity of sand is taken not greater that a poppy-seed, and suppose that it contains not more than 10,000 grains of sand. The diameter of the poppy-seed is not less than 1/40th of a fingerbreadth. Since spheres are to one another in the triplicate ratios of their diameters, one may compute the volume of ever increas-

1. Ibid., p. 222.
2. Ibid., p. 227.

ing spheres in terms of grains of sand. Making the necessary calculations, Archimedes is able to show that the number of grains of sand which could be contained in a sphere of the size of our "universe" (i.e., the sphere of the earth whose centre is the sun) is less than 10^{51} also referred to as 1,000 units of the seventh order.[1] From this, Archimedes further proves that a sphere of the size attributed by Aristarchus to the sphere of the fixed stars would contain a number of grains of sand less than 10^{63} or 10,000,000 of the eighth order of numbers or 10^{56+7}.

Archimedes' conclusion that 10^{63} represents the number of grains of sand which would be contained in a sphere of the size attributed by Aristarchus to the sphere of the fixed stars is of startling significance for our understanding of the "*asaṅkhyeya*-cosmology." Mr. Joinville reports that the value of an *asaṅkhyeya* is precisely equal to one followed by 63 ciphers or 10^{63}.[2] The *Kośa* provides another computation of the value of an *asaṅkhyeya* in conjunction with the three *asaṅkhyeyakalpas* which constitute the career of the bodhisattva, and which, according to La Vallée Poussin is found in a number of other Buddhist texts as well.[3] The value assigned by the *Kośa* is that of the sixtieth member of a series which begins with one and not two, and increases by multiples of ten. The sixtieth member of this series is an *asaṅkhyeya* whose value is taken to be 10^{59}. However, in the list of sixty numbers found in the *Kośa* as well as in a number of other texts, eight numbers or eight members of the series are missing.[4] The consistency with which eight members of this series are found lacking forces us to consider the possibility that under some circumstances, the series is in fact eight members shorter than indicated. Such a reduction

1. Ibid., p. 231.
2. Mr. Joinville, "On the Religion and Manners of the People of Ceylon," *Asiatick Researches* 7 (1801) : 399-448, esp. 405-8. Mr. Joinville adds the following intriguing observation : "Thirty-two, represents the number of his (the Buddha's) great qualities, as well as of his middling ones, which, added together, amount to 64, the number of cyphers of the *asanke* (*asaṅkhyeya*).—In fine, to be short, we shall only observe that 4 *asankes*, 100,000 *mahākalpas*, and 32 great qualities of Bouddha, compose mystically, if not arithmetically, the *kali* (*yuga*) of the *Brahmins* of 432,000 years." Ibid., p. 408.
3. La Vallée Poussin, *Kośa*, chap. iii, p. 190, n. 1.
4. Ibid.

in the value of an *asaṅkhyeya* leaves us with the figure of 10^{51}. This latter figure is no less striking because the fourth step in Archimedes calculation is the determination that it is precisely 10^{51} which is the number of grains of sand which could be contained by the sphere of the earth whose centre is the sun.[1]

Having had the good fortune to find a non-Buddhist equivalent for an *asaṅkhyeya* which corresponds to the volume of the universe expressed in terms of an infinitesimal, we are prompted to search for similar images within the Buddhist tradition. Lest we react too quickly and regard a concern with the volume of the universe as something altogether alien to Buddhism, we should remember that in the single world system discussed in Chapter II, each of the heavens of the Brahmaloka is given an extension (diameter) as well as a height or thickness. According to the *Kośa*, each heaven is as thick as the top of the preceding heaven is above the level of the *cakravāla*.[2] Kirfel also reminds us that a preoccupation with the volume of the cosmos was one of the major concerns of Jain cosmology.[3] Finally, the following passage from the *Lotus Sūtra* provides what appears to be an almost exact duplication of Archimedes exercise:

> ...Suppose some man was to reduce to powder the whole mass of the earth element as much as is to be found in this whole universe; that after taking one atom of dust from this world he is to walk a thousand worlds farther in an easterly direction to deposit that single atom; that after taking a second atom of dust and walking a thousand worlds farther he deposits that second atom, and proceeding in this way at last gets the whole of the earth element deposited in eastern direc-

1. If we increase this figure of 10^{51} by the value assigned by Buddhaghosa to the Buddha's "authority realm," i.e., $10{,}000^3$ or 10^{12}, we again arrive at the figure of 10^{63}. Moreover, it should be remembered that Archimedes begins his calculations based on a 10,000 world-system, i.e., the sphere of the earth which is not greater in diameter than 10,000 diameters of the earth.

2. La Vallée Poussin, *Kośa*, chap. iii, pp. 167-68, 167, n. 2. Also, see above, Chapter II, Figure 8, p. 38.

3. Willibald Kirfel, *Symbolik des Buddhismus* (Stuttgart : A. Hierseman, 1959), p. 55. A Hindu effort to calculate the circumference of the universe can be found in Burgess, *Sūrya Siddhānta*, pp. 250-55. See also Sachau, *Alberuni's India* 2:62-80.

tion. Now, monks, what do you think of it, is it possible by calculation to find the end or limit of these worlds ? They answered: Certainly not, Lord; certainly not, Sugata. The Lord said: On the contrary, monks, some arithmetician or master of arithmetic might, indeed, be able by calculation to find the end or limit of the worlds, both those where the atoms have been deposited and where they have not, but it is impossible by appealing to the rules of arithmetic to find the limit of those hundred thousands of myriads of Aeons; so long, so inconceivable, so immense is the number of Aeons which have elapsed since the expiration of that Lord, the Tathāgata Mahābhijñājñānābhibhū.[1]

There can be little doubt that the *Lotus Sūtra* at least is familiar with the type of reasoning found in Archimedes.

Sands of the Gaṅgā

As has already been noted, an image which recurs frequently in the context of the "*asaṅkhyeya*-cosmology" is that of the "sands of the Gaṅgā." Repeatedly we are told that the Buddhas and their fields in the ten regions of space are "as numerous as the sands of the Gaṅgā" (*gaṅgānadīvālukopama*). Elsewhere, the riddle is posed as to whether the Tathāgatas are as rare as the blooming of an *udumbara* plant or as numerous as the sands of the Gaṅgā. As we have seen, this riddle poses the essential difference between the "*sāhasra*- cosmology" and the "*asaṅkhyeya*-cosmology."

But how are we to understand the meaning of the sands of the Gangā in this context ? First, it is necessary to understand just what the Gaṅgā is. To be sure, it is a river flowing through the region where Gautama was born and where his disciples circulated. The Gaṅgā is further regarded as one of the four rivers flowing from the lake Anavatapta, a lake described in the *Mppś* as filled with lotuses of the colour of gold and made out of the seven jewels as large as the wheels of a chariot.[2] Certainly the jewel-lotuses of Anavatapta are suggestive of celestial imagery. Whether we insist on the precise significance of this imagery or not, it is clear from this passage alone that the Gaṅgā

1. Kern, *Lotus*, pp. 153-54, 155, 299.
2. Lamotte, *Traité*, p. 450.

begins to take on cosmic dimensions. Moreover, we know from other sources that the Gaṅgā was in fact regarded as a cosmic river. Kirfel informs us that

> Die Gaṅgā tritt aus dem Fuss des Nārāyaṇa hervor tritt dann in den Mond ein und kommt von diesem in den Sternenkreis. In einer Ausdehnung von 84 Yojana geht sie in Eile an der südlichen Seite des Meru vorbei. Von einem feurigen Wind in vier Teile geteilt, stürzt die auf die vier höchsten Kuppen des Meru und von diesen durch den Luftraum auf die nach den vier Himmelsrichtungen liegende Stützgebirge.[1]

Here the Gaṅgā is regarded as a river which commences at the boundary of the cosmos, extends throughout the breadth and radius of the cosmos to the centre of the world, which is to say the tip of Mt. Meru. From there, it comes in contact with the earth element, the realm of desire, etc. So, the Gaṅgā is a river through the sky, not unlike the Milky Way, made up of countless (innumerable) worlds, not unlike grains of sand.[2]

Thus, we are encouraged to speculate that the "sands of the Gaṅgā" may be a number of some precision as well, as opposed to simply a very large number. Archimedes was attempting to demonstrate that that which is essentially infinite may nevertheless be known and measured by that which is essentially infinitesimal: a fundamental principle of the infinitesimal calculus.

1. Kirfel, *Kosmographie*, p. 109.
2. The symbolism of the Gaṅgā is exceptionally elaborate throughout a broad spectrum of Indian literature. For a valuable bibliography of Buddhist sources, see Lamotte, *Traité*, p. 450, n. 1. Hindu materials describing the descent of the Gaṅgā from heaven to earth are found in Zimmer, *Myths and Symbols*, pp. 109-21. Beyond these sources, the idea of a cosmic river insinuates itself in countless places. The *Śrāvaka* becomes a "Stream-winner" when he enters the "river of *nirvāṇa*." La Vallée Poussin, *Kośa*, chap. vi, p. 200. The bodhisattva undertakes his infinite labor in order to rescue beings from the "great river of suffering." Ibid., chap. iii, p. 191. Elsewhere, the mental flux is likened to the water in a river. Ibid., chap. ii, p. 199. Warren relates a story from the *Jātakas* about an ascetic, the ego and the Gaṅgā : "If you except the water, the sand, the hither bank and the further bank, where can you find any Gaṅgā ? . . .Although he wander a long time, he will not find such a Gaṅgā or Ego as he is looking for." Warren, *Buddhism*, pp. 153-55. Finally, I will simply recall that the waters of the river Lethe play a key role in the rebirth of the soul for Plato.

Because the image which he chose to represent his infinitesimal was a grain of sand, and because the number at which he arrived must be taken to be at least one of the values of *asaṅkhyeya,* we are driven unavoidably to the conclusion that the value of an *asaṅkhyeya* is precisely that of the number of sands in the Gaṅgā river understood in its cosmic sense. Since the world is essentially a speck of sand in the perspective of the fixed stars, each of the grains of sand which make up the cosmic river must also be a world, a universe unto itself.

The Act of Mind Which is the Universe

The important relationship which exists between an *asaṅkhyeya* and the use of the grain of sand as an infinitesimal also encourages us to re-examine some of the temporal constructs of the "*sāhasra*-cosmology." In this connection, we recall from the discussion of the various destructions at the end of the Kalpa that the final destruction is by wind and reduces the world to dust, i.e., the world is reduced into its atomic nature. The precise ontological status of these atomic particles is cause for considerable debate. The fascination with the atomic nature of material reality dominates a broad range of Classical thought from Lucretius to the Vaiśeṣika and Sarvāstivādins among others. The major issues appear to have been whether matter was infinitely divisible, whether the atoms touched, whether atoms were eternal, were they destroyed at the end of the Kalpa or simply dispersed, and if they were dispersed, did they have any adhesive quality which brought about the formation of a new world; were they seeds (*bīja*) of a new world?

The position of the *Kośa* appears to be that the atoms do not touch because if they did, matter would be a solid irreducible mass, that the atoms are eternal and are scattered at the end of the destructions and that they have no adhesive qualities. As indicated above, the Buddhists explicitly distinguish themselves from the Sāṅkhyan position that the world emerges from the transformation (*pariṇāma*) of primordial matter (*prakṛti*). The Buddhists maintain that it is the acts of beings which bring about the new world.

The scattering of the dust atoms resulting from the destruction by wind further stirs our interest when we recall that it is the 64th destruction which is by wind; that destruction which is the 64th term of a series. As we have just seen, the figure which Archimedes claims to equal the number of grains of sand contained in the universe and which is one value assigned for an "*asaṅkhyeya*" is 10^{63}. Expressed in other terms, 10^{63} is the 64th term of a series beginning with one and increasing by tens. Moreover, Archimedes uses an alternative representation of 10^{63} in the form 10^{56+7}. The manner in which this is expressed cannot fail to remind us of the fact that in the series of 64 destructions, 56 are by fire and 7 are by water. The destruction by wind is a single destruction which for its part destroys the unit.

With all of the remarkable parallels which occur in these numerologies, we may at least consider the possibility that it is the cycle of 64 destructions which is intended by the term *asaṅkhyeyakalpa*. Perhaps the final destruction can be regarded as the *asaṅkhyeyakalpa*. It is, after all, the 64th term of the series as is the value of *asaṅkhyeya* which we have just discussed. And it is this destruction which reduces the world to dust atoms, an image not overly distant from Archimedes' grains of sand. Of course, this still would not explain why or in what sense the career of the *bodhisattva* encompasses three *asaṅkhyeyakalpas*. Nor does it illuminate the problem of the 100 supplementary Kalpas which belong to this career for the purpose of developing the marks, though the relationship between these and the life of Brahmā which encompasses 100 years of days and nights each equal to a *kalpa* is suggestive.

Another area in which this insight into the meaning of the *asaṅkhyeya* is illuminating is with regard to its relationship to the mind. As has been stated, the literal meaning of *asaṅkhyeya* is "innumerable." However, the *Kośa* asks, if the word "*asaṅkhyeya*" signifies an "innumerable" or an "incalculable," how is it possible to speak of three "incalculables," i.e., in conjunction with the career of the *bodhisattva*.[1] And in fact we have just seen the possibilities for interpretation of one of the values of *asaṅkhyeya*. Elsewhere the *Kośa* is quite emphatic: "The *asaṅkhyeya* does not receive its name from the fact that it is incalculable."[2]

1. La Vallée Poussin, *Kośa*, chap. iii, p. 189.
2. Ibid., p. 191.

What sense can be made out of a number which is named an "innumerable" and yet has specific values assigned to it? The use of the infinitesimals and the juxtaposition of these images with those of a world suggest that the *asaṅkhyeya* is at the heart of complex speculations relating the infinitesimal to the infinite, and it is this relationship which provides a clue to the dual meaning of "*asaṅkhyeya*" as an "innumerable" on the one hand and an "enumerable" on the other. While it designates what is innumerable or infinite from one perspective, it is nevertheless knowable or enumerable by means of the divine science of mathematics, i.e., from the perspective of the divine eye and from the perspective of the first *abhijñā*, the *ṛddhi* of *nirmāṇa*, or multiplication and unification. Thus, the importance of the "*asaṅkhyeya*" emerges not in its specific value, but rather in its relational value, i.e., as that which relates the infinite to the infinitesimal.

Clearly, it is in the mind of the cosmic Buddha that the vastness of the cosmos is enumerated. Quite by chance, I have found a use of "*asaṅkhyeya*" in a Jain text, the *Pravacanasāra*, which shows a relationship between an "*asaṅkhyeya*" and the limits of the mind's powers of knowledge. There we find "*asaṅkhyeya*" apparently defined as the number of limited spatial units which the mind can know.[1] The *Mppś* firmly establishes this relationship within Buddhism by stating that the number of sands of the Gaṅgā are known only to the Buddha and bodhisattvas of the Dharmakāya. They are capable of counting the quantity of atoms (*paramāṇu*) which are born and perish in all of Jambudvīpa, a fortiori, the number of grains of sand of the Gaṅgā.[2]

From what we have seen, the term *asaṅkhyeya* derives its significance from two facts. First, it describes a relationship between that which is infinite and that which is infinitesimal. Second, it apparently has implications for the idea of omniscience

1. The intricacies of Jain metaphysics cannot occupy us here, but the text in question apparently maintains that the soul possesses only "innumerable" (*asaṅkhyeya*) infinitesimal spatial units. See Barend Faddegon, trans., *The Pravacana-sāra of Kunda-kunda Ācārya, Together with the Commentary, Tattva-dipikā by Amṛtacandra Sūri* (London : Cambridge University Press, 1935), pp. 108-9.

2. Lamotte, *Traité*, p. 451.

by virtue of the fact that it characterizes the limits of the mind to know. Moreover, the second notion is clearly implicit in the first since both the infinite and the infinitesimal are relationships established by the mind, i.e., they constitute the mind's limit to know. Following this insight one step further, we must conclude that from the perspective of the "*asaṅkhyeya*-cosmology," a "world" or "universe" must be understood as an act of knowing in which the mind establishes a relationship between the infinite and the infinitesimal. *Nirvāṇa*, then, must be understood as a going beyond this world or a destruction of this act of the mind.

Meditations of the Buddha

It is clear that Archimedes' calculations are occasioned by a recognition that the universe is infinitely larger than generally imagined. The sphere of the stars is at a distance from the earth which approaches infinity. From this perspective, the earth appears no larger than the centre of a circle; a mere point occupying relatively no space; a speck of dust. While the precise value of the *asaṅkhyeya* is not of particular significance for the remainder of this discussion, the implications of the great distances to the fixed stars are of paramount importance.

If the stars are infinitely remote, they must not be part of a continuous material substance which makes up the single *buddhakṣetra*. If there is a discontinuity in substance between the earth and the stars, we are no longer able to speak about a universe in the sense of a single *buddhakṣetra*, but about innumerable *buddhakṣetras*. The teaching is no longer performed by a single Buddha or by a single *dharmacakra*, but rather by the Buddhas of the ten regions (*daśadigbuddhas*). Moreover, because of the radical discontinuity between this world and the sphere of the fixed stars, it is necessary to postulate the reality of empty space (*ākāśa*) and the possibility of a void (*śūnyatā*). Finally, if the sphere of the stars is discontinuous with the earth, we may speculate that the "wheel of the dharma" which constitutes the realm of the teaching and the realm of purity no longer bears the same relationship to this world. Our final task then will be to analyze the meaning of the drama of the "*asaṅkhyeya*-cosmology" in terms of the implications of this numerology.

In the discussion of the "*sāhasra*-cosmology," the "wheel of the dharma" or the "wheel of Brahmā" played a critical role in the progress of the *śrāvaka* toward the state of *arhat*. Furthermore, the four *dhyānas* of the Brahmaloka which mark the progress of the *śrāvaka* clearly constitute the realm of purity. Buddhaghosa characterizes the progress of the *śrāvaka* through the four *dhyānas* as the "path of purity," and in the *Mppś*, we are told that the Brahmaloka is the "realm of purity and renunciation."[1] The "wheel of Brahmā" is also "pure" in nature. As the *śāstra* puts it, "the *brahmacakra* is pure because it belongs to Brahmā."[2] The goal of the *śrāvaka* then is to gain access to the *dharmacakra* which is at once the wheel of the law, or the teaching, symbolized in the perfect circular motion of the sphere of the stars and the realm or path of purity.

The "*asaṅkhyeya*-cosmology" on the other hand, ascribes all these attributes to the ten regions. Clearly it is access to the regions which affords access to the teaching and to the pure realm. The regions obviate karmic necessity and are pure "like space." Having access to the regions the asssemblies are now able to hear the dharma being preached in these "pure" lands. As a result of the access to these pure lands, the assemblies acquire the *abhijñās* just as the *arhat* who has successfully mastered the pure realm of Brahmā. Just as the *śrāvaka* who has completed the sixteenth moment of the *darśanamārga* which is identified with the *brahmacakra* becomes a stream-winner (*srota-āpanna*) and is assured of deliverance,[3] so those assemblies who have access to the regions are "fixed" in *anuttarasamyaksambodhi*. Finally, we must add that just as the *śrāvaka* who has mastered the pure realm and achieved the state of *arhat* is able to extend his life, so those who have access to the pure lands and are reborn in them enjoy prolonged life.[4]

1. Ibid., p. 605. On the importance of the gods for Buddhism, see ibid., p. 141 n. On the importance of being reborn in the Brahmaloka, see ibid., pp. 1264, n. 2; 1266, n. 1.
2. Ibid., pp. 467, n. 2; 1598-1603.
3. La Vallée Poussin, *Kośa*, chap. vi, p. 200.
4. Genshin provides the following summary of the Pure Land's superior conditions for rapid progress to Buddhahood : "(1) The power of Amida Buddha's compassionate vows constantly embracing those reborn, (2) the constant illumination of the Buddha's light encouraging their

Finally, we have already seen that the "super-kalpic" life of Brahmā is transferred to the regions in the "*asaṅkhyeya*-cosmology." Just as the stars and planets are instrumental in computing the duration of a *caturyuga*, one thousand of which equals one *kalpa* and constitutes a daytime in the 100 year life of Brahmā, so we read that in the pure land Sukhāvatī, one day and one night is the equivalent of one[1] *kalpa* in Sahā. Clearly, the regions in the "*asaṅkhyeya*-cosmology" are the equivalent of the Brahmaloka in the "*sāhasra*-cosmology." Clearly, the pure lands of the "*asaṅkhyeya*-cosmology" are not considered as part of this universe. We must speculate that this pure realm does not belong to this universe because it is regarded as infinitely remote just as Aristarchus' postulate regarding the stars. The grains of sand of the river Gaṅgā are not grains of sand at all, but entire worlds infinitely remote from this Sahā world, separated by the emptiness of space.

Because the starry heavens are separated from this Sahā world by an unbridgeable discontinuity, the drama of salvation is dramatically reinterpreted. No longer are the *dharmacakra* and the *dhyānas* a part of this universe, this *buddhakṣetra*. An individual cannot gain access to the realm of purity and enter the stream of *nirvāṇa* by follwing the *darśanamārga*. In short, the meditations of the *arhat* are no longer sufficient to afford access to the Brahmaloka, the realm of purity. What is required is a force far greater, a force equivalent to the combustion of the world at the end of the age.

As such, we must conclude that the copious displays of light exhibited by Śākyamuni in his cosmic form absorbed in meditation are intended for this purpose. As indicated in the previous Chapter, the texts themselves draw the closest parallels between these concentrations and the combustion of the world at the end of the Kalpa. Just as the meditations of the *arhat* enabled the *arhat* to be reborn in Brahmā's pure realm, so the

'enlightened mind,' (3) the sounds of the Land's birds, leaves, bells, and other adornments constantly inducing them to reflect on the Buddha, Dharma, and *saṅgha*, (4) the constant companionship of Bodhisattvas, and (5) their *long and uninterrupted lives* (emphasis added). Thus, for both the pleasures it affords and the Buddhahood it offers, we are urged to long for the Pure Land of Amida Buddha." Andrews, *Teachings*, p. 50.

1. La Valleé Poussin, "Cosmogony," p. 138.

meditations of the Buddha enable beings to be reborn in the pure lands. This insight is central to an understanding of the drama of the "*asaṅkhyeya*-cosmology" and is probably at the heart of the extensive literature on the "Great Concentrations" of the Buddha/bodhisattva of the tenth stage.[1] As the *Lotus Sūtra* states so succinctly:" . . . he does not teach a particular Nirvāṇa for each being; he causes all beings to reach complete Nirvāṇa by means of the complete Nirvāṇa of the Tathāgata."[2]

Clearly, we are in a milieu where the significance of the concentrations of the *arhat* have been superseded by the concentrations of the Buddha in his cosmic form, by the "other-power" of the Buddha; motifs which are at the heart of the Pure Land traditions as they were to develop in China and Japan.

Seeds of Rebirth

The ultimate form of access to the pure realm is rebirth in that realm. The ideal of rebirth in the *dhyāna* realms resulting from the meditations of the *śrāvaka* was the goal of the Hīnayāna. In the "*asaṅkhyeya*-cosmology", however, the goal is rebirth in other worlds as a result of the meditations of the cosmic Buddha. The images used to convey the idea of rebirth in the Hīnayāna revolve around taking possession of the four fruits of the religious life, viz., *srotāpanna, sakṛdāgāmin, anāgāmin, arhat* or *aśaikṣa*. Moreover, karma is repeatedly represented in agrarian terms. Karma is like the grain covered with its chaff.[3] The world of karma belongs to the "series of rice"[4]; the *ārūpyas* to the "mental series."[5] We are also informed that a world is related to its fruit,[6] and in the discussion of the single world system, we proposed that the significance of the Jambu tree after which Jambudvīpa receives its name derived from some association with the various mechanisms for rebirth.

1. For a discussion of the bodhisattvas of the tenth stage, see above, Chapter IV, p. 83, n. 1; Chapter V, p. 92, n. 3.

2. Kern, *Lotus*, p. 81.

3. La Vallée Poussin, *Kośa*, chap. iii, pp. 116-17, 116, n. 2.

4. Ibid., p. 33.

5. Lamotte, "Marche," p. 16; La Vallée Poussin, *Kośa*, chap. iii,, pp. 5ff.

6. "Des devaputras, installés dan les chateaux, y mangent le fruit de leurs actes," La Vallée Poussin, "Vasubandhu et Yaçomitra,"pp. 307-8.

But where are the mechanisms for rebirth in the "*asaṅkhyeya*-cosmology"? How is rebirth achieved in the pure lands and not merely visual access? In order to formulate a possible solution to this problem, we must recall the agrarian imagery of the *paramapuṇyakṣetra*, the supreme field of merit made up of the Buddhas of the ten regions, so integral to the drama of the "*asaṅkhyeya*-cosmology" as presented in the *Śāstra*. The Buddhas of the ten regions constitute a supreme field of merit. In it the seeds of merit are brought to maturity and fruition. As a result, the repeated admonition of the *Śāstra* is to "plant your merits in this supreme field of merit."

As we have seen, the regions are not accessible to the meditations of the individual. They are, however, accessible as a result of the concentrations of the Buddha. One of the powers associated with these concentrations is that of *gamana* or displacement. The *Śāstra* is explicit in stating that the rays of light issued by Śākyamuni provide the power which enables the bodhisattvas to travel or to displace themselves to Sahā. It is not inconceivable that these rays also provide the means by which the seeds of merit are displaced to other worlds to be planted and brought to fruition.[1]

A second possibility regarding the mechanism of rebirth in the "*asaṅkhyeya*-cosmology" relates this process back to the numerology which is at the heart of this drama. As we saw in the "*sāhasra*-cosmology," the result of the 64th *mahākalpa* or the "*asaṅkhyeya*" *kalpa* is to reduce the world to dust and to scatter the dust atoms. It is from these dust atoms that a new world is eventually formed. The imagery of dust atoms or grains of sand which are instrumental in the formation of a new world is not overly distant from that of seeds which are transplanted to other worlds in the ten regions. Moreover, several textual references make a close association. Certain Buddhists argued that the wind was the seed (*bīja*) of the new universe; the wind being that which accomplished the 64th

1. Examples of the phenomenon of "catasterism" or "translation to the stars" are provided in Cumont, *Astrology*, pp. 65, 97. We have already touched on this possibility in discussing the power of the rays to transport the bodhisattvas to different worlds. See above, Chapter V, p. 106, n. 3.

destruction. The Mahīśāsikas apparently held the position that the wind carried seeds from one universe to another.[1] Therefore, we must speculate that the concentrations of the Buddha with their "kalpic" force have the effect of reducing the world to dust, to infinitesimals, to seeds of merit which are scattered to the ten regions. There they will be brought to fruition by the Buddhas of the ten regions who preach the dharma in the present. If we follow the significance of the predictions (*vyākaraṇa*) so characteristic of the *Lotus*, they will not only be brought to fruition, they will become Buddhas in other worlds.

There can be no doubt that this imagery of seeds either forming new worlds or being transplanted to new worlds to ripen to maturity extended beyond the limits of India. The Christian Apologist Origen, to cite just a single but striking example, argued against the notion that world followed identical world in an endlessly repetitious manner in these terms:

> If, two times in a row, one planted in a field a measure of wheat, it would be possible that the second time the grains would fall in exactly the same manner as the first, to the extent that the grains of the second measure are spread about in the same order and in the same places as the grains of the first measure. Certainly, that would not be possible with a quantity of grains which was innumerable, even though, during the centuries of immense duration, one were to undertake such sowings endlessly. In the same manner, it appears impossible to me that the world could be recreated in such manner that the births and deaths and actions of all sorts would be repeated in the same order and in the same manner.[2]

The "*asaṅkhyeya*-cosmology" seems to increase even this certainty of freedom in the cosmic process by depicting a drama which continues from aeon to aeon, but in which the seeds are scattered to innumerable worlds at the limits of space. Moreover, it is all but stated that this is an endless process, that these limits are only provisional and that additional innumerables of worlds exist beyond these limits.[3]

1. La Vallée Poussin, *Kośa*, chap. iii, p. 210.
2. Duhen, *Système*, 2 : 450.
3. It is possible that a similar vision is at the heart of the writings of Suhrawahrdi, the medieval Islamic mystic (d. 1191). Corbin informs

The fact that the seeds of merit which are transplanted to new worlds are so closely related to the rays of light exhibited by the Buddha as well as to a numerology which has as its basis a statement about the distance to the sphere of the fixed stars prompts us to make one further association. The seeds of merit perform the function of what elsewhere would be the soul. They are the continuity in the process of transmigration; they make rebirth possible and in the context of the "*asaṅkhyeya*-cosmology" even desirable. Furthermore, the continuity between these Buddhist speculations and those of the Hellenistic world has surfaced repeatedly in the course of this dissertation. From the affinities already apparent between the seed/soul and the rays of light, it is the smallest of steps to see in them the "particles of light" which constitute the soul, the divine spark which has descended from the realm of light and longs to return.

> The Pythagoreans . . . believed that the glittering particles of dust which danced ceaselessly in a sunbeam were souls descending from the ether, borne on the wings of light. They added that this beam, passing through the air and through water down to its depth, gave life to all things here below. . . . Souls descended upon the earth, and reascended after death toward the sky, thanks to the rays of the sun, which served as the means of transport.[1]

While the "*asaṅkhyeya*-cosmology" is part of a continuum with other Hellenistic cosmologies, it nevertheless bears uniquely

us that "Suhrawahrdi and the philosophers of Ishraq, in Iran, could not be satisfied with a single sphere for the multitude of fixed stars; through the "dimensions" of their new angelology they foreshadowed the limitless spaces of an astronomy that would shatter the traditional schemata, but that had not depopulated the infinite spaces of their celestial 'presences.' " Corbin, *Avicenna*, p. 98.

1. Cumont, *Astrology*, p. 103. It should be recalled that Buddhist uses of the image of the flame to represent a "soul" are found even in the Pāli sources. In the *Milindapañha* (71, 5), Nāgasena is asked : "How does rebirth take place without anything transmigrating ?" He responds with another question : "Suppose . . a man were to light a light from another light; pray, would one light have passed over (transmigrated) to the other light ? . . . In exactly the same way does rebirth take place without anything transmigrating." T. W. Rhys Davids, trans., *The Questions of King Milinda* 2 vols. (New York : Dover Publications, Inc., 1963), 1 : 111.

Buddhist markings. Nowhere do we find the existence of a soul affirmed. All notions of self and world are ultimately held to be "empty" like space. There is no creator and no creation apart from the acts of beings. Time too, as we have suggested, is ultimately illusory as is its corollary motion.[1] Motion in the last analysis, of course, is animation and so its denial leads us back to the doctrine of the emptiness of the self (*ātma-śūnyatā*). The focus of the drama of salvation is cast in terms of meditation; clearly an Indian if not only a Buddhist characteristic. Finally, it seems impossible that the sense of grandeur and of the miraculous which explodes in this cosmology, could be rivalled by any other tradition. The combination, then, of a truly cosmic vision with a rigor and precision we have only begun to decipher, must be taken as the watchword of this most spectacular and most successful of all the theological cosmologies of Antiquity.

1. Eliade, "Time and Eternity," p. 80.

CHAPTER VII

CONCLUSION: MOTION AND LIGHT

"Mother of Buddhas"

Perhaps it is to be expected that the question of perspective would be such a critical issue in viewing the Buddhist cosmologies since it is precisely a metaphysics of perspective or measurement which is at the heart of these speculations. The question of perspective has occurred on three levels. First, within Buddhism, the various strands of cosmological speculation have been seen to stand out in sharpest relief when they are juxtaposed. This is true to such an extent that it is a firm if unexpected conclusion of this research that it is impossible to grasp the intention of these cosmologies in isolation. What we have discovered is an exhaustive theological idiom, precise in every detail. Each particular cosmological system weighs numerous alternatives on a wide range of issues; affirming one, excluding others and qualifying still others. Thus the meaning of a single cosmology cannot be understood unless we understand what is excluded as well as what is affirmed. Our work accomplishes this by juxtaposing the two strands of the mathematical cosmologies one to another and by moving to interpret all phases of Buddhist speculation from this perspective.

Expanding our perspective beyond the boundaries of Buddhism, but within India, one finds corresponding Hindu and Jain cosmologies for each of the strands to be found in Buddhism. This is most obvious in the case of the *cakravāla* where similar circular world disks provide clear equivalents in other traditions. As we have seen, the "*sāhasra*-cosmology" constitutes the Buddhist commentary on pan-Indian themes of cosmic time which play a large role in both Hinduism and Jainism. Hindu and Jain equivalents for the "*asaṅkhyeya*-cosmology" are less apparent although concern for the *asaṅkhyeya* seems to be a preoccupation of Jain cosmological speculation, particularly in conjunction with the Jain vision of mind.

Finally, the discovery of the continuity of these Buddhist cosmologies with a broad spectrum of Hellenistic cosmological speculation has presented yet another perspective, providing key insights into the single world system as well as the numerology of thousands and the significance of the innumerable world systems of the Mahāyāna. To a large extent, the Hellenistic materials have provided access to the scientific setting of these speculations in terms of the concern for motion and for mathematics as the means for measuring and comprehending the implications of these motions.

By bringing all these perspectives to bear on our materials, we have come to an appreciation of the drama implicit in the strands of the mathematical cosmologies. Each of these dramas is really the expression of what we might call a "journey of the soul." While the "journey of the soul" is a theme with wide currency, its subordination to the techniques and powers of meditation provides its characteristically Buddhist markings. The two dramas upon which we have concentrated differ in a number of ways. The precise nature of the journey is at issue as well as when and how beings become "oriented" or "fixed" in the path of enlightenment. The precise status of the Buddha and the relationship of the Buddha to the world is also a major concern and cause for controversy. In the "*sāhasra*-cosmology," the individual is "fixed" in the path of enlightenment after mastering the teaching or the four holy truths, which, as we have seen, is identified with the wheel of the dharma (*dharmacakra*). As a result of our research, we have shown that the *dharmacakra* may be identified cosmologically with the realm of the fixed stars which move "as in a whirlpool" about Mt. Meru. As such, while images of light are not prominent in the "*cakravāla*-cosmology," even here it is evident in conjunction with the teaching. In the "*asaṅkhyeya*-cosmology," on the other hand, all beings are "fixed" in the state of enlightenment when touched by the rays of light issued by the Buddha. Here there is a dramatic identification between light and the teaching. In this context, however, it is the teaching itself which is efficacious, and not the ability of beings to master and comprehend it. Indeed, we are reminded repeatedly that the teaching is infinite (*apramāṇa*) and unlimited (*ananta*), i.e., it cannot be mastered as such.

The journey of the "*sāhasra*-cosmology" is one which moves arduously and laboriously through each of the abodes of the cosmography. It is made up of seemingly endless paths (*mārga*) and its duration extends indefinitely in time. The journey of the "*asaṅkhyeya*-cosmology", on the other hand, occurs in an instant as a result of the Buddha's miraculous power of displacement (*gamana*). In the "self-power" cosmologies, the journey is possible because the world is a universe; a unified, contiguous whole. In the "other-power" cosmologies there are many worlds separated by the void of infinite space. The manner in which salvation occurs differs as well. In the "*sāhasra*-cosmology," individuals realize *nirvāṇa* one by one, while in the "*asaṅkhyeya*-cosmology" all beings are saved by the single *nirvāṇa* of the Tathāgata. In this manner, the Buddha/bodhisattva fulfills his vow to work for the salvation of all beings.

Finally, the status of the Tathāgata is ultimately at issue in these cosmologies. Every indication is that the Buddha of the "*sāhasra*-cosmology" is totally extinct. As we have seen the appearance of a Buddha in a *trisāhasramahāsāhasralokadhātu* is as rare as the blooming of an *udumbara* plant. Magical or fictional Buddhas (*nirmāṇabuddha*) appear, but they are related to the Buddha-nature only as a plant to a seed. The "*asaṅkhyeya*-cosmology," on the other hand, relentlessly affirms the reality of the Buddhas in the ten regions (*daśadigbuddha*) and asserts the importance of their appearance. Indeed, they are "as numerous as the sands of the Gaṅgā." In the first case, the *nirvāṇa* of the Tathāgata is one of quiescence; in the second, we are confronted with what we might term an active *nirvāṇa*.

In short, it is apparent that the single *buddhakṣetra* of the "*sāhasra*-cosmology" casts the drama of salvation in a temporal framework, emphasizing the gradualism of self-discipline. The innumerable *buddhakṣetras* of the "*asaṅkhyeya*-cosmology" on the other hand rely on spatial categories to assert the suddenness of rebirth resulting from the "other-power" of the cosmic Buddha.

In selecting the mathematical cosmologies as the focus of our research, we recognized that they were the least understood aspect of Buddhist cosmological speculation. While our research has not been conclusive in this regard, it strongly suggests that all of Buddhist cosmological speculation falls into one of these two traditions. Those which accept time as the fundamental cosmological reality belong to the "*sāhasra*-cosmology." These cosmologies belong to the Hīnayāna and as such have their philosophical basis in the emptiness of the self (*ātmaśūnyatā*). Those cosmologies which accept space as the fundamental cosmological reality belong to the "*asaṅkhyeya*-cosmology." These cosmologies belong to the Mahāyāna and as such have their philosophical basis in the emptiness of the *dharmas* (*dharmaśūnyatā*) as well as in the emptiness of the self.

As a result of having uncovered the major issues involved in the mathematical cosmologies, we have also come to a more complete understanding of the *cakravāla* and the Pure Land cosmologies. In the case of the *cakravāla*, we have come to understand not only how it is used as the unit of cosmic measurement, but we may speculate that the entire cosmography of the *cakravāla* is intended to point up the fact that the world is a constantly measuring entity whose measurements are ultimately void. In short, we have caught a glimpse of the intention behind the metaphysics of measurement expressed in the *cakravāla* and understood that it is more than so many mountain rings and oceans cluttered with arbitrary detail.

In the case of the Pure Land cosmologies, we have seen that the simplicity of these cosmologies of faith really presupposes a history of cosmological speculation which includes all the refinements of the "*asaṅkhyeya*-cosmology." The existence of countless real Buddhas in the ten directions of space, the transportation at the moment of death to another Buddha-field where the teaching is heard without difficulty or interruption due to shortness of life, the famous eighteenth vow of the Buddha/bodhisattva to work for the salvation of all beings, the attention to the "other-power" of the Buddha; all these themes cohere only in a cosmology of such scope. Repetition of the name of the Buddha in the context of the cosmologies of faith is simplicity itself. But in order to prepare the stage for this "popular" religion, the doctors drew on nothing less refined than the drama of the "*asaṅkhyeya*-cosmology."

If the mathematical cosmologies are in fact the two basic strands containing all the complexities of the Buddhist cosmological materials, we may speculate that the *cakravāla* cosmology and the Pure Land cosmologies actually constitute shorthands or simplifications of these two great traditions. The *cakravāla* or single world system is an abbreviation of the "*sāhasra*-cosmology" for the benefit of the monastic vocation. The Pure Land cosmologies, on the other hand, are simplifications of the *asaṅkhyeya*-cosmology" for the benefit of the devotional traditions of the Mahāyāna. Thus, the three phases of speculation with which we began our research can best be resolved into two discrete strands, each with a simplified version.

Not only are these two strands expressed in terms of a mytho-philosophic drama, but each has a discrete scientific basis. Each constitutes a critique of the goal of gnostic science to embrace the infinite—in one case the eternity of time; in the other, the infinity of space. To accomplish this critique, both strands analyze the universe in terms of its relationship to the mind. As such, it is apparent that the mathematical cosmologies of Buddhism represent a critique of the mind's apprehension of reality and of the mind's ability to analyze reality; to divide it without end and to aggregate it into unities. At one extreme of its abilities, the mind analyzes or divides reality into infinitesimals. At the other extreme, it aggregates reality into infinities.

In the temporal cosmologies, this process of aggregation produced the aeon (*kalpa*) while the process of division resulted in the instant (*kṣaṇa*). This process of analysis was likewise applied to the world of extension. In its totality, the world of extension was expressed in terms of the infinity of space (*ākāśa*), while its smallest logical entity found expression in the atom (*paramāṇu*) whose size, shape and manner of combination were all matters of extensive controversy.

Since all of the speculations on time, space and soul relied heavily on the multiplication and division of observable reality up to the largest possible aggregates (aeon, universe, total number of beings, world soul, etc.) and down to the smallest possible unit (instant, atom, individual soul), they were closely associated with the science of mathematics.

It is clear that questions related to the beginning and end of the world as well as to the limited or unlimited extent of the universe—sometimes expressed in terms of the total numbers of worlds—cannot be known to experience. They are conceived of by the mind, and their answers belong to the capacity of the mind to know. To the extent that these systems rely solely on the powers of the mind, albeit aided by the divine science of mathematics, they are gnostic. As a result, the question of omniscience occurs naturally within the context of these speculations.

We have already seen one expression of this concern in the scholastic dilemmas recorded in the *Mppś*. If the universes are limited in number, and since each of the innumerable Buddhas saves by himself an immense (*aprameya*) and incalculable (*asaṅkhyeya*) number of beings, the totality of beings will be exhausted in the course of time. If, on the other hand, the universes are infinite in number, the Buddha is not omniscient.

While it is observations of the motions of the planets which enable us to subdivide and measure time, it is the mind alone which is able to come to terms with eternity. In a similar manner, it is the void which separates man from the heavens which conveys a sense of non-differentiated and infinite space, of world without end (*ananta*) which can be grasped and comprehended only by the mind free from discrimination. Thus, time and space emerge as the great abstracts of philosophical and theological cosmology.

The "infinities" of time and space are thus unique categories of the mind and do not belong to the realm of experience as such. Moreover, we have seen that it is the divine science of mathematics which is the tool of the mind in its quest for knowledge. In the most general sense, then, we can say that all of the metaphysical and theological systems grounded in such speculations are gnostic in one degree or another.

Having completed our survey of the mathematical cosmologies, we have seen that the "thousands" and "innumerables" of the Buddhist speculations are inextricably related to these gnostic cosmologies, to the use of measurement as the basis for a metaphysics, to the power of the mind to extend measurement to the limits of the universe, however vast, and to the notion that salvation is a function of knowledge. Indeed, it is the perfection of wisdom (*prajñāpāramitā*) which is the highest of the virtues of the bodhisattva. However, the Buddhist cosmologies confront us with one important difference. Briefly stated, it is that they are agnostic rather than gnostic.

In a similar way we noted a striking contradiction between those traditions within Buddhism which rejected and condemned speculation on the limited or unlimited nature of the universe, the numbers of beings and the existence of the Tathāgata, and the seemingly unrestrained enthusiasm for just such. speculation as expressed in what we have called the mathematical cosmologies. However, the further we have probed into the Buddhist materials, the more inclined we are to conclude that there is no discontinuity between this Buddhist agnosticism and the cosmologies we have explored. The Buddhist cosmologies appear more and more as a critique of all those speculations relying in one way or another on certain knowledge regarding the "infinities" of time and space; certainly those of the *Sāṅkhya*, and, we may suspect, those of the Classical world in general. The fact that the *triṣāhasramahāsāhasrulokadhātu* has emerged in this study as the "ever-measuring" universe is certainly a cosmological statement of a familiar Buddhist theme, namely that all knowledge grounded in the discriminating powers of the mind is ultimately void. The implications of the "*asaṅkhyeya*-cosmology" are such that it too constitutes a critique of the discriminating powers of the mind with regard to its apprehension of space. The mind is capable of analyzing reality down to the level of the infinitesimal and aggregating it up to the level of the infinite. But the infinite and the infinitesimal are not realities in and of themselves. Rather, they constitute the limits of the mind's ability to know. Everything between these two limits constitutes a universe. Within these limits, the mind is omniscient, but this is not to say that these limits exhaust reality. Nor is this knowledge based on discrimination, the knowledge which results in salvation.

Thus, it appears that all of the symbolism of these mathematical cosmologies is intended to point up the ultimate emptiness of the cosmos. The cosmos is the stage for salvation. However, salvation occurs only when the cosmos is correctly apprehended, and its correct apprehension is devoid of any meaning which the mind brings to it using the powers of discrimination. Just as the outer mountain which surrounds the universe is known as the "mother of mountains," i.e., the basis of all discrimination, and just as we saw that the *cakravāla* was the basic unit of cosmic measurement both temporally and spatially, so the Prajñāpāramitā, the great teaching of emptiness, is known as the "mother of Buddhas," Thus, we must conclude that the systematic agnosticism of the Fourteen questions is the watchword of both the "*sāhasra*-cosmology" and the "*asaṅkhyeya*-cosmology." The agnosticism of these systems with regard to the "infinities" of time and space is thus clearly established.

* * * *

The perspective we have gained by placing the Buddhist cosmologies in their scientific setting has allowed us to understand the basic intention behind them. But it has also raised many questions, most notably the troublesome question of motion. More than once we have remarked on the absence of references to motion in all the Buddhist cosmologies. The great motions of the planets and stars have seemingly gone all but unnoticed. We have found them hidden in the seven ring mountains and in the great wheel of the *dharma* (*dharmacakra*). Another important example of a veiled or disguised reference to motion is to be found in repeated statements about the "trembling" of the world system. The 10,000 world system is said to tremble in six directions at various stages in the Buddha's life. The *Lotus Sūtra* informs us that when the Buddha entered into meditation, the whole Buddha-field shook in six ways: "it moved, removed, trembled, trembled from one end to the other, tossed, tossed along."[1] In the *Mppś*, we are told that the Buddha shakes the *trisāhasramahāsāhasralokadhātu* in six directions.[2]

We must assume that the six directions mentioned above constitute an allusion to the six linear directions. As such, no mention is made to the rotational motion of cosmic bodies. This is consistent with one strand of Classical science which argued against the existence of the motion of rotation. While there were defensible scientific reasons for such a position, the primary motivation for denying rotational motion was most likely the great theological significance attached to the regular motion of the starry heavens—the *dharmacakra*. If the regular motion of the heavens was not inherent in the fixed stars, but was caused by the rotation of the earth, this Sahā world, the teaching of the immortality of the soul would no longer be credible. While the "*sāhasra*-cosmology" is most closely associated with those traditions which acknowledge only the six linear

1. Kern, *Lotus*, pp. 6-7.
2. Lamotte, *Traité*, pp. 472-76.

directions, it is my feeling that the cosmology of the Mahāyāna accepts the motion of rotation. That the Mahāyāna does accept this motion is indirectly supported by Eitel's definition of Sahā as the "capital of the chiliocosmos." We may take this in the most provisional sense to mean that it is the earth which dictates the laws of the heavens.

If, as we have postulated, the "*asaṅkhyeya*-cosmology" accepts the illusory nature of the teaching and of the motions of the *dharmacakra*, we must ask what has become of the teaching in the Mahāyāna. What we find is that this illusion is one with a purpose since it nevertheless constitutes a teaching which attracts beings beyond the world. But it is a teaching through deception. Therefore, we must conclude that the Mahāyāna accepts the motion of rotation and incorporates it theologically through the doctrine of *upāya* or skill in means. Thus, the great teaching, the setting in motion of the wheel of the law (*dharmaparyāya*) occurs as a result of the great skill in means of the Buddha/bodhisattva, a teaching through a kind of deception. We may speculate additionally that the Buddha/bodhisattva is both Buddha and bodhisattva because he is extinct in the Akaniṣṭha heaven, the pinnacle of the world, which we observe at the centre of the great wheel of the *dharma*, but nevertheless remains active in presenting the teaching through his great skills of deception.

We may speculate additionally that the fact that there are innumerable *buddhakṣetras* in the "*asaṅkhyeya*-cosmology," each understood as a *trisāhasramahāsāhasralokadhātu* also has to do with the scientific premisses accepted by the Mahāyāna for the purpose of theological interpretation. These include the non-geocentric nature of the universe, the infinite remove of the fixed stars and the rotational motion of the earth and other heavenly bodies. The last two premisses apparently were not accepted by the framers of the "*sāhasra*-cosmology," since if the earth were to rotate on its axis, the motion of the fixed stars—the teaching of the *dharmacakra*—would be an illusion. The reasons for regarding the heavens as proximate and continuous with the earth, i.e., as part of a universe have already been reviewed. However, if, as the Mahāyāna apparently maintained, the wheel of the *dharma* is the product of the rotational motion of the earth, and if all heavenly bodies, or innumerable heavenly bodies possess this same motion, there is a wheel of the *dharma* for each world possessing such motion. Thus, for each there is an "ever-measuring universe," a teaching of immortality and of the infinities of space and time. This is only a provisional teaching, however, since it is the emptiness of all dharmas or all motions which is the great perfection of wisdom, the great teaching of universal emptiness.

If we accept the three premisses of non-geocentrism, infinite remove of the fixed stars and rotation of the earth as the scientific basis for the theology of the Mahāyāna, we are confronted with nothing less than a theology with roots in the pre-Christian era which has embraced all of the fundamental tenets of the Copernican revolution.

* * *

Having thus extricated the great motions from their theological captivity in the Buddhist cosmologies, it remains to account for the denial of these motions, although this can only be done in the most suggestive manner at this point. Our research has shown that in addition to the denial of motion in these cosmologies, there has been a persistant preference for spatial categories rather than temporal ones; a preference which culminates in the Mahāyānist emphasis on *diś—direction*, or the regulator of position in space. Even in the "*sāhasra*-cosmology" we saw the ambiguous and qualified status accorded to time with the *caturyuga* of Purāṇic chronometry transposed into the *caturdvīpa* of Sarvāstivādin cosmography. The thousands of Purāṇic kalpas are likewise transposed into the thousands of *cakravālas*. In the Mahāyāna, we have noted the outright rejection of the reality of time.[1] Time, of course, is a corollary of motion. In Plato's words, "time is the moving image of eternity."

This denial of motion or animation and the subsequent denial of time, or the measurements afforded by motion, together with the consistent preference for spatial categories is undoubtedly related to the Buddhist denial of "soul." Realization of the emptiness of the self (*ātmaśūnyatā*) is the fundamental teaching of the Hīnayāna and is tantamount to salvation. The cosmologies of the Hīnayāna are apparently intended to facilitate

1. Lamotte, *Traité*, pp. 1694-96.

this insight in conjunction with an analysis of the arising and falling of the *dharmas*—in short, the momentariness or limits of the *dharmas*. The cosmologies of the Mahāyāna, on the other hand, add to this the emptiness of the *dharmas* (*dharma-śūnyatā*) through its denial of time and motion—in short, the denial of the reality of all *dharmas* or motions. It should simply be noted in passing that the identification of motionlessness with the liberated state is explicit in Jainism.

> According to the Jains, the world is eternal, without beginning or end. Loka is that place in which happiness and misery are experienced as results of virtue and vice. It is composed of three parts, *ūrdhva* (where the gods reside), *madhya* (this world of ours), and *adho* (where the denizens of hell reside). The mundane universe (*lokākāśa*) is pervaded with dharma which makes all movement possible. Beyond the lokākāśa there is no dharma and therefore no movement, but only space (*ākāśa*). Surrounding this lokākāśa are three layers of air. The perfect soul rising straight over the ūrdhva-loka goes to the top of this lokākāśa and (there being no dharma) remains motionless there.[1]

Finally, we must note that motion and light are really corollary realities since it is light which reveals or makes known the motions of the heavens. Those cosmologies emphasizing the motions of the cosmos are grounded in a vision of time. The teaching is the pure motion of the heavens—the law of heaven. Those cosmologies emphasizing light on the other hand are grounded in a vision of space. The rays of light which reveal the motions of the heavens are the teaching because they suggest the questions of limits and the emptiness of those limits to the mind.

The Classical cosmologies of motion are the basis for a theology of God as Prime Mover. We cannot doubt that these themes are taken up in Buddhism albeit in a negative or agnostic manner. As we have seen, the cosmos "trembles" in the six directions at the birth of the Buddha. Since we have seen the repeated negations regarding the relationship between the Buddha and the cosmos as well as the general agnosticism of

1. Surendranath Dasgupta, *History of Indian Philosophy*, 5 vols. (Cambridge : University Press, 1920-1955), 1 : 199.

the Buddhist cosmologies to the general goals of Classical cosmology, we may wonder if the birth of the Buddha is not in fact tantamount to the death of the deity.

As we have noted more than once, all motion is animation and it is motion which is the fundamental characteristic of the soul in the "*sāhasra*-cosmology." The heavens are displaced or animated by the great soul and the individual by the individual soul fallen from heaven. Although the soul is likened to light or the flame of a candle, these themes remain in the background of Hīnayāna speculation. Instead, it is the journey of this flame from one candle to the next and from one body to the next which is important. The soul passes arduously along the various paths through the planetary spheres, into the heavens and beyoud until its ultimate liberation. We may speculate that on one level at least, the seven destructions by fire correspond to seven conjunctions of the planetary spheres and that the fire of the soul passes through the planetary heavens in this manner as it is transmitted from one sphere to the next by virtue of the conjunction—like a flame passing from one candle to another.

In the "*asaṅkhyeya*-cosmology," however, it is not the heavens which are displaced or animated by the soul, but rather the light of the heavens which reveals the limits of the world as the limits of knowledge to the soul and in so doing, displaces the soul by freeing it of all knowledge grounded in discrimination. The teaching is thus an active teaching, salvific in and of itself, constantly efficacious, and not a passive teaching to be mastered. These rays of light are the teaching and have replaced all speculations on motion. Moreover, it is not motion which is the fundamental characteristic of the soul in the "*asaṅkhyeya*-cosmology" but light. When the soul is touched by light which is its true nature, it is displaced to other worlds. We have seen that the rays of light which are the teaching and which fix beings in the path of enlightenment are a result of the extinction of the Tathāgata in meditation. With this thought in mind, we are extremely close to the idea of a cosmic drama which has as its basis a sacrificial and redemptive death. The cosmos is not the product of a Prime Mover, but of the extinct being who creates light. The world and the teaching are identical and are possible only as a result of the sacrifice of the deity.

CHAPTER VIII

BIBLIOGRAPHICAL RESOURCES

Because our survey of the Buddhist materials has brought us into contact with so many new and unexpected areas, it is appropriate to conclude by providing a bibliographical summary which may be of value in assisting future research. It is not an overstatement to say that there is hardly an article or monograph on Indian religion which does not make reference to cosmology; either to the formal systems as such, one or more images associated with the cosmology, or one isolated aspect of Indian religion or culture which is treated or recognized in one way or another by the formal cosmological systems. Nevertheless, relatively few works are dedicated to discussions of the "formal" cosmological systems of India as such.

Willibald Kirfel's *Die Kosmographie der Inder* (Bonn : K. Schroeder, 1920) is the most notable exception to this statement. Its three basic units draw together a vast amount of material relating to the variations in detail of the Hindu, Buddhist and Jain cosmographies. Since its appearance in 1920, this work has been the standard resource for Western scholarship in the area. While Kirfel's work remains an invaluable resource, it suffers from three main shortcomings. First, as the title makes clear, it is restricted to cosmography and does not embrace the full range of cosmology. Second, it is totally lacking in interpretation of the materials which it presents. In a word, we may say that Kirfel has overlooked the "drama of salvation" which, as we have seen, constitutes the coherence and raison d'être of these systems. Third, we should simply note that as far as the Buddhist materials are concerned, Kirfel limits himself to the Pāli materials, dismissing the Sanskrit traditions as the "fantastic speculations of a later period." Thus, while Kirfel is a useful resource in reconstructing the variations in detail of the cosmography of the "*cakravāla*-cosmology," it is of little value in discerning the outlines of the two mathematical cosmologies which have been the primary concern of this work. An excellent review of Kirfel's *Kosmographie*, particularly with regard to his assumptions about the earliest Indian representations of the cosmos, can be found in Walther Schubring, "Anzeige," *zeitschrift der deutschen Morgenländischen Gesellschaft* 75 (1921) : 254-75.

As we have noted more than once, the materials of this research fall logically into three categories: Buddhist, Indian and extra-Indian. In organizing the remaining bibliographical materials, I will begin with some general works on the subject of cosmology and then follow this outline.

General

Among the many works which include Buddhism as part of a comparative survey on cosmological speculation, I will simply note the following: Carmen Blacker and Michael Loewe, eds., *Ancient Cosmologies* (London : George Allen & Unwin Ltd., 1975), Edwin Oliver James, *Creation and Cosmology* (Leiden : E.J. Brill, 1969), and Samuel George Frederick Brandon, *Man and His Destiny in the Great Religions* (Manchester: Manchester University Press, 1962). Much useful information can also be obtained in James Hastings, ed., *Encyclopaedia of Religion and Ethics* (Edinburgh: T & T Clark, 1908-1927). Pertinent articles in the *ERE* include "Ages of the World"; "Agnosticism"; "Blest, Abode of the"; "Cosmogony and Cosmology"; "Dead, State of"; "Damned, Abode of the"; "Docetism"; "Hyperboreans"; "Incarnation"; and "Transmigration." All of these articles contain useful information, generally without interpretation, relating to the cosmologies of a number of traditions in addition to Buddhism.

Buddhism

Our survey of the Buddhist materials has fallen into three general areas, i.e., the single world system, the mathematical cosmologies and the Pure Land speculations. It is convenient to arrange the bibliographical materials relating to these cosmologies in this way as well.

Single World System (Cakravāla)

Diagrams of the "*cakravāla*-cosmology" can be found in the following works : Daniel John Gogerley, *Ceylon Buddhism* (London: Kegan Paul, Trench, Trubner & Co, Ltd., 1908);

Dineschandra Sircar, *Cosmography and Geography in Early Indian Literature* (Calcutta: D. Chattopadhyaya, 1967), Plates I and II; Alicia Matsunaga, *The Buddhist Philosophy of Assimilation* (Tokyo : Charles E. Tuttle Co., 1969) ; Laurence Austine Waddell, *The Buddhism of Tibet or Lamaism* (Cambridge: W. Heffer & Sons, Ltd., 1934), p. 79; and Kirfel, *Kosmographie*, Plates. Many diagrams and much valuable information are available in Francesco Lorenzo Pullé, "La cartografia antica dell' India," *Studi Italiani di Filologia Indo-Iranica* 4 (1901), 5 (1905), 10 (1932). An exhaustive compilation of detail relating to all the Indian cosmologies can also be found in Adolf Bastian, *Ideale Welten*, 3 vols. (Berlin: Emil Felber, 1892). A Russian title inaccessible to me can be found in Jozef Szczepan Kowalewski, *Buddiiskaia Kosmologiia* (1837).

As we have seen, materials providing descriptions of the *cakravāla* are legion, albeit lacking in interpretation. Kirfel's *Kosmographie* and Louis de La Vallée Poussin's "Cosmogony and Cosmology (Buddhist)" in the *ERE* provide ample introduction to the Indian materials. The materials found in Louis de La Vallée Poussin, trans., *L'Abhidharmakośa de Vasubandhu* (Brussels: Mélanges chinois et bouddhiques, 1971), Vol. 16 and in particular Chap. 3 have formed the basis for the descriptions of the *cakravāla* contained in this work. We have also seen that cosmological structures which are all but identical to the *cakravāla* are to be found throughout the Classical world. Bibliography on these materials will be found under "Extra-Indian Resources." One fact to which we have alluded but which was not stressed is that the *cakravāla* is turned to many uses within the Buddhist tradition. While the basic structure of the cosmos remains the same, the drama which occurs there finds a variety of expressions. Thus the hells receive greater or lesser emphasis depending on the context as does the role of the *cakravartin*, the role of the Buddha, the drama of the *kāmadhātu* and the manner of rebirth in heaven. To a large extent, these variations occur from one cultural context to another. A selected bibliography on the *cakravāla* by cultural area follows.

Tibet

A brief survey of the Tibetan cosmological materials is available in Laurence Austine Waddell, *The Buddhism of Tibet or*

Lamaism (Cambridge: W. Heffer & Sons, Ltd., 1934), pp. 77-100. A similar brief description of the *cakravāla* can be found in Walter Yeeling Evans-Wentz, *The Tibetan Book of the Dead* (New York: Oxford University Press, 1960), pp. 61-66. The book as a whole is most interesting, however, for its focus on that aspect of the drama of salvation known as the "intermediate-state," i.e., the period between death and rebirth. For a recent discussion of this topic, see Alex Wayman, "The Intermediate-State Dispute in Buddhism," in L. Cousins, A. Kunst and K. R. Norman, eds., *Buddhist Studies in Honour of I. B. Horner* (Boston: D. Reidel Publishing Co., 1974), pp. 227-39. The *Kośa* discusses the "intermediate-state" at length in chap. iii, pp. 31-60. The Tibetan text of the verses (*kārikā*) of Chapter III of the *Abhidharmakośa* together with a translation of Vasubandhu's *Abhidharmakośabhāṣya* or commentary on the verses can be found in Louis de La Vallée Poussin, "Vasubandhu et Yaçomitra; Troisième Chapitre de l'Abhidharmakoca: Kārikā, Bhāṣya et Vyākhyā," *Mémoires de l'académie royale de Belgique*, 2e sér., Tome 6, Fasicule II (January, 1919). Most of the important information in these texts is footnoted in La Vallée Poussin's complete translation of the *Kośa.*

China

See Jean Pierre Abel-Rémusat, "Essai sur la cosmographie et la cosmogonie des bouddhistes d'après les auteurs chinois," *Journal des savants* 16, 2e sér. (October, 1831): 596-610; 16 (November, 1831): 668-74; 16 (December, 1831): 716-31. This work is also available in Rémusat's *Mélanges posthumes d'histoires et de literature orientales* (Paris: Imprimerie royale, 1843), pp. 65-131. Samuel Beal, *A Catena of Buddhist Scriptures from the Chinese* (London: Trübner & Co., 1871) contains extensive descriptions of the Buddhist cosmos. A more recent work is that of Wolfgang Bauer, *China and the Search for Happiness* (New York: Seabury Press, 1976) which contains a lengthy discussion of the role played by the islands at the ends of the world disk in Chinese Utopian thought.

A description of the *cakravāla* by the Chinese pilgrim is contained in Thomas Watters, trans., *On Yuan Chwang's Travels in India* (Delhi : Munshi Ram Manohar Lal, 1961), 1: 30-38. A description of the Chinese hells strongly influenced by Buddhism can be found in Wolfram Eberhard, *Guilt and Sin in Traditional China* (Berkeley: University of California Press, 1967), pp. 24-59.

Japan

A good sense of the role of cosmology in Japan as well as in Buddhism in general is provided in August Karl Reischauer, *Studies in Japanese Buddhism* (New York: AMS Press, 1971), pp. 183-267. Genshin's descriptions of the *cakravāla*, and particularly its hells, can be found in August Karl Reischauer, "Genshin's Ojo Yoshu: Collected Essays on Birth into Paradise," *Transactions of the Asiatic Society of Japan* 7, 2d ser. (1930): 16-98. Japanese interest in the hells of Buddism is also reflected in Daigan and Alicia Matsunaga, *The Buddhist Concept of Hell* (New York: Philosophical Library, 1972).

Ceylon

A long bibliography on Ceylonese cosmology is possible, though most of it is dated and little surpasses Kirfel's compilation of the Pāli materials. The primary source document, of course, is Buddhaghosa's *Visuddhimagga* available in Bhikku Ñāṇamoli, trans., *The Path of Purification* (Kandy: Buddhist Publication Society, 1975). The relationship between right conduct and meditation and the cosmology are at the heart of this document. In addition, the famous "cosmological" sections (414 ff) include a lengthy description of the full cycle of sixty-four destructions of the world by fire, water and wind together with the relationship of these destructions to the 10,000 world system. Secondary sources of value include Daniel John Gogerley, *Ceylon Buddhism* (London: Kegan Paul, Trench, Trubner & Co., Ltd., 1908); Robert Spence Hardy, *A Manual of Buddhism* (London: Partridge & Oakey, 1853); and Mr. Joinville, "On the Religion and Manners of the People of Ceylon, "*Asiatick Researches* 7 (1801): 399-448. A promising, though not readily available explanation of a number of Buddhist theories relating to the universe can be found in C. P. Ranasinghe, *The Buddha's Explanation of the Universe* (Colombo: Lanka Buddha-Mandalaya Fund, 1957).

Thailand

The following recent works treat the "*cakravāla*-cosmology" in Thailand: George Coedes and Charles Archaimbault, *Les trois mondes* (*Traibhūmi Brah R'van*) (Paris: Publications de l'école française d'Extrême-Orient, 1973); George Coedes, "The Traibhumikatha Buddhist Cosmology and Treaty on Ethics," *East and West* 7, No. 4 (January, 1957): 349-52; Robert Heine-Geldern, *Conceptions of State and Kingship in Southeast Asia* (Ithaca: Cornell Southeast Asia Program Data Paper No. 18, 1956); Craig Reynolds, "Buddhist Cosmography in Thai History with Special Reference to Nineteenth Century Cultural Change," *Journal of Asian Studies* 35 (1976): 203-30; Frank Reynolds and Mani Reynolds, trans., *Three Worlds According to King Ruang* (Palo Alto and Bangkok: Stanford University Press, and the Siam Society, 1977). See also S. J. Tambiah, *Buddhism and the Spirit Cults in North-East Thailand* (Cambridge: Cambridge University Press, 1970), pp. 32-52 and idem, *World Conqueror and World Renouncer* (Cambridge: Cambridge University Press, 1976), pp. 9-18 for the outlines of a Buddhist cosmogony, the so-called "Buddhist Genesis," details of which are available in *Kośa*, chap. iii, pp. 204-7. In general, Thai representations of the "*cakravāla*-cosmology" tend to be structured about the role of the *cakravartin* or "world ruler."

Burma

The cosmology of Burmese Buddhism is reliably described in Winston L. King, "Worlds Without End" in his *A Thousand Lives Away* (Cambridge: Harvard University Press, 1964), pp. 85-113.

The Mathematical Cosmologies

As we have noted more than once, apart from a long series of pejorative remarks, virtually no systematic treatment of the mathematical cosmologies is to be found. For the most part, the mathematical cosmologies are coterminus with what have been called the "*buddhakṣetra*-cosmologies." Because, as we have seen, these cosmologies are primarily concerned with limits, they are directed toward defining the "field" (*kṣetra*) of a Buddha; in particular his field of knowledge, or his omniscience. Use of the term *kṣetra* in this context finds several important counterparts in the Indian literature. The great battle of the *Mahābhārata* takes place at Kurukṣetra which is characterized as the "field of dharma." The limits of the powers of a *cakravartin* are sometimes characterized as a *cakravarti-kṣetra.*[1] More suggestive still is the distinction found in *Bhagavadgītā* XIII between the field (*kṣetra*) and the field-knower (*kṣetrajña*). The distinction is essentially Sāṅkhyan in nature and amounts to a distinction between the body and the soul. A discussion of this distinction as a possible parallel to the *buddhakṣetra* can be found in Teresina Rowell, "The Background and Early Use of the Buddha-Kṣetra Concept," *The Eastern Buddhist*, 6 : 204. For a characterization of Brahmā as *kṣetra-jña*, see Madeleine Biardeau, "Études de mythologie hindoue: Cosmogonies purāṇiques," BEFEO, Pt. I, 54 (1968): 31, 42. For discussions of the omniscience of the Buddha which we must assume is the essential element in the establishment of a "field of knowedge," see Lamotte, *Traité*, pp. 1743-54 and Padmanabh S. Jaini, "On the *Sarvajñatva* (Omniscience) of Mahāvīra and the Buddha" in L. Cousins, A. Kunst, and K. R. Norman, eds., *Buddhist Studies in Honour of I. B. Horner* (Boston: D. Reidel Publishing Co., 1974), pp. 71-90; and Chapter 1, p. 2, n. 1 of this work.

The resources for interpreting the materials of the mathematical cosmologies are distributed throughout this work. However, several introductory works provide some additional insights. Among these are "Butsudo" in *Hôbôgirin; dictionnaire encyclopédique du Bouddhisme d'après les sources chinoises et japonaises*, ed. Paul Demiéville (Tokyo: Maison francojaponaise, 1929-37), pp. 198-203; Note I—"Les buddhakṣetra" in Étienne Lamotte, trans. and ann., *L'enseignement de Vimalakīrti* (*Vimalakīrtinirdeśa*) (Louvain: Bibliothèque du Muséon, 1958), pp. 395-404; Louis de La Vallée Poussin, "Cosmogony and Cosmology (Buddhist)," *ERE*, especially the section on the "Great Cosmology," pp. 137-38; and Teresina Rowell, "The Background and Early Use of the Buddha-Kṣetra Concept," *The Eastern Buddhist* 6 (1934): 199-246, 279-430; 7 (1935): 131-61.

A 10,000 world system is occasionally referenced in the Pāli Canon and in a more systematic way in Sections 414 ff. of

1. See Dineschandra Sircar, *Cosmography and Geography in Early Indian Literature* (Calcutta : D. Chattopadhyaya, 1967), p. 19.

Buddhaghosa's *Visuddhimagga*. Sources for the *trisāhasramahāsāhasralokadhātu* which we have taken as the primary expression of the "cosmology of thousands" are cited in Étienne Lamotte, "Note I—Les buddhakṣetra" in his *L'enseignement de Vimalakīrti* (*Vimalakīrtinirdeśa*) (Louvain: Bibliothèque du Muséon, 1962), 5 : 395. The "cosmology of innumerables" dominates the Mahāyāna and its fullest expression seems to be in conjunction with the mytheme whose structure and contents are analyzed in Chapters V and VI.

To our surprise, we have seen the importance of atomistic speculations in the context of the "mathematical-cosmologies." This suggests that a more comprehensive examination of Indian atomism may be valuable. Some works of use in such a pursuit include: Hermann Jacobi, "Atomic Theory (Indian)," *ERE*, 2 : 199-200; Arthur Berriedale Keith, *Indian Logic and Atomism; An Exposition of the Nyāya and Vaiśeṣika Systems* (Oxford: Clarendon Press, 1921); Surendranath Dasgupta, *History of Indian Philosophy* (Cambridge: Cambridge University Press, 1922), esp., 1:274-366; Sadananda Bhaduri, *Studies in Nyāya-Vaiśeṣika Metaphysics* (Poona: Bhandarkar Oriental Research Institute, 1947); Camille Bulcke, *The Theism of Nyāya-Vaiśeṣika; Its Origin and Early Development* (Delhi: Motilal Banarsidass, 1968); and Umesh Mishra, *Conceptions of Matter According to Nyāya-Vaiśeṣika* (Benares: Krishna Das Gupta, 1936). See also Richard H. Robinson, "The Emptiness of Divison into Parts" in his *Early Mādhyamika in India and China* (Madison: University of Wisconsin Press, 1967), pp. 191-96. Like the single world system, the innumerables of worlds which dominate these cosmologies and the atomistic philosophies associated with them have important parallels in the Classical world. These resources are outlined under "Extra-Indian Resources."

The Pure Land Traditions

While much has been written about the vows of the bodhisattva and the elements of faith which result in rebirth in the pure land Sukhāvatī, virtually nothing has been written which recognizes the cosmological setting of these "dramas of faith." The themes of "faith" can be found adequately outlined in Hans Haas, *Amida Buddha: Unsere Zuflucht* (Göttingen: Vandenhoeck und Ruprecht, 1910); Alfred Bloom, *Shinran's Gospel of Pure*

Grace (Tucson: University of Arizona Press, 1965); and Harper Havelock Coates and Ryugaku Ishizuka, *Honen, the Buddhist Saint* (Kyoto: Chion-in, 1925). Details of the cosmography of Sukhāvatī are discussed in Henri de Lubac, *Amida* (Paris: Éditions du Seuil, 1955), though de Lubac's goal is not to understand the philosophical precision of these images, but rather to see in them a general "nostalgia" for paradise. A Pāli source for the images associated with the pure lands is discussed in Mr. Dwijendralal Barua, M. A., "'Buddhakhetta' in the Apadāna" in D. R. Bhandarkar et al., eds., *B. C. Law Volume*, 2 vols. (Poona: Bhandarkar Oriental Research Institute, 1946), 2:183-90.

We have begun to see that the cosmological background of these traditions lies more precisely in the T'ien-t'ai/Tendai school. As a result, Genshin's *Ōjōyōshū* previously cited again catches our interest. An exceptionally interesting and cogent work on Genshin and the Pure Land traditions is found in Allan A. Andrews, *The Teaching Essential for Rebirth* (Tokyo: Sophia University, 1973). Leon Hurvitz, "Chih-I," *Mélanges chinois et bouddhiques*, vol. 12 (1960-62) also provides some useful insights into the T'ien-t'ai concept of the "interpenetration" of all worlds or all dharmas as well as to the specific understanding of the *trisāhasramahāsāhasralokadhātu* in this context to mean 3,000 Great Worlds. The relationship between techniques of meditation and visualization and the images of the pure lands is apparent in Julian F. Pas, "Shan-tao's Interpretation of the Meditative Vision of the Buddha Amitāyus", *History of Religions Journal* 14, No.2 (November,1974):96-116.

A useful, if dated, summary of scholarship relating to this Sahā world can be found in Eugène Burnouf, "De l'expression *Sahālokadhātu*" in his *Introduction à l'histoire du buddhisme indien* (Paris: Imprimerie royale, 1844), 1:594-97. However, Sahā and Sukhāvatī are not the only *buddhakṣetras* which achieve prominence. Themes and materials associated with Abhirati, the field of the Buddha Akṣobhya, are summarized in Étienne Lamotte, *L'enseignement de Vimalakīrti* (*Vimalakīrtinirdeśa*) (Louvain: Bibliothèque du Muséon, 1958), pp. 360-67 and idem, "La marche de la concentration héroïque (*Śūraṅgamasamādhisūtra*)," *Mélanges chinois et bouddhiques* 13 (1965): 189, n. 178; 191, n. 181.

Miscellaneous Subjects

Solar Mythological School

It is well known that the "solar mythological" school produced some important if controversial works on Buddhism before the turn of the century. Most important among these was Émile Senart, *Essai sur la légende du Buddha* (Paris: Libraire de la Société Asiatique, 1882). In this work, Senart concludes that

> . . . la description du Mahāpurusha est, non pas le portrait réaliste d'un chef de religion, mais, sous cette forme affaiblie *où* aboutit le conte, l'héritage de vieilles conceptions cosmogoniques qui seules rendent raison de sés étrangetés persistantes.[1]

The focus of our research has been on the formal cosmological systems of Buddhism and not on the biography of the Buddha as such. However, we have seen that the changing image of the Buddha corresponds in large part to a changing understanding of the relationship between the Buddha and the cosmos together with changing views as to the precise role which the Buddha plays in the drama of salvation.

Time/Motion/Soul

In our reviews of the "*sāhasra*-cosmology" and the "*asaṅkhyeya*-cosmology" we saw the ambiguous and qualified status accorded to time, and the preference for spatial categories even in the "*sāhasra*-cosmology." Motion or animation which permits the measurement of time, is all but denied by Buddhism, a fact which is undoubtedly related to the Buddhist denial of "soul." In the Mahāyāna, we have noted the outright rejection of the reality of time.[2] We have also noted that the identification of motionlessness with the liberated state is explicit in Jainism.

The following works provide an introduction to Buddhist concepts of time : André Bareau, "The Notion of Time in Early Buddhism," *East and West* 7, No. 4 (January, 1957):

1. Émile Senart, *Essai sur la légende du Buddha* (Paris : Libraire de la Société Asiatique, 1882), p. xv.
2. See Chapter V, p. 91, n. 5.

353-64; Lilian Silburn, *Instant et cause, le discontenu dans la pensée philosophique de l'Inde* (Paris: Librarie philosophique J. Vrin, 1955); Kumar Kishore Mandal, *Comparative Study of the Concepts of Time and Space in Indian Thought* (Varanasi: Chowkhamba Sanskrit Series Office, 1968); Stanislaw Schayer, "Contributions to the Problem of Time in Indian Philosophy," *Polska Akademia Umiejetnosci*, 31 (1938): 1-76; and Louis de La Vallée Poussin, "La controverse du temps et du pudgala dans le Vijñānakāya," in G. Van Oest, ed., *Études Asiatiques*, 2 vols. (Hanoi: Publications de l'éçole française d'Extrême-Orient, 1925), 1:343-76.

Cosmology and Meditation

It has long been recognized that there is a close relation between the Buddhist techniques of meditation and the Buddhist cosmologies. Particularly in connection with the meditation realms (*dhyānas*) or the *cakravāla*, this relationship is unmistakable. While it is premature to offer a comprehensive interpretation of Buddhist techniques of meditation on the basis of this work, we may say that what appears are three basic classes of meditations which closely parallel the three types of cosmologies we have distinguished. The techniques of meditation associated with the *cakravāla* or single world system are those of the individual; the arduous method of the paths resulting in the salvation of a single "being" at the end of an immeasurably long period of time. The meditative techniques which parallel the "*buddhakṣetra*-cosmologies" are the meditations of the Buddha or the bodhisattvas of the tenth stage. These are the Great Concentrations performed by the Buddha which result in the salvation of all beings or at least of "innumerable" beings. Finally, a third type of meditation may be seen which in a general way is related to the Pure Land cosmologies. These are the simplified methods of "visualization," "*nembutsu*" and in short all the "sudden" techniques of enlightenment which are opposed to the arduous *dhyānas*. These are techniques practiced by individuals which are efficacious only as a result of the Great Concentrations performed by the Buddha or bodhisattva.

The meditations of "self-power" are described in Edward Conze, *Buddhist Meditation* (London: George Allen & Unwin, Ltd., 1956); Giulio Cesare Andrea Evola, *The Doctrine of*

Awakening; A Study on the Buddhist Ascesis (London : Luzac & Co., Ltd., 1951); Marie Beauzeville Byles, *Journey into Burmese Silence* (London: George Allen & Unwin, Ltd., 1962); G. Constance Lounsbery, *Buddhist Meditation in the Southern School* (London: Kegan Paul, Trench, Trubner & Co., 1950); and Nyanaponika Thera, *Satipatthana. The Heart of Buddhist Meditation* (Colombo : Word of Buddha Publishing Co., 1954). Bhikku Ñāṇamoli, trans., *The Path of Purification* (*Visuddhimagga*) (Colombo: R. Semage, 1956) provides the most comprehensive compendium of the scholasticism of the Theravāda with regard to meditation. Additional resources for understanding the techniques of "self-power" in the Sanskrit traditions are found in Chapter IV, p. 76, n. 2.

The Great Concentrations of the Buddha/bodhisattva which emerge in conjunction with the "*buddhakṣetra*-cosmologies" are discussed in Étienne Lamotte, "La concentration de la marche héroïque (*Śūraṅgamasamādhisūtra*)," *Mélanges chinois et bouddhiques*, vol. 13 (1965) and idem, "Mañjuśrī," *T'oung Pao* 48 (1960) : 1-96.

Our research has strongly suggested that the simplified "meditations" of the third type are dependent upon the Great Concentrations of the Buddha/bobhisattva for their efficacy. The relationship between meditation and "visualization" is discussed in Julian F. Pas, "Shan-tao's Interpretation of the Meditative Vision of the Buddha Amitāyus," *History of Religions Journal* 14, No. 2 (November, 1974): 96-116. Techniques of visualization related to the marks of the Buddha as well as a wide range of *nembutsu* techniques are discussed in Allan A. Andrews, *The Teachings Essential for Rebirth* (Tokyo: Sophia University, 1973). The "sudden" method of the Southern school of Zen is discussed in William Barrett, ed., *Zen Buddhism; Selected Writings of D. T. Suzuki* (Garden City, N. Y. : Doubleday & Co., Inc., 1956), esp. pp. 111-226.

The techniques of the T'ien-t'ai which played an important role in the formation of Pure Land doctrine are also informative. See Leon Hurvitz, "Chih-I," *Mélanges chinois et bouddhiques*, Vol. 12 (1960-1962) and Bruno Petzold, "On Buddhist Meditation," *The Transactions of the Asiatic Society of Japan* 1, 3rd ser. (1948): 64-100. Additional materials relating to the T'ien-t'ai are available in K'uan Yü Lu (Charles Luk), *The Secrets of Chinese Meditation* (London: Rider & Co., 1964). Materials relating to all phases of Buddhist meditation can be found in Stephan Beyer, *The Buddhist Experience* (Encino, Calif.: Dickenson Publishing Co., 1974).

Periodizations of the Teaching

The "ages of the law" during which the dharma experiences a successive decline is a topic to which we have only alluded. However, it is an important theme of Buddhist cosmological speculation, particularly with regard to its use in defining the need for salvation by the "other-power" of the Buddha in this "evil age." Robert Lingat, "Time and the Dharma," *Contributions to Indian Sociology,* No. 6 (December, 1962), pp. 7-76 relates the discussion of the decline of the *yugas* in the *Laws of Manu* to this Buddhist theme. Also of value are Paul O. Ingram, "Honen's and Shinran's Justification for their Doctrine of Salvation Through 'Other power'," *Contemporary Religions in Japan* 9, No. 3 (September, 1968): 233-51, and Rowell, "Background," "Appendix D—The Buddha-Field in Relation to the Cosmic Cycle" 7 (1935): 164-69.

The "ages of the law" are structured in a number of ways. According to the *Vinaya*, the Buddha himself fixed at 500 years the length of time which the Good Law was to endure. The *Milindapañha* agrees and notes that there are three manners in which the law disappears, i.e., the disappearance of the acquisition of degrees of sanctity; the disappearance of the observance of the precepts; and the disappearance of the outward signs that show this observance.

Buddhaghosa states that the Good Law will endure for 5,000 years and that it will experience five stages of decline each of which lasts 1,000 years. The five stages are :

(1) the disappearance of the acquisition of the degrees of sanctity;

(2) the disappearance of the observance of the precepts;

(3) the disappearance of the knowledge of the Scriptures;

(4) the disappearance of the outward signs that show the observance of the precepts; and

(5) the disappearance of the corporeal relics of the Master.

After Buddhaghosa, the sequence of items two and three

is generally reversed while the five-fold structure of 5,000 years is generally accepted in the Therevāda tradition.

The *Kośa* on the other hand makes reference to a period of 1,000 years during which the Law endures.[1] A standard Mahāyāna formula divides the effectiveness of the dharma into five periods of 500 years each. In this context, reference is made to the Buddha who will come "at the end of time" (*paścime kāle*) "in the last period" (*paścime samaye*). A brief outline of the Theravādin materials relating to the decline of the law can be found in G. Coedes, "The Traibhumikatha Buddhist Cosmology and Treaty on Ethics," *East and West* 7, No. 4 (January, 1957): 349. A more comprehensive discussion of the Indian materials is available in Étienne Lamotte, *Histoire du bouddhisme indien* (Louvain: Bibliothèque du Muséon, 1958), pp. 210-22.

The Chinese Pure Land patriarch Tao-ch'o (562-645) emphasized a five-fold scheme taught by the Buddha.[2]

> The first five hundred years after my Nirvana my disciples will be sure of attaining deliverance according to my right Law. The second five hundred they will be sure of attaining *samadhi*; the third five hundred, of reading and reciting the Sutras; the fourth five hundred, of building temples and pagodas; the fifth five hundred, of being at variance with themselves and bringing right Law to ruin.

Since it was believed at that time that the Buddha entered *nirvāṇa* at about !000 B.C., Tao'ch'o could reason that he lived at the beginning of the fourth period. Finally, we should mention a three-fold scheme which was important in the Japanese schools of the Kamakura period consisting of the following divisions:[3]

(1) a correct doctrine (*saddharma/shōbō*) with a duration of 500 years;

(2) a counterfeit doctrine (*pratirūpakadharma/zōbō*) with a duration of 1,000 years;

1. See La Vallée Poussin, *Kośa*, chap. viii, pp. 218; 219, n. 2; 220 n. 2.
2. Bloom, *Shinran*, p. 12.
3. Paul O. Ingram, "Honen's and Shinran's Justification for Their Doctrine of Salvation and Faith Through Other Power," *Contemporary Religions in Japan* 9 (1970) : 244.

(3) the latter days of the law (*paścimadharma/mappō*) with a duration of 10,000 years.

In the case of Metteya, we are told that he appears when human life has a duration of 80,000 years. When he enters into *parinirvāṇa*, he leaves behind (1) a torch of the Dhamma, (2) a ship of the Dhamma, (3) a mirror of the Dhamma, and (4) a healing plant. It is said that Metteya's teaching lasts 180,000 years.[1]

The Chinese theory of the five periods of Gautama's preaching should be included among these various periodizations of the dharma although no reference is made to an eventual disappearance of the law. In this scheme, Gautama was imagined to have given forth the most diverse doctrines as part of a consolidated teaching plan. The first was represented by the *Buddha-avataṃsaka Sūtra.* The second included the *Āgamas* of the Sarvāstivādins; the third the *Laṅkāvatāra* and *Suvarṇaprabhāsa Sūtras*; the fourth the *Prajñāpāramitā Sūtras*; and the fifth the *Saddharmapuṇḍarīka Sūtra.* This theory was first set forth by Chih-I, the founder of the T'ien-t'ai school.

For a theory which regarded Aśvaghoṣa as arising in the "remnant of the True Dharma" and Nāgārjuna as being born at the end of the Counterfeit Dharma, see Richard H. Robinson, *Early Mādhyamika in India and China* (Madison: University of Wisconsin Press, 1976), p. 23. For a suggestion that the Buddhist ages of the law are related to Iranian speculations, see Hendrik Kern, trans., *The Lotus of the True Law* (*Saddharmapuṇḍarīka*) (New York: Dover Publications, Inc., 1963), p. 68, n. 1.

The "Lesser" Beings

The beings whose lot it is to participate in the structures of time and space are treated in many places, including Kirfel. However, it is not only gods and saviour figures who are significant. Several works are worth mentioning which are devoted to "lesser" beings who are often not regarded as playing a role in the overall drama of salvation and tend to be left out of discussions of the formal cosmological systems. Among these

1. Emil Abegg, *Der Messiasglaube in Indien und Iran* (Berlin : Walter de Gruyter & Co., 1928), p. 176.

are Ananda Coomaraswamy, *Yakṣas* (Washington, D.C.: Freer Gallery of Art, 1931); S. Sen, "On Yakṣa Worship" in J. Ensink and P. Gaeffke, eds., *India Maior; Congratulatory Volume Presented to J. Gonda* (Leiden: E. J. Brill, 1972), pp. 187-95; Lowell Bloss, "The Buddha and the Nāga; A Study in Buddhist Folk Religiousity," *History of Religions Journal* 13 (1973): 36-53; B. C. Law, *The Buddhist Conception of Spirits* (London: Luzac & Co,. 1936); and Paul Mus, *La lumière sur les six voies* (Paris: Institut d'Ethnologie, 1939) treating as it does those traditions within Buddhism which include the *asuras* among the *gatis*.

Other Indian Resources

Vedas

The literature on Vedic cosmology is vast, and most works on the subject also treat the Purāṇic materials as well. The following limited bibliography provides several avenues to the Vedic materials: Henry White Wallis, *Cosmology of the Rigveda* (London: Williams & Norgate, 1887); Ramchandra Narayan Dandekar, "Universe in Vedic Thought" in J. Ensink and P. Gaeffke, eds., *India Maior; Congratulatory Volume Presented to J. Gonda* (Leiden: E. J. Brill, 1972), pp. 91-114 and idem, *Universe in Hindu Thought* (Bangalore : Bangalore University, 1972). The works of Jan Gonda have been cited more than once in this work. His philological approach to cosmology includes such works as *Loka: World and Heaven in the Veda* (Amsterdam: Noord-Hollandsche U. M., 1966), and *The Meaning of the Sanskrit Word Dhāman* (Amsterdam : Noord-Hollandsche U. M. 1967). *Loka* in particular is useful in providing a sense of the interchangeability of "soul" and "world," as well as for non-Buddhist uses of the plurality of worlds; particularly in conjunction with techniques of meditation as in the Upaniṣadic idea that one who has attained spiritual insight is afforded "access to all the worlds."

In addition to Kirfel's *Kosmographie*, a number of works belonging to what I have termed the Indian "cosmographic" school include much on the Vedas. Works belonging to this school include Dineschandra Sircar, *Cosmography and Geography in Early Indian Literature* (Calcutta: D. Chattopadhyaya, 1967); and Hemchandra Raychaudhuri, *Studies in*

Indian Antiquities (Calcutta: University of Calcutta, 1932). According to Sircar, Indian cosmography has been the subject of compulsory papers for M.A. candidates in Ancient Indian History and Culture at the University of Calcutta for the past fifty years.[1] While one of the goals of this school is the questionable one of identifying place names in the early cosmographies with actual regions of India, these works nevertheless contain some useful insights into the detail of these cosmologies.

Mahābhārata

The *Mahābhārata* contains several large sections which reflect cosmological themes in the sense that we have come to understand them. The *Sabhāparvan* provides lengthy descriptions of the palaces (*sabhā*) of the four world-guardians (*lokapāla*) and Brahmā. Images common to the Pure Land traditions abound in these descriptions and we may wonder if the *sabhā* of Brahmā is not simply the universe. The early sections of the *Bhīṣmaparvan* contain a well-developed cosmography, similar to that of the Purāṇas involving the continents and mountains surrounding Mt. Meru. The famed "white isle" of the *Mahābhārata* is described in an excellent article by Kasten Rönnow, "Some Remarks on Śvetadvīpa," *Bulletin of the School of Oriental Studies* (University of London) 5 (1929) : 253-84. The journey of the Pāṇḍavas at the end of the *Svargārohaṇaparvan* may well correspond to a drama of salvation in the sense that we have come to understand this term (see Chapter IV, p. 76, n. 2).

The focus of the *Mahābhārata*, of course, is the great battle which takes place at Kurukṣetra, the "field of dharma." The idea that the cosmos is the stage for a great battle finds many expressions. The Mazdean materials provide but a single example. There we find:

> Les douze signes du Zodiaque sont, la religion nous apprend, douze généraux aux côtés d'Ormuzd. Les sept planètes sont, comme il est dit, sept généraux aux côtés d'Ahriman. Les sept planètes violentent toutes les créatures et les livrent à la mort et à toutes sortes d'afflictions. Des sept planètes aussi

1. See Sircar, *Cosmography*, "Preface."

> bien que des douze signes du Zodiaque dépendent le sort et le gouvernement de ce monde-ci.[1]

In this context, it is important to keep in mind that the word "cosmos" may have had the meaning of order in the sense of troops arrayed for battle.[2]

The setting of the great battle of the *Mahābhārata* within the overall structure of the *yugas* is an important theme in Alf Hiltebeitel, *The Ritual of Battle—Krishna in the Mahābhārata* (Ithaca: Cornell University Press, 1976). The importance of the *yugas* to the overall structure of "epic eschatology" can also be found in Alf Hiltebeitel, "*Mahābhārata* and Hindu Eschatology," *History of Religions Journal* 12 (1972): 95-135; and Madeleine Biardeau, "Études de mythologie hindoue: Bhakti et avatāra, "Pt. 4, *BEFEO* 43 (1976): 111-263.

The dynastic histories of the *Mahābhārata* present another possible correspondence to cosmological themes we have noted. Basically, the story of the *Mahābhārata* extends over four generations, a structure which is potentially reminiscent of the *caturyuga* and of the four islands of the Buddhist cosmos. While the parallel is not rigorous, it is most striking in the case of the fourth generation of the Kuru dynasty inaugurated by the marriage of Uttarā and Abhimanyu of the Kuru dynasty. The union marks the onset of the troubled *kaliyuga* whose duration is said to be 1,000 years. We have already noted that the Buddhist island of the North is Uttarakuru where the duration of life is said to be 1,000 years.

Insights into many of the cosmological images of the *Mahābhārata* can be found in a series of articles published by E. Washburn Hopkins in the *Journal of the American Oriental Society,* including his "Remarks on the Form of Numbers, the Method of Using Them, and the Numerical Categories Found in the Mahābhārata", *JAOS* 23 (1902): 109-55; "Phrases of Time

1. Henrik Samuel Nyberg, "Questions de cosmogonie et de cosmologie mazdéenes," *Journal asiatique* 214, No. 2 (1929) : 199.

2. See Gregory Vlastos, *Plato's Universe* (Seattle : University of Washington Press, 1975), p. 3 and Zaehner, *Zurvan*, pp. 158-63. On the meaning of "cosmos" in general, see also Charles H. Kahn, *Anaximander and the Origins of Greek Cosmology* (New York : Columbia University Press, 1960) and Jula Kerschensteiner, "Kosmos," *Zetemata*; *Monographien zur klassischen Altertumswissenschaft*, Heft 30 (München : Beck, 1962).

and Age in the Sanskrit Epic," *JAOS* 23 (1902): 350-57; "Epic Chronology," *JAOS* 24 (1903) : 7-56; and "Mythological Aspects of Trees and Mountains in the Great Epic," *JAOS* 30 (1909): 347-74. A careful analysis of the cosmography contained in the *Bhīṣmaparvan* can be found in Walther Schubring, "Anzeige," *Zeitschrift der deutschen morgenländischen Gesellschaft* 75 (1921): 254-75.

Purāṇas

The *Kośa* repeatedly characterizes the Sāṅkhyan doctrine of creation as resulting from the transformation of a primordial substance. The Purāṇas present at least two different cosmogonies of this sort in mythological terms. The first involves the issuance of a lotus from the navel of Viṣṇu. The lotus is the universe. Its petals constitute the islands of the world disk and its seed vessel or pericarp is Mt. Meru. The second mythological cosmology of transformation is that of the "churning of the ocean." As a result of the constant churning of the primordial waters, a variety of substances emerges which constitutes the diversity of the world. By contrast, the *Kośa* states that the variety of the world is born from the act, i.e., the collective merit of all beings. More specifically, it is the merit of beings which sets the wind in motion which wind churns the waters of the *ābmaṇḍala* producing foam. The foam in turn solidifies forming the golden earth.

Purāṇic cosmography is documented in detail in Kirfel, *Kosmographie* and idem, *Purāṇa Pañcalakṣaṇa* (Bonn: K. Schroeder, 1927). The 1840 translation and annotation of the *Vishṇu Purāṇa* by Horace Hayman Wilson (4th edition. Calcutta: Punthi Pustak, 1972) is still the single most useful document in English. Dated secondary sources include F. Wilford, "An Essay of the Sacred Isles in the West," *Asiatick Researches,* 8 (1805): 245-367; 9 (1807): 32-115; 11 (1808): 27-157 and V. Venkatachellam Iyer, "The Seven Dwipas in the Purāṇas," *The Quarterly Journal of the Mythic Society*, 15 (1924-25) : 62-75, 119-27, 238-45; 16 (1925-26): 116-24, 268-83; 17 (1926-27): 30-45, 94-105. A more recent study which identifies the seven Purāṇic islands with contemporary regions of the earth can be found in S. Muzafer Ali, *The Geography of the Purāṇas* (New Delhi: People's Publishing House, 1966). A recent work on the distribution of the *janapadas* or "tribes" can be found in M. R. Singh, *Geographical Data in the Purāṇas* (Calcutta: Punthi Pustak, 1972). The seven heavens which extend above the Purāṇic cosmos are distributed in such a way that a clear distinction exists between the lower three and the upper four which constitute the realms of the liberated souls. To this extent we may see a parallel between the four liberation realms and the four meditation realms in Buddhism.

The most coherent and plentiful works on Purāṇic cosmology have to do with the measurements of time; *yugas* and *kalpas*. Reliable accounts can be found in John Faithfull Fleet, "The Kaliyuga Era of B.C. 3102," *Journal of the Royal Asiatic Society* (1911), pp. 479-96; 675-98 ; Dolarray Rangildas Mankad, *Purāṇic Chronology* (Anand: Gangajala Prakashan, 1951); and Cornelia Dimmit Church, "The Purāṇic Myth of the Four Yugas," *Purāṇa* 13, No. 2 (July, 1971): 151-59. The parallels between the *caturyuga* and the *caturdvīpa* have been noted more than once as have those between the thousands of Purāṇic chronometry and the Buddhist *trisāhasramahāsāhasralokadhātu*. The integration of chronometric themes with those of liberation has been a major interpretive key provided by Madeleine Biardeau's study of the *pralayas* in "Études de mythologie hindoue: Cosmogonie purāṇiques," Pt. 3, *BEFEO* 58 (1971): 17-89.

The doctrine of *avatāras* or "incarnations" associated with the mythology of Viṣṇu is accessible in Jan Gonda, *Aspects of Early Vishṇuism* (Utrecht: A. Oosthoek, 1954) and Deborah A. Soifer, "Toward an Understanding of Viṣṇu's Avatāras," *Purāṇa* 18 (1976): 128-48. Sources for studying the related phenomenon of the appearances of the Buddha are outlined in Chapter IV, p. 87, n. 1. The appearances of the Tīrthaṅkaras are set forth in *The Kalpa Sūtra* in Hermann Jacobi, trans., *Jaina Sutras,* 2 vols. (New York: Dover Publications, Inc., 1968), 1 : 217-85. Another Jain structure accounting for the appearance of Tīrthaṅkaras, *cakravartins* and heroes totalling 63 in number can be found in Helmuth V. Glasenapp, "Die Triṣaṣṭilaksaṇamahāpurāṇa der Digambaras" in *Beiträge zur Literaturwissenschaft und Geistesgeschichte Indiens* (*Festschrift Hermann Jacobi*), ed. Willibald Kirfel (Bonn: Kommissionsverlag Fritz Klopp, 1926), pp. 331-45. Again it is the work of Madeleine Biardeau which provides the most recent and comprehensive treatment of the mythology of the *avatāras* in "Études de mythologie hindoue : Bhakti et avatāra," Pt. 4, *BEFEO* 63 (1976): 111-263.

Siddhānta *Literature*

The cosmological literature of Buddhism consists only of a "religious" tradition. There is no "secular" or "profane" cosmological tradition within Buddhism so far as I am aware. By contrast, it may be possible to characterize the Hindu *siddhānta* literature as "secular," focusing as it does on the accurate measurement of the movements of the planets. According to al-Biruni, the word *siddhānta* means "accuracy without crookedness"; a fact which we may take to mean the time when the planets were all in a straight line, i.e., the moments of creation and destruction which the astronomers attempted to reach with their calculations. Most literally, the term means simply "astronomical system" of which five were known to the sixth century astronomer Varāhamihira. Summaries of the major texts of this tradition may be found in Arthur Llewelyn Basham, *The Wonder That Was India,* 3rd rev. ed. (New York: Taplinger Publishing Co., 1968), Appendix II—Astronomy, pp. 491-94; and Kirfel, *Kosmographie*, pp. 173-77.

The major texts of this astrological and astronomical literature include Ebenezer Burgess, trans., *Sūrya-Siddhānta, A Text-Book of Hindu Astronomy* (New Haven: American Oriental Society, 1860); Hendrik Kern, trans., *Bṛhat-Saṃhitā or Complete System of Natural Astrology of Varāha-Mihira* (London: Royal Asiatic Society of Great Britain and Ireland, 1869); Swami Vijnanananda, trans., *The Bṛhajjātakam of Varāha Mihira* (Allahabad: The Sacred Books of the Hindus, Vol. 12, 1912); and David Pingree and Otto Neugebauer, trans., *The Pañcasiddhāntikā* (Copenhagen: Munksgaard, 1970).

Additional resources for understanding the extent of Hindu astronomical speculation include George Frederick William Thibaut, *Astronomie, Astrologie und Mathematik* (Strassburg: Karl J. Turner, 1899); Sukumar Ranjan Das, "The Scope and Development of Indian Astronomy," in George Sarton, ed., *Osiris: Studies on the History and Philosophy of Science, and on the History of Learning and Culture* (Bruges: Saint Catherine Press Ltd., 1936), 2:197-219; P. Sengupta, "Hindu Astronomy" in the *Cambridge History of India,* Vol. 2; and Roger Billard, *L'astronomie indienne* (Paris: Publications de l'école français d'Extrême-Orient, 1971). See also D.A. Somayaji, *A Critical Study of Ancient Hindu Astronomy in the Light and Language of the Modern* (Dharwar: Karnatak University, 1971).

The most recent and thorough researches into the Sanskrit astrological literature have been by David Pingree who has apparently set himself the task of cataloging this literature in the manner of the *Catalogus Codicum Astrologorum Graecorum* (Bruxellis: Mauritii Lamertin, 1898-1936) edited by Franz Cumont and others. Among Pingree's works are "Sanskrit Astronomical Tables in the United States," *Transactions of the American Philosophical Society,* new series, Vol, 58, Pt. 3 (1968); and *Census of the Exact Sciences in Sanskrit* (Philadelphia: American Philosophical Society, 1970). An extremely valuable summary of mathematical themes found in the *siddhānta* literature can be found in his "History of Mathematical Astronomy in India," in Charles Coulston Gillespie, ed., *Dictionary of Scientific Biography* (New York : Charles Scribner's Sons, 1970-1978), XV, Supplement I (1978), pp. 533-633.

Jainism

The cosmological resources of the Jain traditions are without peer. In addition to Kirfel, *Kosmographie*, pp. 208-339, several excellent summaries are available. These include Walther Schubring, *Die Jainas* (Tübingen: Mohr, 1927), and idem., *The Doctrine of the Jainas Described After the Old Sources,* trans. from the revised German edition by Wolfgang Beurlen (Delhi: Motilal Banarsidass, 1962).

Al Biruni

In addition to the astrological and astronomical literature of India, al-Biruni (973-1048) has preserved a considerable body of the Hindu sciences in his writings. English translations of al-Biruni's major works are available in Edward C. Sachau, trans., *The Chronology of Ancient Nations* (London: W. H. Allen & Co., 1879); R. Ramsay Wright, trans., *The Book of Instruction in the Elements of the Art of Astrology* (London: Luzac & Co., 1934); Mohammed Saffouri and Adnan Ifram, trans., *On Transits* (Beirut : American University of Beirut,

1959); and Edward C. Sachau, trans., *Alberuni's India* (London: Trubner & Co., 1888). A recent study is available in Seyyed Hossein Nasr, *An Introduction to Islamic Cosmological Doctrines,* 2nd ed. (London: Thames and Hudson, 1978).

Other

Under this sub-heading, I will simply note Arthur Llewelyn Basham, *History and Doctrine of the Ājīvikas: A Vanished Indian Religion* (Motilal Banarsidass, Delhi, 1981) which we have had occasion to cite more than once in the course of our research. It is especially noteworthy for its coherent presentation of Ājīvika cosmology which embraces the position that there are a limited number of souls, and the Ājīvika understanding of the bodhisattva as a liberated soul which re-enters the world of rebirth in order that the world/teaching may continue.

Extra-Indian Resources

The extra-Indian literature which shows parallels and similarities to the Buddhist cosmologies is vast and probably inexhaustible. This bibliography will attempt only to indicate a limited number of resources for each of the main strands of our research.

The Single World System

Among those works which provide substantial insight into the role which the single world system played in Hellenistic thought, the most comprehensive is undoubtedly Pierre Duhem, *Le système du monde histoire des doctrines cosmologiques de Platon à Copérnic* (Paris : Hermann, 1971). Volumes 1-2 in particular are useful in explaining the relationship between measurement and metaphysics in these cosmologies. The single world system can be found in Plato's *Timaeus* and "The Myth of Er" as well as in Aristotle's *De Caelo.* Useful commentaries are available in Francis MacDonald Cornford, *Plato's Cosmology* (New York: Liberal Arts Press, 1957); George Maximilian Anthony Grube, "The Gods" in his *Plato's Thought* (Boston: Beacon Press, 1958), pp. 150-78; Paul Friedländer, "Plato's Geography" in his *Plato: An Introduction* (New York: Harper & Row, 1958), pp. 261-85; Gregory Vlastos, *Plato's Universe* (Seattle: University of Washington Press, 1975). See also,

Charles Kahn, *Anaximander and the Origins of Greek Cosmology* (New York: Columbia University Press, 1960). An older, though still useful survey of Greek cosmological speculation, particularly as concerns the figure of Aristarchus, is Thomas Little Heath, *Aristarchos of Samos* (Oxford: Clarendon Press, 1913).

Information on the single world system in Islam is available in a number of articles in Hamilton Alexander Resskeen Gibb and Johannes Hendrik Kramer, eds., *The Shorter Encyclopedia of Islam* (Ithaca: Cornell University Press, 1953) under such listings as "Barza*kh*," "*D*janna," etc., and in "Islamic Cosmology" in Carmen Blacker and Michael Loewe, eds., *Ancient Cosmologies* (London: George Allen & Unwin Ltd., 1975). The journeys associated with the single world system in Islam and their possible influence on Dante are found in Miguel Asin Palacios, *Islam and the Divine Comedy* (London: Frank Cass & Co., Ltd., 1968).

Mazdean use of the single world system is accessible in Henrik Samuel Nyberg, "Questions de cosmogonie et de cosmologie mazdéenes," *Journal asiatique* 214, (1929): 193-310; 219 (1931): 1-134, 195-244. The philosophy of time which dominates this cosmology is examined in detail in Henry Corbin, "Cyclical Time in Mazdaism and Ismailism" in Joseph Campbell, ed., *Man and Time; Papers from the Eranos Yearbooks No.* 3 (New York: Pantheon Books, 1954), pp. 115-72; and Robert Charles Zaehner, *Zurvan: A Zoroastrian Dilemma* (Oxford: Clarendon Press, 1955).

Multiple World Systems

That Multiple world systems exist outside of Buddhism and outside of India is clear. However, the purpose or intention of these systems is not nearly so well documented as is the single world system. Nevertheless some resources are available. Pierre Duhem, *Le système du monde; histoire des doctrines cosmologiques de Platon à Copernic* (Paris: Hermann, 1971), 1:230-41 provides an indication of the existence of multiple world systems and that the issue of one world—a universe—as opposed to many worlds was an issue of controversy and a subject of philosophical speculation. As we have seen, the issue of whether empty space exists and whether or not the stars are infinitely remote were factors in this discussion. The role of multiple world systems in the thought of Anaximander is well documented. For a discussion, see William Keith Chambers Guthrie, *A History of Greek Philosophy*, 4 vols. (Combridge : Cambridge University Press, 1962, 1965, 1969, 1975), 1: 106-15. Guthrie's discussion of the Atomists is also extremely useful in understanding the role of these systems; see ibid., 2: 404-13. We have already cited the mystical cosmology of Suhrawahrdi (Chapter VI, p. 129, n. 3) which appears to incorporate a multiple world system. For references to multiple world systems in Iran and in Kabbalism, see Henry Corbin, *L'homme de lumière* (Paris: Éditions Presence, 1971), p. 162, n. 116.

Infinitesimals/Seeds/Souls

The use of infinitesimals in Greece receives considerable illumination in Guthrie's discussion of the Atomists (*History of Greek Philosophy*, 2:382-507) as well as in his discussion of Zeno's attack on infinitesimals (*History*, 2:97). Among other things, Zeno uses the logic of infinitesimals to prove that motion is unreal (*History*, 2:94). See also, Gregory Vlastos, "Minimal Parts in Epicurean Atomism," *Isis* 56 (1965): 121-47.

For the role played by seeds in Anaxagoras, see Vlastos, *Plato's Universe*, p. 20. Recall that the seeds of merit are to be planted in the supreme field of merit (paramapuṇyakṣetra), and that the *Gītā* recommends a path to salvation which involves detachment from the fruits of karma (*karmaphala*). Presumably it is legitimate to sow the seeds of karma as long as one does not harvest the fruit. The *śrāvaka* on the other hand gradually takes possession of each of the four fruits of the path. Finally, I will simply point out that Senart in his treatment of the biography of the Buddha maintains that the association of the Buddha with the Bo-tree borders on outright identification. The Buddha is the cosmic tree: "Nos récits mêmes semblent présenter le Buddha et l'arbre comme des notions corrélatives, des termes inséparables."[1]

Hellenistic speculation on the nature of the soul integrates many of the above themes. We are told that Plato maintained that there were a limited number of souls.[2] Moreover, Plato

1. Senart, *Essai*, p. 209.
2. Werner Jaeger, *Paideia : The Idea of Greek Culture* (Oxford : Basil Blackwell, 1944), 2:368.

regarded the number of souls as being equal in number to the stars; each soul having one star for its habitation.[1] Elsewhere we are told that the Orphics regarded the Milky Way as the "Land of Souls."[2] Finally, in Plato's theory of education, reference is made to "that part of the soul which is kindled to flame by mathematics."[3] Additional materials for studying Hellenistic conceptions of the soul can be found in Erwin Rohde, *Psyche: The Cult of Souls and Belief in Immortality Among the Greeks* (New York: Harper & Row, 1966).

India and Antiquity

The interactions between India and the Hellenistic world and their relationship to Buddhism are still largely unexplored. Babylonian influences are explored in Jean Przyluski, "La ville de cakravartin," *Rocznik Orientalistyczny* 5 (1927): 165-85. Iranian influences are found in Maria Thérèse de Mallman, *Introduction à l'étude d'Avalokiteśvara* (Paris: Annales du Musée Guimet, 1948), esp. pp. 85-95, and we have indicated a relationship between the *trisāhasramahāsāhasralokadhātu* and the combinations of tri-millenia which are the basis for Mazdean chronography. Greek influences on the emergence of the Buddha figure are found in Alfred Foucher, *L'art gréco-bouddhique de Gandhâra-étude sur les origines de l'influence classique dans l'art bouddhique de l'Inde et de l'Extrême-Orient* (Paris: E. Leroux, 1905-1922). Other works of interest include: Donald F. Lach, *Asia in the Making of Europe*, 2 vols. (Chicago: University of Chicago Press, 1965), esp. Bk. I, Vol. 1; H. G. Rawlinson, "Early Contacts between India and Europe" in Arthur Llewelyn Basham, ed., *A Cultural History of India* (Oxford: Clarendon Press, 1975), pp. 425-41. Similarities between Buddhism and the Gnostic traditions can be found in Edward Conze, "Buddhism and Gnosis" in Ugo Bianchi, ed., *The Origins of Gnosticism. Colloquium of Messina* 13-18 *April* 1966 (Leiden: E. J. Brill, 1967), pp. 651-67, reprinted in Edward Conze, *Further Buddhist Studies* (Oxford: Bruno Cassirer Publishers Ltd., 1975), pp. 15-32; and idem, "Prajñā and Sophia"

1. Vlastos, *Plato's Universe*, p. 36, n. 30.
2. W. K. C. Guthrie, *Orpheus and Greek Religion* (New York: W. W. Norton & Co., Inc., 1966), p. 185.
3. Jaeger, *Paideia*, 2 : 304-5.

in his *Thirty Years of Buddhist Studies* (Columbia: University of South Carolina Press, 1968), pp. 207-9. Works by Classicists approaching the problem of influences can be found in Jula Kerschensteiner, *Platon und der Orient* (Stuttgart : W. Kohlhammer Verlag, 1945); Andrá Marie Jean Festugière, "Platon et l'Orient," *Revue de Philologie* 21 (1947): 5-45; and Martin Litchfield West, *Early Greek Philosophy and the Orient* (Oxford: Clarendon Press, 1971).

BIBLIOGRAPHY

Texts and Translations

L'Abhidharmakośa de Vasubandhu. Translated by Louis de La Vallée Poussin. 7 vols. Originally published 1923-1931. Brussels: Mélanges chinois et bouddhiques, 1971.

Abhidharmakośa. "Vasubandhu et Yaçomitra; Troisième Chapitre de l'Abhidharmakoça: Kārikā, Bhāṣya et Vyākhyā; Avec une analyse de la Lokaprajñapti et de la Kāraṇaprajñapti de Maudgalyāyana." Translated by Louis de la Vallée Poussin. *Mémoires de l'académie royale de Belgique*, 2e sér. Tome 6, Fascicule II (January, 1919).

Alberuni's India. Translated by Edward C. Sachau. London: Trubner & Co., 1888.

Aṅguttara-nikāya. *The Book of Gradual Sayings or More-Numbered Suttas.* Translated by Frank Lee Woodward. Pāli Text Society, Vols. 22, 24, 25, 26, 27. London: Oxford University Press, 1932-1936.

Amitāyur Dhyāna Sūtra. *Buddhist Mahāyāna Texts.* Translated by Junjiro Takakusu. Edited by Edward Byles Cowell. Sacred Books of the East, Vol. 49. Originally published 1894. New York: Dover Publications, Inc., 1969. Rept. 1970, Motilal Banarsidass.

Atthasālinī. *The Expositor, Buddhaghosa's Commentary on the Dhammasangaṇī, the First Book of the Abhidhamma Piṭaka.* Translated by Maung Tin. Pāli Text Society, Vols. 8, 9. London: Oxford University Press, 1920-1921.

Bodhicaryāvatāra. *Introduction à la pratique des futurs Bouddhas, poème de çantideva.* Translated by Louis de La Vallée Poussin. Paris: Bloud et Cie, 1907.

Bodhicaryāvatāra. *La marche à la lumière.* Translated by Louis Finot: Paris: Classiques de l'Orient, No. 2, 1920.

The Book of Instruction in the Elements of the Art of Astrology (al-Biruni). Translated by R. Ramsay Wright. London: Luzac & Co., 1934.

The Bṛhajjātakam of Varāha Mihira. Translated by Swami Vijnanananda. Allahabad: The Sacred Books of the Hindus, Vol. 12, 1912.

Bṛhat-Saṃhitā or Complete System of Natural Astrology of Varāha-Mihira. Translated by Hendrik Kern. London: Royal Asiatic Society of Great Britain and Ireland, 1869.

Buddhism in Translations. Translated by Henry Clarke Warren. Originally published 1896. New York: Atheneum, 1968.

The Chronology of Ancient Nations (al-Biruni). Translated by Edward C. Sachau. London: W. H. Allen & Co., 1879.

De Caelo (Aristotle). *On the Heavens.* Translated by William Keith Chambers Guthrie. Cambridge: Harvard University Press, 1939.

Digha-nikāya. *Dialogues of the Buddha.* Translated by Thomas Williams Rhys Davids. 3 vols. London: Oxford University Press, 1899-1921.

The Kalpa Sūtra of Bhadrabāhu. Translated by Hermann Jacobi. Sacred Books of the East, Vol. 22. Originally published 1884. *Jaina Sutras.* New York: Dover Publications, Inc., 1968.

Mahāprajñāpāramitāśāstra. *Traité de la grande vertu de sagesse de Nāgārjuna.* Translated by Étienne Lamotte. Louvain: Bibliothèque du Muséon, Vol. 18, 1949; Publications de l'Institut Orientaliste de Louvain, Vols. 2, 12, 1970, 1976.

Majjima-nikāya. *The Collection of the Middle Length Sayings.* Translated by Isaline Blew Horner. Pāli Text Society, Vols. 29, 30, 31. London: Luzac & Co. Ltd., 1954.

Milindapañha. *The Questions of King Milinda.* Translated by Thomas William Rhys Davids. Sacred Books of the East, Vols. 35, 36. Delhi, Motilal Banarsidass, 1975.

On Transits (al-Biruni). Translated by Mohammed Saffouri and Adnan Ifram. Beirut : American University of Beirut 1959.

The Pañcasiddhāntikā (Varāhamihira). Translated by David Pingree and Otto Neugebauer. Copenhagen: Munksgaard, 1970.

The Pañcaviṃśatisāhasrikā-Prajñāpāramitā. Edited by Nalinaksa Dutt. London: Calcutta Oriental Series, No. 28, 1934.

Pañcaviṃśatisāhasrikā-Prajñāpāramitā. *The Large Sūtra on Perfect Wisdom, With the Divisions of the Abhisamayālaṅkāra.* Translated by Edward Conze. Part I. Motilal Banarsidass, Delhi, 1979. Part II. Madison: College Printing and Typing Co., 1964.

The Pravacana-sāra of Kunda-kunda Ācārya, Together with the Commentary Tattva-dīpikā by Amṛtachandra Sūri. Translated by Barend Faddegon. London : Cambridge University Press, 1935.

The Republic (Plato). Translated by Sir Henry Desmond Pritchard Lee. Baltimore: Penguin Books, 1955.

Saddharmapuṇḍarīka (Burnouf). *Le lotus de la bonne loi.* Translated by Eugéne Burnouf. 2 vols. Originally published 1852. Paris: Maisonneuve frères, 1925.

Saddharmapuṇḍarīka (Hurvitz). *Scripture of the Lotus Blossom of the Fine Dharma.* Translated by Leon Hurvitz. New York: Columbia University Press, 1976.

Saddharmapuṇḍarīka (Kern). *The Lotus of the True Law.* Translated by Hendrik Kern. Sacred Books of the East, Vol. 21. Originally published 1884. New York: Dover Publications, Inc., 1963.

The Sand Reckoner (Archimedes). *The Works of Archimedes.* Translated by Thomas Little Heath. New York: Dover Publications, Inc., 1912.

Sukhāvatīvyūha. *Buddhist Mahāyāna Texts.* Translated by F. Max Müller. Edited by Edward Byles Cowell. Sacred Books of the East, Vol. 49. Motilal Banarsidass, Delhi, 1975.

Śūraṃgamasamādhisūtra. "La marche de la concentration héroïque." Translated by Étienne Lamotte. *Mélanges chinois et bouddhiques,* Vol. 13 (1965).

Sūrya-Siddhānta, A Text-Book of Hindu Astronomy. Translated by Ebenezer Burgess. New Haven: American Oriental Society, 1960.

Timaeus (Plato). *Plato's Cosmology.* Translated by Francis MacDonald Cornford. New York: Liberal Arts Press, 1957.

Vijñaptimātratāsiddhi. *La Siddhi de Hiuan-tsang.* Translated by Louis de La Vallée Poussin. 2 vols. Paris: Librairie Orientaliste Paul Geuthner, 1928-1948.

Vimalakīrtinirdeśa. *L'enseignement de Vimalakīrti.* Translated by Étienne Lamotte. Louvain: Bibliothèque du Muséon, 1958.

Visuddhimagga (Buddhaghosa). *The Path of Purification.* Translated by Bhikku Ñāṇamoli. Kandy: Buddhist Publication Society, 1975.

On Yuan Chwang's Travels in India. Translated by Thomas Watters. Delhi: Munshi Ram Manohar Lal, 1961.

Other Works Consulted

Abegg, Emil. *Der Messiasglaube in Indien und Iran.* Berlin: Walter de Gruyter & Co., 1928.

Abel-Rémusat, Jean Pierre "Essai sur la cosmographie et la cosmogonie des bouddhistes d'après le auteurs chinois." *Journal des savants*, 2e sér., 16 (October, 1831): 596-610; 16 (November, 1831): 668-74; 16 (December, 1831): 716-31. Republished in Abel-Rémusat, J. P. *Mélanges posthumes d'histoires et de literature orientales.* Paris: Imprimerie royale, 1834. pp. 65-131.

Ali, S. Muzafer. *The Geography of the Purāṇas.* New Delhi: People's Publishing House, 1966.

Andrews, Allan A. *The Teachings Essential for Rebirth.* Tokyo: Sophia University, 1973.

Auboyer, Jeannine. *Le trône et son symbolisme dans l'Inde ancienne.* Paris: Presses Universitaires de France, 1949.

Bareau, André. "The Notion of Time in Early Buddhism." *East and West* 7 (1957): 353-64.

Barua, Mr. Dwijendralal. "'Buddhakhetta' in the Apadāna." *B. C. Law Volume.* Edited by D. R. Bhandarkar et al. Poona: Bhandarkar Oriental Research Institute, 1946. 2: 183-90.

Basham, Arthur Llewelyn. *History and Doctrine of the Ājīvikas: A Vanished Indian Religion.* Motilal Banarsidass, Delhi, 1981.

———. *The Wonder That Was India.* 3rd rev. ed. New York: Taplinger Publishing Co., 1968.

Bastian, Adolf. *Ideale Welten.* 3 vols. Berlin: Emil Felber, 1892.

Bauer, Wolfgang. *China and the Search for Happiness.* New York: Seabury Press, 1976.

Beal, Samuel. *A Catena of Buddhist Scriptures from the Chinese.* London: Trübner & Co., 1871.

Beyer, Stephan. *The Buddhist Experience.* Encino California: Dickenson Publishing Co., 1974.

Bhaduri, Sadananda. *Studies in Nyāya-Vaiśeṣika Metaphysics.* Poona: Bhandarkar Oriental Research Institute, 1947.

Bhattacharyya, Benoytosh. *Introduction to Buddhist Esoterism.* Motilal Banarsidass, Delhi, 1980.

Bhattacharyya, Narendra Nath. "Brahmanical, Buddhist and Jain Cosmography." *Journal of Indian History* 47 (1969): 43-64.

———. *History of Indian Cosmogonical Ideas.* New Delhi: Munshiram Manoharlal, 1971.

Biardeau, Madeleine. "Études de mythologie hindoue: Cosmogonies purāṇiques," Pts. 1-3, *Bulletin de l'école français d'Extrême-Orient* 54 (1968): 19-45; 55 (1969): 59-105; 58 (1971): 17-89; "Bhakti et avatāra," Pt. 4, *Bulletin de l'école français d'Extrême-Orient* 63 (1976): 111-263.

Billard, Roger. *L'astronomie indienne.* Paris: Publications de l'école français d'Extrême-Orient, 1971.

Blacker, Carmen and Loewe, Michael, eds. *Ancient Cosmologies.* London: George Allen & Unwin Ltd., 1975.

Bloom, Alfred. *Shinran's Gospel of Pure Grace.* Tucson: University of Arizona Press, 1965.

Bloss, Lowell. "The Buddha and the Nāga: A Study in Buddhist Folk Religiousity." *History of Religions Journal* 13 (1973): 36-53.

Brandon, Samuel George Frederick. *Man and His Destiny in the Great Religions.* Manchester: Manchester University Press, 1962.

Bulcke, Camille. *The Theism of Nyāya-Vaiśeṣika; Its Origin and Early Development.* Delhi: Motilal Banarsidass, 1968.

Burnouf, Eugène. *Introduction à l'histoire du bouddhisme indien.* 2 vols. Paris: Imprimerie royale, 1844.

———. *Le lotus de la bonne loi.* 2 vols. Originally published 1852. Paris: Maisonneuve frères, 1925.

Byles, Marie Beauzeville. *Journey into Burmese Silence.* London: George Allen & Unwin, Ltd., 1962.

Church, Cornelia Dimmit. "The Indian Yugas and the Magnus Annus in Iran and Greece." International Congress of Orientalists, 29th, Paris, 1973. *Inde ancienne.* Edited by Jean Filliozat. 6 vols. Paris: L'Asiathèque, 1976. 3: 236-43.

———. "The Purāṇic Myth of the Four Yugas." *Purāṇa* 13 (1971): 151-59.

Coates, Harper Havelock and Ishizuka, Ryugaku. *Honen, the Buddhist Saint.* Kyoto: Chion-in, 1925.

Coedes, George. "The Traibhumikatha Buddhist Cosmology and Treaty on Ethics." *East and West* 7 (1957): 349-52.

Coedes, George and Archaimbault, Charles *Les trois mondes* (*Traibhūmi Brah R'van*). Paris: Publications de l'école française d'Extrême-Orient, 1973.

Conze, Edward. "The Buddha's lakṣaṇas in the Prajñāpāramitā." *Journal of the Oriental Institute* (Baroda) 14 (1965): 225-29.

———. *Buddhism: Its Essence and Development.* New York: Harper & Row Publishers, 1959.

———. "Buddhism and Gnosis." *The Origins of Gnosticism. Colloquium of Messina* 13-18 *April* 1966. Edited by Ugo Bianchi. Leiden: E. J. Brill, 1967. Pp. 651-67. Reprinted in Conze, Edward. *Further Buddhist Studies.* Oxford: Bruno Cassirer Publishers Ltd., 1975. Pp. 15-32.

———. *Buddhist Meditation.* New York: Harper & Row Publishers, Inc., 1969.

———. *Buddhist Thought in India.* Ann Arbor : University of Michigan Press, 1967.

———. "Prajñā and Sophia." *Thirty Years of Buddhist Studies.* Edited by Edward Conze. Columbia: University of South Carolina Press, 1968.

Coomaraswamy, Ananda K. "Kha and Other Words Denoting 'Zero' in Connection with the Metaphysics of Space." *Bulletin of the School of Oriental Studies* (University of London) 7 (1933-1935): 487-97.

Corbin, Henry. *Avicenna and the Visionary Recitals.* Originally published 1952-1954. Translated by Willard R. Trask. New York: Pantheon Books, Inc., 1960.

———. "Cyclical Time in Mazdaism and Ishmailism." *Man and Time. Papers from the Eranos Yearbooks No.* 3. Edited by Joseph Campbell. New York: Pantheon Books, 1957.

Corbin, Henry. *L'homme de lumière dans le soufisme iranien.* Paris: Éditions Presence, 1971.

———. *Terre céleste et corps de resurrection.* Paris: Buchet-Chastel, 1961.

Cornford, Francis MacDonald. *Plato's Cosmology.* New York: Liberal Arts Press, 1957.

Cullmann, Oscar. *Christ and Time.* Philadelphia: Westminster Press, 1964.

Cumont, Franz. *After Life in Roman Paganism.* Originally published 1922. New York: Dover Publications, Inc., 1959.

———. *Astrology and Religion Among the Greeks and Romans.* Originally published 1912. New York: Dover Publications, Inc., 1960.

———. *Catalogus Codicum Astrologorum Graecorum.* 12 vols. Bruxellis: Mauritii Lamertin, 1898-1936.

———. *The Mysteries of Mithra.* Originally published 1902. New York: Dover Publications, Inc., 1956.

———. *Oriental Religions in Roman Paganism.* Originally published 1911. New York: Dover Publications, Inc., 1956.

———. "Virgile et les morts prematurées." *Conferences.* Paris: Librairie E. Droz, 1945.

Dandekar, Ramchandra Narayan *Universe in Hindu Thought.* Bangalore: Bangalore University, 1972.

———. "Universe in Vedic Thought." *India Maior; Congratulatory Volume Presented to J. Gonda.* Edited by J. Ensink and P. Gaeffke. Leiden: E. J. Brill, 1972. Pp. 91-114.

Das, Sukumar Ranjan. "The Scope and Development of Indian Astronomy." *Osiris : Studies on the History and Philosophy of Science, and on the History of Learning and Culture.* Edited by George Sarton. 2 vols. Bruges : Saint Catherine Press Ltd., 1936. 2 : 197-219.

Dasgupta, Surendranath. *History of Indian Philosophy.* 5 vols. Cambridge : Rep. Motilal Banarsidass, Delhi, 1975.

Dayal, Har. *The Bodhisattva Doctrine in the Buddhist Sanskrit Literature.* Delhi, Motilal Banarsidass, 1978.

Demiéville, Paul, ed. *Hôbôgirin; dictionnaire encyclopédique du Bouddhisme. de' après les sources chinoises et japonaise.* Tokyo: Maison franco-japonais, 1929.

Deussen, Paul. *The Philosophy of the Upanishads.* Originally published 1908. New York : Dover Publications, Inc., 1966.

Duhem, Pierre. *Le système du monde; Histories des doctrines cosmologiques de Platon à Copernic.* Originally published 1913-1959. 10 vols. Paris : Hermann, 1971.

Dutt, Nalinaksha. "The Brahmajāla Sutta in the Light of Nāgārjuna's Expositions." *Indian Historical Quarterly* 8 (1932) : 706-46.

Duyvendak, J. J. L. "A Chinese 'Divina Commedia'." *T'oung Pao* 41 (1952) : 255-316.

Eberhard, Wolfram. *Guilt and Sin in Traditional China.* Berkeley : University of California Press, 1967.

Eitel, Ernest John. *Handbook of Chinese Buddhism; A Sanskrit-Chinese Dictionary.* 2nd Edition. Tokyo : Sanshusha, 1904.

Eliade, Mircea. "Briser le toit de la maison." *Studies in Mysiism and Religion Presented to Gerhsom G. Scholem.* Jerusalem : Hebrew University, 1967. Pp. 131-39.

———. *Cosmos and History.* Translated by Willard R. Trask. Originally published 1949. New York : Harper & Brothers, 1959.

———. *Images and Symbols; Studies in Religious Symbolism.* Translated by Philip Mairet. Originally published 1952. New York : Sheed & Ward, 1961.

———. *Myths, Dreams and Mysteries; The Encounter Between Contemporary Faiths and Archaic Realities.* Translated by Philip Mairet. Originally published 1957. New York : Harper & Row, Publishers, 1967.

———. *Patterns in Comparative Religion.* Translated by Rosemary Sheed. Cleveland : World Publishing Co., 963.

——— *The Sacred and the Profane : The Nature of Religion.* Translated by Willard R. Trask. Originally published 1957. New York : Harper & Brothers, 1961.

———. *Shamanism : Archaic Techniques of Ecstasy*. Translated by Willard R. Trask. New York : Pantheon Books, 1964.

———. "Spirit, Light and Seed." *History of Religions Journal* 11 (1971) : 1-30.

———. "Time and Eternity in Indian Thought." *Man and Time. Papers from the Eranos Yearbooks No.* 3. Edited by Joseph Campbell. New York : Pantheon Books, 1957. Pp. 173-200. Reprinted in *Images and Symbols*.

———. *The Two and the One*. Translated by J. M. Cohen. Originally published 1962. New York : Harper & Row, Publishers, 1969.

———. *Yoga : Immortality and Freedom*. Translated by Willard R. Trask. Originally published 1954. Princeton : Princeton University Press, 1970.

Evans-Wentz, Walter Yeeling. *The Tibetan Book of the Dead*. Originally published 1927. New York : Oxford University Press, 1960.

Evola, Giulio Cesare Andrea. *The Doctrine of Awakening; A Study on the Buddhist Ascesis*. London : Luzac & co., Ltd., 1951.

Festugière, André Marie Jean. "Platon et l'Orient." *Revue de Philologie* 21 (1947) : 5-45.

Fleet, John Faithfull. "The Kaliyuga Era of B. C. 3102." *Journal of the Royal Asiatic Society* (1911), pp. 479-96, 675-98.

Foucher, Alfred. *L'art gréco-bouddhique de Gandhâra; étude sur les origines de l'influence classique dans l'art bouddhique de l'Inde et de l'Extrême-Orient*. Paris : E. Leroux, 1905-1922.

Friedländer, Paul. *Plato : An Introduction*. Translated by Hans Meyerhoff. Originally published 1954. New York: Harper & Row, 1958.

Gibb, Hamitton Alexander Rosskeen and Kramers, Johannes Hendrik, eds. *The Shorter Encyclopedia of Islam*. Ithaca : Cornell University Press, 1953.

Glasenapp, Helmuth V. "Die Trisastilaksanamahapurana der Digambaräs." *Boiträge zur Literaturwissenschoft und Gesesgeschichte Indiens* (*Festschrift Hermann-Jacobi*). *Edited* by Willibald Kirfel. Bonn : Kommissionsverlag Fritz Klopp, 1926. Pp. 331-45.

Gogerley, Daniel John. *Ceylon Buddhism.* London : Kegan Paul, Trench, Trubner & Co., Ltd., 1908.

Gonda, Jan. *Aspects of Early Vishnuism.* Utrecht : A. Oosthoek, 1954.

———. *Loka : World and Heaven in the Veda.* Amsterdam : Noord-Hollandsche U. M., 1966.

———. *The Meaning of the Sanskrit Term Dhāman.* Amsterdam: Noord-Hollandsche U.M., 1967

Grube, George Maximillian Anthony *Plato's Thought.* Originally published 1935. Boston : Beacon Press, 1958.

Guthrie, Willian Keith Chamber *The Greeks and Their Gods.* Originally published 1950. Boston: Beacon Press, 1955.

———. *A History of Greek Philosophy.* 4 vols. Cambridge : Cambridge University Press, 1962-1975.

———. *Orpheus and Greek Religion.* Originally published 1935. Rev. 1952. New York : W. W. Norton & Co., Inc., 1966.

Haas, Hans. *Amida Buddha : Unsere Zeflucht.* Göttingen : Vandenhoeck und Ruprecht, 1910.

Hardy, Robert Spence. *A Manual of Buddhism.* London : Partridge & Oakey, 1853.

Hastings, James. ed. *Encyclopaedia of Religion and Ethics.* 13 vols. Edinburgh : T & T Clark, 1908-1927.

Heath, Thomas Little. *Aristarchos of Samos.* Oxford : Clarendon Press, 1913.

———. *The Works of Archimedes.* New York : Dover Publications, Inc., 1912.

Heine-Geldern, Robert. *Conceptions of State and Kingship in Southeast Asia.* Ithaca : Cornell Southeast Asia Program Data Paper No. 18, 1956.

Hiltebeitel, Alf. "*Mahābhārata* and Hindu Eschatology." *History of Religions Journal* 12 (1972) : 95-135.

———. *The Ritual of Battle; Krishna in the Mahābhārata.* Ithaca : Cornell University Press, 1976.

Hiriyanna, M. *Outlines of Indian Philosophy.* London : George Allen & Unwin, Ltd., 1975.

Hopkins, E. Washburn. "Epic Chronology." *Journal of the American Oriental Society* 24 (1903): 7-56.

———. "Mythological Aspects of Trees and Mountains in the Great Epic." *Journal of the American Oriental Society* 30 (1909) : 347-74.

———. "Phrases of Time and Age in the Sanskrit Epic." *Journal of the American Oriental Society* 23 (1902) : 350-57.

———. "Remarks on the Form of Numbers, the Method of Using Them, and the Numerical Categories Found in the Mahābhārata." *Journal of the American Oriental Society* 23 (1902) : 109-55.

Hurvitz, Leon. "Chih-I." *Mélanges chinois et bouddhiques* Vol. 12 (1960-62).

Ingram, Paul O. "Honen's and Shinran's Justification for Their Doctrine of Salvation and Faith Through Other Power." *Contemporary Religions in Japan* 9 (1970): 233-51.

Iyer, V. Venkatachellam. "The Seven Dwīpas in the Purāṇas." *The Quarterly Journal of the Mythic Society* 15 (1924-25) : 62-75, 119-27, 238-45; 16 (1925-26) : 116-24, 268-83; 17 (1926-27) : 30-45, 94-105.

Jacobi, Hermann. "Ages of the World (Indian)." *Encyclopaedia of Religion and Ethics* 1 : 200-202.

Jaeger, Werner. *Paideia : The Idea of Greek Culture.* 2 vols. Oxford : Basil Blackwell, 1944.

Jaini, Padmanabh S. "On the Sarvajñatva (Omniscience) of Mahāvīra and the Buddha." *Buddhist Studies in Honour of I. B. Horner.* Edited by L. Cousins, A. Kunst and K. R. Norman. Boston : D. Reidel Publishing Co., 1974. Pp. 71-90.

James, Edwin Oliver. *Creation and Cosmology.* Leiden : E. J. Brill, 1969.

Jayatilleke, Kullatissa Nanda. "The Buddhist Conception of the Universe." *The Message of the Buddha.* Edited by Ninian Smart. London : George Allen & Unwin Ltd., 1975. Pp. 90-103.

Joinville, Mr. "On the Religion and Manners of the People of Ceylon." *Asiatick Researches* 7 (1801) : 399-448.

Kahn, Charles. *Anaximander and the Origins of Greek Cosmology.* New York : Columbia University Press, 1960.

Keith, Arthur Berriedale. *Indian Logic and Atomism; An Exposition of the Nyāya and Vaiśeṣika Systems.* Oxford : Clarendon Press, 1921.

Kennedy, Edward Stewart. "Ramifications of the World Year Concept in Islamic Astrology." *Ithaca. Actes du Dixième Congrès Internationale d'Histoire des Sciences* 1 (1964) : 23-43.

Kerschensteiner, Jula. "Kosmos." *Zetemata; Monographien zur klassischen Altertumswissenschaft*, Heft 30 (München: Beck, 1962.

———. *Platon und der Orient*. Stuttgart : W. Kohlhammer Verlag, 1945.

King, Winston L. *A Thousand Lives Away*. Cambridge : Harvard University Press, 1964.

Kirfel, Willibald. *Kosmographie der Inder*. Bonn : K. Schroeder, 1920.

———. *Purāṇa Pañcalakṣaṇa*. Bonn : K. Schroeder, 1927.

———. *Symbolik des Buddismus*. Stuttgart : A. Hiersemann, 1959.

Kowalewski, Jozef Szczepan. *Buddiiskaia Kosmologiia*. 1837.

Lach, Donald F. *Asia in the Making of Europe*. 2 vols. Chicago : University of Chicago Press, 1965.

Lamotte, Étienne. *Histoire du Bouddhisme Indien des origines à l'ère Śaka*. Louvain : Bibliothèque du Muséon, 1958.

———. "Mañjuśrī." *T'oung Pao* 48 (1960) : 1-96.

———. "Les premières relations entre I'Inde et l'Occident." *La Nouvelle Clio* (Brussels) 5 (1953) : 83-118.

La Vallée Poussin, Louis de. "Adibuddha." *Encyclopaedia of Religion and Ethics*, 1 : 93-100.

———. "Ages of the World (Buddhist)." *Encyclopaedia* of *Religion and Ethics*, 1:187-90.

———. "Agnosticism (Buddhist)." *Encyclopaedia of Religion and Ethics*, 1:220-25.

———. "Bodhisattva." *Encyclopaedia of Religion and Ethics*, 1:739-53.

———. "Le Bouddha et les Abhijñās." *Le Muséon* (Louvain) 44 (1931) : 335-42.

———. "La controverse du temps et du pudgala dans le Vijñānakāya." *Études Asiatiques*. Edited by G. Van Oest. 2 vols. Hanoi : Publications de l'école français d'Extrême-Orient, 1925. I :343-76.

———."Cosmogony and Cosmology (Buddhist)." *Encyclopaedia of Religion and Ethics*, 2:129-38.

———. "Magic (Buddhist)." *Encyclopaedia of Religion and Ethics*, 8:255-57.

———. "Les neuf Kalpas qu'a franchi Śakyamuni pour devancer Maitreya." *T'oung Pao*, 2d ser. 26 (1929) : 17-24.

———. *Nirvāṇa*. Paris : Gabriel Beauchesne, 1925.

Law, Bimala Churn. *The Buddhist Conception of Spirits*. London : Luzac & Co., 1936.

———. *Geography of Early Buddhism*. Varanasi : Shri V. S. Singh, 1973.

Lévy, Paul. *Buddhism : A Mystery Religion* ? New York : Schocken Books, 1968.

Lingat, Robert. "Time and the Dharma." *Contributions to Indian Sociology* 6 (1962) : 7-76.

Lounsbery, G. Constance. *Buddhist Meditation in the Southern School*. London : Kegan Paul, Trench, Trubner & Co., 1950.

Lubac, Henri de. *Amida*. Paris : Éditions du Seuil, 1955.

Luk, Charles (K'uan Yü Lu). *The Secrets of Chinese Meditation*. London : Rider & Co., 1964.

Mallmann, Maria Thérèse de. *Introduction à l'étude d'Avalokiteśvara.*: Paris Annales du Musée Guimet, 1948.

Mandal, Kumar Kishore. *Comparative Study of the Concepts of Time and Space in Indian Thought*. Varanasi : Chowkhambha Sanskrit Series Office, 1968.

Mankad, Dolarray Rangildas. *Purāṇic Chronology*. Anand : Gangajala Prokashan, 1951.

Matsunaga, Alicia. *The Buddhist Philosophy of Assimilation*. Tokyo : Charles E. Tuttle Co., 1969.

——— and Matsunaga, Daigan. *The Buddhist Concept of Hell*. New York : Philosophical Library, 1972.

McGovern, William Montgomery. *A Manual of Buddhist Philosophy, Vol. 1 : Cosmology*. New York : E. P. Dutton & Co., 1923.

Mishra, Umesh. *Conceptions of Matter According to Nyāya-Vaiśeṣika*. Benares : Krishna Das Gupta, 1936.

Murti, Tirupattur Ramesshayyer Venkatachala *The Central Philosophy of Buddhism; A Study of the Mādhyamika System*. London : George Allen and Unwin. Ltd., 1955.

Mus, Paul. *Barabadur; esquisse d'un histoire du Bouddhisme.*

2 vols. Hanoi : Bulletin de l'école français d'Extrême-Orient, 1935.

———. *La lumière sur les six voies.* Paris : Institute d'ethnologie, 1939.

Nasr, Seyyed Hossein. *An Introduction to Islamic Cosmological Doctrines.* 2nd edition. London : Thames and Hudson, 1978.

Nyanaponika, Thera. *Satipaṭṭhāna. The Heart of Buddhist Meditation.* Colombo : Word of the Buddha Publishing Co., 1954.

Nyanatiloka, Bhikku. *Guide Through the Abhidhamma-Piṭaka.* London : Luzac & Co., 1938.

Nyberg, Henrik Samuel. "Questions de cosmogonie et de cosmologie mazdéenes." *Journal asiatique* 214 (1929) : 193-310; 219 (1931) : 1-134, 195-244.

Obermiller, Eugen. "The Doctrine of the Prajñā-pāramitā as Exposed in the Abhisamayālaṅkāra of Maitreya." *Acta Orientalia* 11 (1932) : 18-26.

Palacios, Miguel Asin. *Islam and the Divine Comedy.* London : Frank Cass & Co., Ltd., 1968.

Pas, Julian F. "Shan-tao's Interpretation of the Meditative Vision of Amitāyus." *History of Religions Journal* 14 (1974) : 96-116.

Petzold, Bruno. "On Buddhist Meditation." *The Transactions of the Asiatic Society of Japan*, 3rd ser., 1 (1948) : 64-100.

Pingree, David. "Astronomy and Astrology in India and Iran." *Isis : An International Review Devoted to the History of Science and Its Cultural Influences* 54 (1963) : 229-46.

———. *Census of the Exact Sciences in Sanskrit.* Philadelphia : American Philosophical Society, 1970.

———. "History of Mathematical Astronomy in India." *Dictionary of Scientific Biography.* Edited by Charles Coulston Gillespie. New York : Charles Scribner's Sons, 1970-1978, XV, Supplement I (1978), pp. 533-633.

———. "Sanskrit Astronomical Tables in the United States." *Transactions of the American Philosophical Society*, new series, Pt. 3, Vol. 58 (1968).

———. *The Thousands of Abū Ma'shar (Kitāb al'ulūf).* Leiden : E. J. Brill, 1968.

Price, Derek John de Solla. *Science Since Babylon.* New Haven : Yale University Press, 1961.

Przyluski, Jean. "Brahmā Sahāṃpati." *Journal asiatique* 205 (1924) : 155-63.

———. "Le symbloismc du pilier de Sarnath." *Études d'orientalisme publiées par le Musée Guimet à la mémoire de Raymonde Linossier.* 2 vols. Paris : Libraire Ernest Leroux, 1932. Pp. 481-98.

———. "Les vidyārāja." *Bulletin de l'école français d'Extrême-Orient* 23 (1923) : 301-18.

———. "La ville de cakravartin." *Rocznik Orientalistyczny* 5 (1927) : 165-85.

Pullé, Francesco Lorenzo. "La cartografia antica dell'India" *Studi; Italiani di Filologia Indo-Iranica* 4 (1901) 5 (1905), 10 (1932).

Ranasinghe, C. P. *The Buddha's Explanation of the Universe.* Colombo : Lanka Buddha-Mandalaya Fund, 1957.

Rawlinson, Hugh George. "Early Contacts between India and Europe." *A Cultural History of India.* Edited by A. L. Basham. Oxford : Clarendon Press, 1975.

Raychaudhuri, Hemchandra. *Studies in Indian Antiquities.* Calcutta : University of Calcutta, 1932.

Reischauer, August Karl. "Genshin's Ojo Yoshu : Collected Essays on Birth Into Paradise." *Transactions of the Asiatic Society of Japan,* 2d ser., 7 (1930) : 16-98.

———. *Studies in Japanese Buddhism.* Originally published 1917. New York : AMS Press, Inc., 1970.

Reynolds, Craig. "Buddhist Cosmography in Thai History with Special Reference to Nineteenth Century Cultural Change." *Journal of Asian Studies* 35 (1976) : 203-30.

Reynolds, Frank and Reynolds, Mani. *Three Worlds According to King Ruang.* Palo Alto and Bangkok : Stanford University Press and the Siam Society, 1977.

Robinson, Richard H. *The Buddhist Religion.* Belmont, Calif. : Dickenson Publishing Co., Inc., 1970.

———. *Early Mādhyamika in India and China.* Madison : Delhi, Motilal Banarsidass, 1978

Rohde, Erwin. *Psyche : The Cult of Souls and Belief in Immortality Among the Greeks.* Originally published 1925. 2 vols. New York : Harper & Row, 1966.

Rõnnow, Kasten. "Some Remarks on Śvetadvīpa." *Bulletin of the School of Oriental Studies* (University of London) 5 (1929) : 253-84.

Rowell, Teresina. "The Background and Early Use of the Buddha-Kṣetra Concept." *The Eastern Buddhist* 6 (1934): 199-246, 379-430; 7 (1935) : 131-69.

Ruegg, David Seyfort. *La theorie du tathāgatagarbha et du gotra; études sur la sotériologie et la gnoséologie du Bouddhisme.* Paris : Publication de l'école française d'Extrême-Orient, 1969.

Russell, David Syme. *The Method and Message of Jewish Apocalyptic.* Philadelphia : Westminster Press, 1964.

Schayer, Stanislaw. "Contributions to the Problem of Time in Indian Philosophy." *Polska Akadeuia Umiejetnosci* 31 (1938) : 1-76.

Schipper, Kenneth. *L'empereur Wou des Han dans la légende taoiste, Han Wou-ti Nei-tchouan.* Paris : Publications de l'école française d'Extrême-Orient, 1965.

Schubring, Walther. "Anzeige (Kirfel, *Kosmographie*)." *Zeitschrift der deutschen Morgenländischen Gesellschaft* 75 (1921) : 254-75.

———. *The Doctrine of the Jainas Described After the Old Sources.* Translated by Wolfgang Beurlen. Delhi : Motilal Banarsidass, 1962.

———. *Die Jainas.* Tübingen : Mohr, 1927.

Sen, S. "On Yakṣa and Yakṣa Worship." *India Maior; Congratulatory Volume Presented to J. Gonda.* Edited by J. Ensink and P. Gaeffke. Leiden : E. J. Brill, 1972.

Senart, Émile. *Essai sur la légende du Buddha.* Paris : Libraire de la Société Asiatique, 1882.

Singh, M. R. *Geographical Data in the Purāṇas.* Calcutta : Punthi Pustak, 1972.

Silburn, Lilian. *Instant et cause, le discontenu dans la pensée philosophique de l'Inds.* Paris : Libraire philosophique J. Vrin, 1955.

Sircar, Dineschandra. *Cosmography and Geography in Early Indian Literature.* Calcutta : D. Chattopadhyaya, 1967.

Söderblom, Nathan. "Ages of the World (Zoroastrian)." *Encyclopaedia of Religion and Ethics*, 1: 205-10.

Soifer, Deborah A. "Toward an Understanding of Viṣṇu's

Avatāras." *Purāṇa* 18 (1976) : 128-48.

Somayaji, D. A. *A Critical Study of the Ancient Hindu Astronomy in the Light and Language of the Modern.* Dharwar, Karnatak University, 1971.

Soymié, Michael. "Le Lo'feou Chan; Étude de géographie religieuse." *Bulletin de l'école français d'Extrême-Orient* 48 (1956) : 1-139.

Suzuki, Daisetz Teitero. *Studies in the Laṅkāvatāra Sūtra.* London : Routledge & Kegan Paul Ltd., 1930.

———. *Zen Buddhism; Selected Writings of D. T. Suzuki.* Edited by William Barrett. Garden City, N. Y. : Doubleday & Co., Inc., 1956.

Takakusu, Junjiro. *Essentials of Buddhist Philosophy.* Delhi, Motilal Banarsidass, 1978

Tambiah, S. J. *Buddhism and the Spirit Cults in North-East Thailand.* Cambridge : Cambridge University Press, 1970.

———. *World Conqueror and World Renouncer.* Cambridge : Cambridge University Press, 1976.

Thibaut, George Frederick William. *Astronomie, Astrologie und Mathematik.* Strassburg : Karl J. Turner, 1899.

Vlastos, Gregory. "Minimal Parts in Epicurean Atomism." *Isis : An International Review Devoted to the History of Science and Its Cultural Influences* 56 (1965) : 121-47.

———. *Plato's Universe.* Seattle : University of Washington Press, 1975.

Waddell, Laurence Austine. *The Buddhism of Tibet or Lamaism.* Cambridge : W. Heffer & Sons, Ltd., 1934.

Waerden, Bartel Leendert van der. "Das Grosse Jahr und Die ewige Wiederkehr." *Hermes* 80, No. 2 (1952) : 129-55.

———. "The World-Year of the Persians." *Journal of the American Oriental Society* 83 (1963) : 315-27.

Wallis, Henry White. *Cosmology of the Rigveda.* London : Williams & Norgate, 1887.

Wayman, Alex. "The Intermediate-State Dispute in Buddhism." *Buddhist Studies in Honour of I. B. Horner.* Edited by L. Cousins, A. Kunst and K. R. Norman. Boston : D. Reidel Publishing Co., 1974. Pp. 227-39.

Welbon, Guy. *The Buddhist Nirvāṇa and Its Western Interpreters.* Chicago : University of Chicago Press, 1967.

Welch, Holmes. *The Practice of Chinese Buddhism, 1900-1950.* Cambridge : Harvard University Press, 1967.

West, Martin Litchfield. *Early Greek Philosophy and the Orient.* Oxford : Clarendon Press, 1971.

Wilford, F. "An Essay on the Sacred Isles in the West." *Asiatick Researches* 8 (1805) : 245-367; 9 (1807) : 32-115; 11 (1808) : 27-157.

Zaehner, Robert Charles. *Zurvan : A Zoroastrian Dilemma.* Oxford : Clarendon press 1955.

Zimmer, Heinrich. *Myths and Symbols in Indian Art and Civilization.* Edited by Joseph Campbell. Princeton : Princeton University Press, 1946.

INDEX